PRAISE FOR *AFFLICTION: GROWING UP WITH A CLOSETED GAY DAD*

"*Affliction* is a loving and tender portrait of a relationship and a family. It's also an important addition to the history of gay parents in America and of the particular challenges faced by gay men and women in the years before Stonewall."
—ALYSIA ABBOTT, author of *New York Times Book Review* Editors' Choice and Stonewall Book Award winner *Fairyland: A Memoir of My Father*

"This moving memoir is about not just a daughter, not just a father, but a whole family, one that's impossible not to love. Hall's writing is honest and insightful and her story a comfort and a gem."
—VICTORIA LOUSTALOT, author of *This is How You Say Goodbye* and *Living Like Audrey: Life Lessons from the Fairest Lady of All*

"This book shares a vital perspective that, until now, was missing from the LGBTQ community's understanding of its own history. Hall finally adds the missing puzzle piece: the voice of the children of gay parents who have always stood in the shadows. We are given a rare and precious gift as she warmly invites the reader into the world of her closeted family and shares a perspective that is deeply loving and raw in its honesty."
—ROBIN MARQUIS, who served as Program Director of COLAGE

AFFLICTION

GROWING UP
WITH A
CLOSETED
GAY DAD

LAURA HALL

SHE WRITES PRESS

Published 2021
Printed in the United States of America
Print ISBN: 978-1-64742-124-3
E-ISBN: 978-1-64742-125-0
Library of Congress Control Number: 2021903411

For information, address:
She Writes Press
1569 Solano Ave #546
Berkeley, CA 94707

Interior design by Tabitha Lahr

She Writes Press is a division of SparkPoint Studio, LLC.

For my parents

CONTENTS

ME THE YEAR MY FATHER CAME OUT TO ME,
AGE TWENTY-FOUR

PROLOGUE

"I knew I was different," he said. "I was also aware of the fact I should conceal it, that it was an affliction."

It wasn't like any other Father's Day, though it started out that way. A wrapped gift sat next to me in our yellow Volkswagen Bug. I don't remember what was inside, but it might have been a macramé wall hanging I made or a collage of shells and twigs I glued onto a piece of driftwood. My father admired the crafts of that era, especially if they were created by one of his four children.

The year was 1975. Jody, my five-year-old daughter, slept soundly in the back seat of our car. The trip was a ninety-minute drive from Sonoma County to San Carlos, the small city on the San Francisco Peninsula where I grew up.

My mother greeted us at the front door of the family house before we even rang the bell. A fresh summer pie, either peach or apricot, would have been cooling on the kitchen island next to a stack of linen cocktail napkins and an open can of See's Fancy Nuts. The dining room table was always set the night before with the fancy pink linen tablecloth and napkins, sterling silver flatware, blue Wedgwood china with white trim, and amethyst-colored crystal stemware. My father would have assembled the centerpiece that morning out of purple statice he had dried in the garage, and long shiny brown seed pods he collected from city sidewalks, a single lavender iris from the front yard, and maybe a fern frond or two.

Caroline, my older sister by eighteen months, home from college, was cloistered at the back of the house in the bedroom she still claimed as her own. Tim, our younger brother, would have been downstairs singing and strumming the music of the Beatles and Neil Young on his guitar. Susan, twenty-one, and the youngest of the four of us, might have been on the phone with her tall and tan surfer boyfriend.

Jody and her grandmother got down to business in the kitchen. I grabbed a handful of salted nuts from the counter. At the sound of yapping and the rustle of a dog leash, I peeked out from the kitchen doorway and saw my father and the family dog.

"Laurie, would you like to come walk Daisy with me?"

Mom waved me on, assuring me she had everything covered, certain to cherish the rare one-on-one time she could spend in the kitchen with her only grandchild. It had been a few months since we'd been down to the Peninsula, and Mom was prepared. A sugar bowl and cinnamon shakers were within Jody's easy reach. She was well-versed in the art of placing the finishing touches on her grandmother's leftover pie dough that had already been cut into narrow strips for her. Mam, as she called her, would soon be sliding them into a *very hot* oven. "Don't touch," she'd warn Jody.

My father and I, and Daisy the yappy terrier, took off up the hills behind the family house. I remember the sky as being a light blue, but the summer haze lower on the horizon partially obscured our view of the San Francisco Bay. Dad and I bantered about not much at all, as I recall, perhaps the long hot summer that year, the dry vegetation surrounding us, and the unnatural-looking pinkish-orange color of the Leslie Salt evaporation ponds in the bay below us.

Behind the small talk, though, my mind churned. I hadn't planned it, but now seemed like as good a time as ever to ask the question that had pressed on me since I was little. I was desperate for the truth, though I already had my suspicions. Still, I hoped hearing it out loud would help me make sense of the mess I'd made of my own life.

At twenty-four, I'd already been through a teen pregnancy, two marriages, multiple extramarital affairs, and was now working on my second divorce. I hoped to finally point the finger at someone other than myself. I'd spent at least two decades following the clues my father left behind. After weighing the evidence and knitting together a story that would hopefully explain away my own shortcomings, I readied myself for the final proof. When we reached the ridgeline and Dad unleashed Daisy, I made my move.

"Have you ever been unfaithful to Mom?"

Looking back now, I am shocked by my boldness. But as soon as the words left my mouth, I could feel my heart pounding against my snug, powder-blue poor-boy top. I regretted saying them. I already knew the answer.

Daisy by then had disappeared into the scrubby manzanitas, her scruffy brown head bobbing up and down like a free-range jackrabbit. I wished I could disappear with her, but it was too late. There was no retracting my question.

Dad alternated his gaze from my eyes to the view of Mount Diablo behind me. When his cheeks turned a reddish-purple and he drew in a large breath, letting it out slowly, I assumed he was stunned by my courage. I'd stunned myself.

He broke out in the same guilty-looking grin he had on his face that scandalous evening on Birch Avenue when I was about six. In the afterhours of a dinner party my parents hosted, I caught him red-handed in the living room with one of the other wives, her bright red, lipsticked mouth pressed conspiratorially up to his left cheek.

"Honey, I'm gay," Dad said, jolting me back to the present. His voice was disturbingly cheery. When I didn't immediately respond, he repeated himself, this time with emphasis. "I've *always* been gay."

My stomach clutched. Behind him stood a glaring sun, but oddly his face wasn't in shadow. Rather, it glowed a shiny bronze, a phenomenon that to this day I can't explain. His big blue eyes sparkled more than usual, and his breath came out in short, staccato bursts. After keeping his secret from nearly everyone for more than five decades, a fact I'd soon glean, he appeared gleeful to unburden himself to me. Even in my state of shock, it was clear to me that the weight of his secret had shifted from his shoulders to mine.

CHAPTER 1: USO DANCE

"As you know, Laurie, it almost didn't happen." Yes, I knew that. My mother told the story of the night they first met so often I could recite it word for word from memory.

I was a teenager at the time, with boys and romance on my mind. I was eager to hear my parents' love story again. My siblings were long gone from the dinner table. Mom's rubber-gloved hands in the soapy dishwater stilled when I asked the question. Dad sat in front of his near-finished dinner, as usual the last one in the family to finish. After wiping his plate clean with what remained of his slice of bread, he brought his dishes over to the sink. He reached for the mug Mom left for him near the coffee pot and filled it to the brim with coffee, cream, and a spoonful of sugar. It was their evening ritual. She didn't even seem to notice him rustling behind her.

Mom's gaze moved to the window and the hills beyond. Feeling his shirt pocket, Dad slipped out the sliding glass door onto the deck to have a smoke while sipping his sweet, steaming coffee. I stood at the kitchen island, facing my mother and relishing the retelling of my favorite story.

1

My father at the time was a twenty-four-year-old private first-class soldier in the US Army. Four months earlier, he had been stationed at Fort Ord in Monterey County when, on December 7, 1941, he and his fellow soldiers were informed that Japanese forces had bombed Pearl Harbor. The following day, December 8, 1941, President Roosevelt declared war against Japan, and the United States officially entered World War II. Dad's orders over the next four months took him first to guard Northern California railway bridges against possible attack. Afterward his unit caravanned to the San Francisco Presidio for staging before deployment overseas. But the Presidio was full. An abandoned country club in Belmont, a city located a few miles from where my mother lived, temporarily housed the soldiers.

It was April 1942. Mom, a high school senior at the time, was a month shy of her eighteenth birthday. She and her best friend, Enid, looked forward to the upcoming USO dance at the San Carlos City Hall. After the bombing of Pearl Harbor, most of the local young men had left to join the armed services. An invitation had gone out to girls in local high schools encouraging their attendance before the "brave soldiers" shipped out to battlefronts and parts unknown.

"Oh, Laurie, we were so excited to meet the soldiers," Mom said, glancing over at me. "I was dancing with Pete, the company cook. Then your dad and a fellow soldier walked in."

I knew what was coming and held my breath.

"The soldiers outnumbered the girls," she said matter-of-factly. "Your dad's buddy shouted, 'Hey, Hall, let's get outta here. There aren't any girls to dance with.'"

At that moment, I heard the front door close with a click. Dad must have finished his cigarette and walked around to the front of the house. He was probably switching into the moccasins he kept at the front entry. Mom peeled back her rubber gloves, draped them over the pots and pans that were dripping onto the plastic drying rack, and turned back toward me.

"I looked over and that's when I first saw your father," she said in a singsong voice. Her whole face was smiling now. "He had the most beautiful blue eyes. He looked like a movie star to me." She added, "And his teeth were *so* white." That last part always made me laugh. Then Dad chimed in.

"And that's when I heard this sweet voice say, '*I'll* dance with you.'" Dad must have been eavesdropping from out in the hallway. His voice was sweet and high like Mom's when he spoke those words, as if that scene in the dance hall were the most wonderful moment of his life. Now standing equidistant from both of my parents, I was filled with a warm rush.

"What I first noticed about your mother was her hair," Dad said, his voice now taking on an almost professorial tone. "Even though her nickname was Rusty at the time, her hair wasn't red. It was Titian blond." For some reason, this clarification was of utmost importance to my father. Perhaps red seemed too common or unsophisticated a term. "And it looked like spun gold," he added.

It was Mom's turn again.

"And then he smiled and walked toward me," she said. "We danced the rest of the night." In that moment my mother looked like a smitten teenager.

"I don't think Pete was very happy with me," Mom added with a giggle. I couldn't tell if she felt bad over her quick dismissal of the company cook or was priding herself for so boldly going after what she wanted.

The story followed the trajectory I knew well. After the dance, Dad walked her the six blocks home. She invited him in for banana cake. This particular layer cake, frosted in vanilla buttercream icing and covered in chopped walnuts, was long a staple in our household. I wondered if she had made her favorite cake that afternoon just in case some handsome soldier offered to walk her home.

"And I pretended to like it!" Dad said with a hearty laugh.

Mom shot him a look. I hadn't heard this part before. This cruel crack seemed out of character for him. I wished he'd stopped with his Titian blond comment. He hustled over to the kitchen sink to rinse his mug out and exit, but Mom had already readied her return taunt.

"Then your father did the strangest thing, Laurie," she said. "He pulled out his wallet and slid out baby pictures of Marsha."

Marsha was Dad's niece, his brother's oldest child. I didn't know where all this was headed, but I sensed it wasn't good. Mom continued.

"And then he laid them all out in front of me on Nana's tiny kitchen table!"

I looked over toward Dad, but he was already out the door and headed down the hallway to their bedroom.

"Your dad thought she was the most *beautiful* baby in *all* the world."

This time her voice was louder than normal. I assumed she wanted Dad to hear her. But her sudden change rankled me.

"I had never known a young man to go on and on like that over babies," she said.

I found it endearing that my father loved children before I was born. I would have expected my mother to feel the same way. After all, it was obvious she'd met a bright, well-spoken, and handsome man with perfect teeth who wanted to settle down and have a family. Strangely, though, she kept up with her taunts.

"There was something else your father did that night," she said.

I sighed.

"When he took out his wallet, I noticed he'd rubbed out the first of three initials engraved on it. Only two remained, *RH*. I couldn't make out the first one. I thought there might be some record of mental illness in his family."

I wondered what a rubbed-out initial on a wallet had to do with mental illness. But Mom seemed delighted to share

MOM, AGE EIGHTEEN, HIGH SCHOOL SENIOR, 1942

DAD, AGE TWENTY-FOUR, FORT ORD, 1942

this detail. It was out of character with her normally generous nature. Even though my grandparents called my father Duane, not Ralph, I hadn't heard this part of the story before, that the D in his initials on his wallet had been erased. Just then the master bedroom door closed with a click.

My mother's suspicions about Dad's character seem to have been aroused early on. Whenever I asked my father why he switched his first and middle names, he gave me a different answer every time. He either said that the Army made a mistake or that he didn't like the name Duane, or he simply hemmed and hawed.

Mom changed the subject.

"You know, Laurie, your father had *so* many girlfriends before we met," she said. "And he was engaged to a lot of them."

I don't know about the "a lot" part, but, yes, I knew this, too. She'd brought it up before. Dad would blush and roll his eyes at this telling. But I couldn't get a read on why she brought it up now. Did his popularity with girls before they were married unsettle her? Or did she take it as a badge of honor? After all, he picked her over all the others.

CHAPTER 2: THE LIGHT UNDER THE DOOR

I'm perhaps eighteen months old. My vantage point is low to the ground. The house is dark except for a thin line of light under the kitchen door, a sign my father hasn't yet left. I toddle down the hallway toward the light. A few feet shy of the kitchen door, I tuck myself under one of the dining room chairs, keeping my eye focused on the bright yellow line.

The gurgling of the percolator and the tick-tick-ticking of the toaster calm me, but my stomach clutches at the sounds of running water and dishes clanking in the sink that follow. The light switch clicks. The light goes out, the back door latches close. He's gone.

I don't know how often I make this trip in the predawn hours before my father leaves for work. But the scene is always the same. Each time I hope the light won't go out. Each time it does.

"It's time for Easter baskets, kids!" Dad calls out from the open front door, three small jackets draped over his elbow.

I drop my Gerber baby doll's pink-and-white scalloped bib, which my tiny fingers had been struggling to snap, and run to my father. He takes his time fastening each metal button on my jean jacket, finishing with a strong tug on the bottom hem. Mom ties red paisley bandanas around Caroline's head and mine. She fits Tim with a snug leather cap complete with earflaps.

After seven years of marriage and four miscarriages, my parents finally became parents in 1949, four years after my father returned from the war. They made up for lost time by having four babies in five years. Caroline was now five. I was four, having arrived eighteen months afterward in 1951. Our younger brother, Tim, was three. Susan, now a toddler, was born a year after him.

I was born in this cottage my parents built at the rural edge of San Carlos. The double Dutch door at the front and the cedar shake roof were of my mother's choosing. My father designed the garden and patio. Though modest, the simple gabled roof and beveled glass windows reminded me of the cottages in storybooks Dad read to us at bedtime. Behind the house, fields of oat grasses grew tall in the spring. By Easter they were above our heads.

Like little ducklings, the three of us older children followed our father in single file through the back gate and onto a path he'd flatten in the grasses before us. I couldn't keep up. At one point, the tall oats enveloped me. I panicked.

"Over here, Laurie," he said. "Come on, sweetie. I'll wait for you."

Breathless from worry, I followed his voice, elbowing my way through the grasses until I saw him. Caroline and Tim stood at his side.

"Okay, kids, stay right where you are and watch."

With this pronouncement, Dad lowered himself down onto the moist grasses and curled up in a big ball, tucking his knees tightly to his chest. He rolled around in one spot until a gigantic basket-shaped space formed, flat in the middle and edged in tall blades of grass. The three of us observers stood by as our baskets, one by one, were readied for occupation. No colored eggs, chocolate bunnies, or speckled jellybeans would inhabit these Easter baskets. Only small, delighted children.

As soon as Dad dropped us down into our giant baskets, making sure not to flatten the basket edges, our pre-occupation voices turned to whispers and then to silence, hushed by the cozy, womb-like chambers. I glimpsed the top half of my father floating above the edges of my basket. His tall slender figure and slow movements reminded me of the lanky sunflowers that grew along our side fence and swayed slowly in the breezes. Secure with him in view, I envisioned pretty little fairies stealing looks at me from behind the blades of tall grasses. My mother's voice from the back stoop of the house jolted me out of my fantasy.

"Ralph! Kids! It's dinner time!"

I rose to my feet. In due time, my father scooped me up and out of my basket. He brushed off the wet grasses that clung to my overalls and dropped me down onto the path leading home. I glanced back and wondered what would become of our fantastic baskets now camouflaged by the tall grasses. Dad led us back up to the rear steps of the cottage where he pulled off our muddy, grass-stained shoes. He lifted me onto a stool at the concrete sink.

"It's warm now, Laurie," he said. "Give me your hands."

Standing on tiptoes, I leaned over the sink as far as I could. From behind, Dad's chest braced me from falling backwards off the wobbly stool.

"Go on now, your hands are all clean," he said. "Your mother is waiting. I'll be right in."

The screen door snapped shut. I turned to see him walk toward the patio edge where he pulled his silver lighter out of his pants pocket. Flipping the top back, he flicked the spark-wheel which emitted a flinty smell I could detect from ten feet away. The tip of his cigarette glowed a bright orange-red as he took a long draw on it.

Full plates of food awaited the three of us kids at the kitchen table. Susan pushed Cheerios around on her highchair tray. Dad soon came in, singing "Catch a Falling Star." Once Mom seated us at our assigned places, she joined him. She had a sweet shy look on her face as she turned toward him and sang the melody. Dad switched to harmony. The effect on me was immediate, my throat tightening so much that it hurt. I never wanted the harmony to end.

"Don't forget to drink your milk," Mom reminded us when the song was over.

This was important to her, along with sturdy lace-up shoes, scarves in the sun, and soft, warm jackets buttoned up to our chins on breezy days. And vegetables. We only got dessert if we finished them. I'd already nudged my mushy, foul-tasting carrots to the edge of my plate with my fork. Then out of nowhere, my father's hand appeared over mine, guiding it. Together we smashed the offensive carrots into the mashed potatoes. Once this more palatable mixture was a uniform light orange, Dad helped me form it into a dome-like shape.

"See, honey," he said. "It's an igloo!"

"It is!"

He wasn't finished, though. Using the fork's tines, together we imprinted dozens of thin ridges all over the outside of the mashed potato-and-carrot igloo.

"Now poke your finger in here to make the front door," he said, positioning my thumb in the correct location.

"Why, look at that!" he boasted.

Retracting his arm, he returned to his own dinner. The bland-tasting mélange in the shape of an Eskimo's shelter was now something I could countenance. I was certain Mom would treat me to one of her chocolate-frosted graham crackers she'd laid out on racks earlier to allow the frosting to harden.

Long before Dad finished his dinner, Mom was out of her chair and standing at the kitchen sink. Long, pink rubber gloves enveloped her hands and arms while steam from the hot water rose and swirled around her flushed face. Caroline and I were now tall enough to bus our own dishes. Mom whisked them out of our hands before they even landed on the countertop and dropped them, *plop*, into the sudsy water.

"That is very good of you girls," she said. "Now go ahead and play until your father finishes his dinner."

Dad always washed his own dishes, afterward running a bath for the three of us older kids. Sometimes he treated us to a bubble bath. After pouring the soapy liquid under running water, he let the large suds float up until they reached the rim of the bathtub. Only three tiny heads were then visible above the thick foam. When the suds dissolved, we begged for more. He obliged us up to a point.

After rinsing us and drying us off, Dad snapped on our pajamas, combed our hair, and had us ready for bedtime stories by seven o'clock, the time Mom set for us to be in bed. Dad struggled to arrange two pillows behind his back on one of our tiny twin beds before all four of his children piled on. He read us fairytales like *Snow-White and Rose-Red*, *Rumpelstiltskin*, and *Jack and the Beanstalk,* though the dark threats inherent in them frightened me, but the sing-song rhymes of *Madeline* and the cute drawings in *The Little House* calmed me. As he clapped a book shut and began to disentangle himself from his children, one of us inevitably begged him not to stop.

"Just one more page, Daddy."

"Okay, fine," he smiled, removing the bookmark he'd inserted. "But just one." I had a feeling he'd planned ahead for this.

One evening before our nighttime routine, Dad let me join him outside in the twilight. I was maybe five or six. I stared at the vapors of his cigarette smoke swirling high above us and at the stars beyond. Our rural neighborhood didn't have streetlights, and the stars lit up the night sky. In my first-grade class, the nuns were already teaching us about a heavenly afterlife for those who were good. I wondered if heaven was out there mixed in with the twinkling stars.

"Where do we go when we die, Daddy?"

He scrunched up his face a little. I could tell he was thinking about my question.

"Well, honey," he said after a long pause. "Try this. Think about a time before you were born."

I closed my eyes and tried to imagine it. I felt myself floating in space in a sort of light-filled ether. I couldn't feel my body. There was no sound. I sensed people all around me although I couldn't make out who they were. It was like watching a movie, but one in which I was the lead.

"Okay, I did it."

"All right now," he said, squinting, as if he were carefully considering his next words. I loved that about him.

"When you imagined it, did you feel as if you *didn't* exist?"

I didn't even have to think about my answer. "No. I was still me."

The slightest of smiles broke out on his face.

"Well, I think that is what happens after we die. I think we still exist."

THE COTTAGE WHERE I WAS BORN

ME, AGE EIGHTEEN MONTHS,
FACING THE KITCHEN DOOR

House on Birch Avenue, 1957

Backyard pool, 1957

CHAPTER 3: BIRCH AVENUE

I n 1957, we moved from the small country cottage where I was born to a larger fixer-upper on Birch Avenue in town. I was six. Caroline was seven, Tim was four, and Susan three.

At first, I didn't realize that the musty old house with the shabby swimming pool was ours. If I thought about it at all, I probably saw it as a remodeling project we visited on weekends. It didn't seem like someone's home, certainly not ours. Dirty wallpaper, yellowed at the edges, was peeling off the living room walls. Spongy white stuffing poked out of the ripped seats of the red, built-in, Naugahyde dinette set in the kitchen. It looked as if someone had taken a knife to them.

Behind the house was a chaotic grouping of backyard elements in various stages of decay: a decrepit swing set; a rusty incinerator, something I didn't know even existed until then; uneven concrete pavement with large patches of sour grass and wild dandelions poking through its cracks; and a large rectangular swimming pool with decaying leaves floating on yellowish-brown water.

A slatted fence around the pool yard swayed so much that when you opened the gate, it seemed certain to collapse at any moment. The front yard was no better. A dry, weedy lawn ran the length of it. Nothing about this new place was like our sweet country cottage with the tall oat fields behind it that swayed in the breeze and became baskets for us every spring.

A few months after we moved in, sharp stomach pains woke me in the middle of the night. The house was still and dark. My little sister in the twin bed next to mine was sound asleep. When the pain wouldn't stop, I panicked and yelled for my parents. Soon my father was at my bedside, lifting me gently out of bed. He carried me in his arms down the hall to the master bedroom where he settled me in between himself and my mother. My pain temporarily subsided. When it returned, I stretched out my arms and legs in my parents' bed in the pitch-black room to confirm that both of them were still beside me. The pain dissipated again.

These nighttime episodes probably only lasted a few weeks, but they felt interminable to me. I couldn't stop the pain, and I didn't understand how my siblings were able to sleep so soundly. I was certain there was something wrong with me.

Mom kept a close eye on me now. When I started sleep-walking during this same period, she was there to comfort me. I'd wake up in the living room not knowing how I got there. There she and my father would be, reading the nightly newspaper under the light of the mustard-colored floor lamp. I can still recall the startled, quizzical look on my mother's face when I suddenly appeared by her side. I was perplexed, too. She'd jump out of her chair and take my hand tightly in hers.

"Oh, Laurie, honey, let's get you back to bed," she said.

Even in my dazed state, I understood her tone of voice to be one of concern. She walked me back to my room and tucked me in tightly. I wonder if she thought that would do the trick. In the morning, I didn't have any memory of my nocturnal walk-abouts unless she reminded me, and then only in vague images.

One day I overheard my mother on the phone sharing her worries with Nana. What if I managed to leave the house one night, clamber over our rickety side-yard fence, and drown in the pool, she posited to her own mother. She may have been worried, but I wasn't. I didn't want to leave our house. My goal was only to be in the comforting presence of both of my parents.

Instead of letting the four of us kids randomly pick a seat at mealtime, my mother now seated me between her and Dad, a position I kept until I left home at seventeen. While Mom kept a close eye on me, I kept an eye on my father. Though on Sundays the six of us attended Mass at our Catholic parish church, Saturdays were for Dad and me. We gardened, cleaned the pool, and hosed down the sidewalk together. I got to see the landscape through his eyes and to use adult-sized garden tools, hoses, and brooms. My siblings weren't excluded in this; they just didn't seem interested.

One Saturday when I skipped over to the pool yard, my father was nowhere to be found. In a panic, I rushed through the screened door into the kitchen. Mom was at the sink, her face pink from the steam of the hot dishwater.

"Where's Daddy?"

"Your father's at work, Laurie," she said.

Her quick response and lifeless tone told me she didn't appreciate my question. I could tell from the way she bit her lower lip that there was more to say and also that she wouldn't be saying it to me. Still, I pressed on. I asked her why he was at work. It was *our* day, I reminded her. I'd searched in vain for him in the front yard, where I would stoop down next to him while he pruned junipers. He'd snip a little off one of the shrubs and place the trimmings in a neat pile. Before snipping again, he'd lean back to eye his work. His movements in the garden mesmerized me.

"See, Laurie, it's not yet in balance," he'd say.

Even at age six, my eyes could see the imbalance, too. Eventually the shape would be just right. Only then would Dad move on to the next juniper. He also taught me how to pull out the sour-tasting oxalis pushing through the fence along our back property line.

"Don't pull on the roots too hard or they'll break right off," Dad said. "And then you will have to start all over again next weekend."

He guided my hand as it dug deep into the moist soil, and together we slowly retrieved a complete set of roots.

"There you go, sweetie. Now they won't grow back."

Once the plants in the front yard were neatly trimmed, we'd move to the pool yard. Using a metal mesh basket attached to one end of a long pole, something I couldn't yet manage myself, Dad skimmed off the yellow leaves and other debris floating in the pool. He told me the trick to capturing everything was to move the skimmer *very* slowly. I stared at him and his silent back and forth movements, feeling at once calmed and bewitched by his impressive skills. Few if any ripples appeared in the water. I didn't know how anyone could do that.

During his smoking breaks, he'd squat down next to a planting bed and flicked his ashes onto the gravel. This act seemed out of character with his tidy nature. He must have noticed the look of surprise on my face.

"Don't worry, Laurie. The ashes turn into dirt."

While he squatted to smoke, I'd sit on the concrete next to him and made paper chains out of the brightly colored wrappers of his empty cigarette packs. He never wanted to throw anything out and often had a creative use for discards.

To make the paper chains, he schooled me, we had to first smooth out the wrinkled wrappers on the hot concrete. Once flattened, we folded them in thirds, making sure each segment was precisely the same size.

"Watch me first, honey," Dad said. "You have to do it slowly to get it perfect."

Doing things slowly was a theme for him. But over time, we accumulated a pile of paper loops that we'd then use to connect one to the other. I considered the colorful, geometric design of the chains and their thick, chunky feel cute and clever. But the final product bewildered me.

"Now what do we do with them, Daddy?"

"It doesn't matter, honey," he said. "They're pretty. That is reason enough to make them."

I loved that answer, perhaps because it sounded like an adult response, but one I could understand too. That was the thing about conversations with my father. He spoke to me as an equal. I missed him and our playful, creative work on that first Saturday he wasn't there, and on subsequent ones.

"Go out and play now, Laurie," Mom said.

She leaned down to put a shiny, copper-bottomed saucepan in the lower cabinet and glanced back at me. Her face looked pale. She turned away and went back to her housework. I closed the screen door behind me.

I wondered why Dad had to work *that* day. I kicked pebbles around and played tetherball by myself on our small patio but kept one eye on the driveway. Dad eventually pulled up in his car, but only after Mom had called us into dinner.

A few weeks or maybe months later, Dad and I were back to spending Saturdays together. We weeded and watered and performed our artistic endeavors as a team again. I stopped being on the lookout for him, and Mom stopped biting her lower lip, at least for a time. Her volunteer duties at St. Charles School Mother's Club, where she helped plan the school's carnival, kept her busy in the evenings while Dad bathed us, got us into our pajamas, and read us bedtime stories. I never asked him where he was on those Saturdays when he went missing. But the homemade layer cakes and chocolate-frosted angel food cakes Mom baked for the carnival that year seemed an optimistic sign.

CHAPTER 4: THE DINNER PARTY

By the following summer, my night terrors had subsided, and our formerly shabby fixer-upper on Birch Avenue was open for barbecues, pool parties, and formal dinner parties. Mom's friends from the Catholic church lugged their large families, swimwear, and potluck fare over for afternoons of swimming, drinking, and socializing. I turned seven that summer.

The adults, with their highballs and gin and tonics, lounged on the wooden patio chaises with the aqua-and-white-striped cushions. Children played in the pool until we were enticed with the typical summer fare: barbecued hamburgers and hot dogs, macaroni salad speckled with chopped sweet pickles, chunky potato-and-egg salad, and store-bought baked beans warmed in their cans over hot coals.

One of my mother's specialties was a lemon Jell-O mold studded with small chunks of canned pineapple, chopped walnuts, and bits of cream cheese. I couldn't understand how she got the embellishments to float in the Jell-O instead of sinking to the bottom.

"Oh, Laurie, it just works that way," she said. I obviously didn't understand the physics of Jell-O, nor did I understand its important role in the 1950s as an inexpensive dessert for large postwar families.

As a contrast to these relaxed, family-friendly pool parties, the adults-only dinner parties my parents threw during this period were formal affairs. As usual, my father fashioned the table displays with flowers he'd grown and dried himself. Standing on a ladder in the garage before the guests arrived, he selected each bloom or stalk carefully from what looked like a fantastic, painted sky of mustard-colored yarrow and bunches of bright purple statice. Months earlier, he'd plucked them from our garden at their peak of color and hung them upside down from the rafters. I watched in silence as he cradled them in his arms on his steep descent down the tall ladder. I somehow knew without looking that the garages of my neighborhood friends didn't look like ours, and that I was the luckier.

Never a gourmet cook, though a good one, my mother tried her hand at chicken cacciatore, veal scaloppini, and Welsh rarebit, fare considered exotic during the bland food era of the 1950s. And with his talent for attractive visuals, food and otherwise, Dad assumed charge of the desserts. On one particular evening, his treat was a fanciful-looking mixture of thinly sliced purple grapes suspended in a frozen mixture of vanilla ice cream and fresh strawberry sauce which he then poured into a rectangular metal mold. He'd shown us an image of it on the cover of one of Mom's *McCall's* magazines weeks earlier and promised he'd one day create it for us. He kept his promise.

Three couples from the church arrived in elegant attire— women in tightly belted, colorful dresses and men in stiff-collared, cufflinked shirts under dinner jackets. My two sisters, brother, and I mumbled our polite hellos in the living room as directed. Our mother then banished us to the stuffy rumpus room at the back of the house that doubled as Tim's bedroom. Our babysitter, an elderly lady from the church, dealt out our coveted Swanson turkey TV dinners on our own TV trays, those stackable plastic tables new to us at the time, and turned on *The Adventures of Ozzie and Harriet*. Before the show ended, Dad called us from the end of the hallway.

"Kids! I'm taking it out now!"

We knew what that meant and stampeded down the hallway. Dad had already submerged the metal mold in a large pan of hot water in the kitchen sink. In a serious voice he informed us of the need to take great care with this particular step so that none of the steaming hot water would spill over the top of the mold and into the dessert. "That would simply *ruin* it," he said while keeping his focus on the complex action at hand.

After counting to ten, he carefully lifted the mold out of the water. He placed a large platter on top of it before flipping it over. In what appeared like slow motion to me, he lifted up the metal container by its thin edges. Four sets of very wide eyes watched in wonder as the pinkish-purple dessert magically slid out onto the platter with a delightful *plop*, wobbling for a minute or two until finally coming to rest.

"Wow!" Dad said.

There was a moment of silence as he stood back to admire his creation before pulling out a knife and running it under hot water. With the warm knife, he slowly cut slices of his attractive dessert, all of which surprisingly looked like the exact same width to me. Next, he slid the fancy sterling silver cake server out of its protective red velvet pouch and used it to gently lay out the slices out on dessert plates, one by one. Miraculously, it seemed to me, the grape slices were spread out evenly throughout the ice cream mixture as if they were floating in pink clouds. I figured he and Mom shared a special secret, one which they alone knew, that allowed them to keep fruit and other tidbits of food indefinitely suspended in desserts.

On top of the slices, Dad scattered a few whole purple and green grapes that he'd previously frozen and briefly let thaw. Tiny droplets of water clung to them like snow-covered jewels.

Before our father returned to host the company, he handed the four of us our own plates of the dessert to take back to the rumpus room. I was happy to find out that it tasted as good as it looked, all at once sweet and tart and creamy. I could feel myself burst with respect and pride for my father.

As the evening wore on, the music in the living room grew louder. *Tennessee Waltz* blared out of our new hi-fi, the same record Dad played when he danced with me perched on top of his shoes. I snuck back down the unlit hallway. The sight of my parents gliding across the living room together kept me planted in the dark. The two of them moved in sync as if they were one. I felt warmth and tenderness deep in my chest as I watched my mother's golden-red hair sway with the music, her spiky, powder-blue high heels floating above the floor. The eyes of the three couples standing off to one side were as fixated on my parents as mine were.

Near the end of the record, I caught my parents staring into each other's eyes, holding their gazes for a moment or two. At age seven, I was already a practiced scout in my own house, ever on the lookout for signs of affection between my parents. I skipped back down the hallway, buoyed by a rare glimpse of my parents' romantic feelings for each other.

Our babysitter's eyes were now glued to *The Lawrence Welk Show*. The Lennon Sisters, clad in their pink chiffon dresses, swayed in sync as they sang one of their sugary sweet songs. Caroline must have retreated to her bedroom. Tim was on the floor playing with Lincoln Logs. Susan was sound asleep, curled up on Tim's green corduroy bedspread.

The music in the living room stopped. With the babysitter distracted by the harmonizing sisters, I snuck back down the hallway for one last look from my darkened lookout. My father was sitting in a dining room chair that was now planted in the middle of the living room. His necktie was uncharacteristically loosened, and his collar hung limply over his unbuttoned shirt. Hanging precariously over one of the chair's stiles was his dinner jacket. The most disturbing part of this picture, though, was Violet, the pretty, olive-skinned Italian friend of my mother's. She sat on his lap with her left arm draped around my father's neck—*all* the way around. She crossed one of her long, toned legs high above the other, twirling one of her glossy, pointy high heels round and round. I hoped it wouldn't fall off and require my father's assistance in retrieving it and sliding her foot back in.

I tiptoed in closer. From there I could make out Violet's dark red lipstick and flushed cheeks. She squealed in a high voice while caressing my father's face. "Oh, Ralph," she said, while petting his balding head. Dad grinned goofily. His eyes darted around, seeking an escape, I thought. I hoped, anyway. I scanned the room for my mother, but she was nowhere in sight. Maybe she was in the kitchen cleaning up. I stomped back down the hall and watched the last few minutes of *Lawrence Welk* with the babysitter, clutching my stomach against a gnawing, familiar pain. Something untoward was going on right there in our living room. I was certain of it.

CHAPTER 5: MORE REVELATIONS

On the day I'd unwittingly nudged my father out of the closet, the weather on the mountain was hot, too hot for me. But as a native of California's Central Valley accustomed to its scorching summer temperatures, Dad seemed to revel in it. He wasn't wearing a hat or even sunglasses that day. Our banter was clipped and casual on the dirt trail up one side of the mountain. I wondered aloud how the perky blue lupines could live in the dry, gravelly earth with the unrelenting heat.

"Over time they adapted to a hostile environment," Dad said. "They had to, or they wouldn't have survived."

With Jody under the loving care of her grandmother, it didn't take long for me to realize the opportunity this private trek with my father offered. When I asked him if he'd ever been unfaithful to Mom, and he answered by telling me he was gay, I wanted to protest. I wanted to tell him that wasn't the question I had asked. But I'd gone mute. By contrast, stories poured out of him. Above the ringing in my ears, which was more like a roar, I caught some clips.

I knew when I was five. I also knew I should conceal it.

I wondered if there was anyone else in the world like me. Should I just throw myself off the plateau?

I ran home every day from school. The other boys stoned me. I didn't dare fall because it would have been worse.

On the one hand, I was hearing a series of awful stories, and on the other hand, I was negotiating in my mind. The narrowest of stereotypes came to me. *The man over whom my mother's girlfriends swooned was gay? The father we begged to flex his bulging biceps was gay?* I must have looked bewildered, but I guessed from Dad's faraway look that he didn't notice. We were each in our own worlds now.

"One of my earliest memories is of seeing my uncle naked," he said.

My eyes scanned the earth beneath me. With one foot, I pushed the loose dirt around, my mind racing with the unwanted image of a young boy staring longingly at a naked adult man. I can still recall every word of this story.

"Uncle Paul was about nineteen at the time," he said. "He was in the Navy and staying at the house for a few days during a furlough. I walked by his room one morning and caught sight of him climbing out of bed. He was completely nude. I had never seen such a beautiful sight. He was tall and muscular. And his skin was the color of gold. I knew at that moment I was attracted to men. But I didn't have a name for it."

The tanned dome of Dad's balding head glistened in the hot sun while his words spilled out of his mouth with a disturbingly delirious joy. I wondered if he was suggesting that Uncle Paul made him gay. Staring at the sharp, brownish-gray rocks not far from my powder-blue sneakers, I batted them around from one foot to the other. As Dad rambled on, my thoughts got louder. Then it came to me. Maybe he's gay, but he's Mom's straight husband *too*. While I was busy hoping for that, Dad kept going.

"The boys in grammar school bullied me and called me a sissy."

I again fell into stereotypes. My father was the manliest of men to me, I thought, a man who just happened to enjoy flower arranging and musicals and styling our hair and selecting our clothes. I'd long told myself he was just more modern than the other dads in the neighborhood, a fact that made me proud of him and our family. It was I who was the lucky child.

"They took off my pants and left me in the middle of the schoolyard. The girls all stared at me. I could tell they pitied me. That was the worst part. It was horrible, honey. I was afraid all the time."

I'd known as a child that my father was taller than the other boys in his class. He was also good-looking and excelled to such a degree that his teachers skipped him a grade. Then they skipped him *again*. He was by all accounts a successful, confident boy and then young man.

However, I knew he wasn't like the others because he told me so. He even appeared boastful when talking about writing poetry while his brother and the other boys roughnecked and played football and baseball. He crocheted, gardened, and arranged flowers for his mother. His favorite flowers, he said, were the black-eyed Susans that lined the drainage ditches near their home.

His paternal grandmother taught him to make lace—to tat—something they did together after school. Of course, he would have been bullied by other boys in the 1920s and 1930s in the conservative Central Valley oil town where he grew up. He was the more sophisticated one. But that was about as far as I'd ever gone with it.

Dad continued.

"I would hike over to the top of that huge plateau outside Fellows after school and look out into the distance and ask God if there was anyone else in the world like me. I didn't want to live."

While my heart was stung by this new story, Dad in contrast thrust his chest out, unable or unwilling to contain the grin on his face while telling me the grimmest of stories. Stuffing my own feelings, I searched for words to match his upbeat demeanor. At twenty-four, I hoped to sound sophisticated, as in, "Of course you're gay, Dad." After all, I'd come of age during the free-spirited sixties. I was familiar with the gay rights parades and protests in nearby San Francisco. As much as I thought about these activities at all, I supported them. I willed myself not to burst my father's bubble.

"I understand, Dad. Grandma Hall was domineering, and Grandpa was distant."

I cringed at his kind but wry smile in response.

"Yes," he said. "I've heard that theory."

His tone was gentle and fatherly, not demeaning. But what I heard beneath his words was, *It's all right, Laurie. One day you'll understand I was born this way.* Embarrassed by my own naïveté, I changed the subject.

"Do you love Mom?"

When he didn't immediately respond to my plaintive plea, I had my answer.

He jingled Daisy's metal leash in his hand. Out she wriggled from under a stand of manzanita shrubs. She must have been hunkering down there all this time, maybe spying a still lizard or camouflaging herself from the birds scratching at the bare earth nearby. Dad cleared his throat. I planted my Keds hard in the soil.

"To be able to say I love you and mean it, and to have someone say the same thing back to you . . . well, I think that is the most important thing in life."

DUANE HALL (YOUNG BOY ON THE RIGHT), SIX YEARS, 1924

DUANE, AGE TWELVE, 1930

His voice was a deep baritone now, the one he used when he was singing, serious, or sad. I grasped hard to my hope, compromised as it was, where he'd say he loved Mom and he loved men, *too*.

"But I don't love your mother that way," he said.

I must have gone numb at that point, because I didn't feel angry or sad.

"Uh," I stuttered. "Does she know?"

I was aware of my voice trailing off. I couldn't even say the word *gay*. Dad lowered his gaze and swallowed repeatedly, his large Adam's apple bobbing up and down. I braced myself.

"Yes, honey." He took a deep breath. "She found out on Birch Avenue. It was 1957."

I didn't make the connection in that moment, but that was the year I started sleepwalking and experiencing stomach pangs in the middle of the night. I was six.

I closed my eyes in order to concentrate. So, Mom had known the truth that day in the kitchen when she retold the details of their romantic first meeting for the umpteenth time. She knew when she'd bragged about how Dad had so many girlfriends before her, too, and had been engaged multiple times.

"It was horrible, honey," Dad said. "Your mother found some photos. She called me at work in hysterics. I thought one of you kids had been hit by a car."

He pursed his lips and dropped his gaze again, as if the memories were too much for him to bear. They were too much for me to bear. His eyes filmed over with a faraway gaze but then abruptly came back to our perch on the mountain. Maybe he decided he had gone far enough with me for one day. I'd have to learn the details of that event another time. I turned toward the view of the murky, reddish-brown salt flats below us.

"Laurie, I'm sorry," Dad said, his voice returning to a familiar fatherly tone. My shoulders relaxed.

The sun was now halfway down the horizon. Elongated shadows from the nearby ancient oak tree covered my shoes. Dinner would be ready soon. Afterward my mother would serve slices of one of her signature fruit pies with a scoop of vanilla ice cream on top.

Dad took a deep breath and slowly blew it out as if he were exhaling cigarette smoke. But he wasn't smoking.

LOOKING AT THE SAND CRABS,
HALF MOON BAY, 1956

PARASOLS FOR EVERYONE, JAPANESE TEA GARDEN,
SAN FRANCISCO, 1955

CHAPTER 6: FAMILY DAYS

Starting when I was seven until I was about nine, our family seemed to move as one. There were summer road trips, bountiful Christmases and birthdays, stylish home improvements, and visits to amusement parks and to adoring grandparents. My nighttime stomach pains ceased.

I couldn't have conjured up more exotic grandparents than Grandma and Grandpa Hall, who lived in the Central Valley. Their warm embraces and sweet Southern drawl from their Missouri farm days stood in contrast to my mother's stern and proper family from New York, Chicago, and Minneapolis.

Santa Claus brought pretty baby dolls in lacy pink dresses for Susan and me. Tim got a BB gun and more Lincoln Logs and Caroline a record player, a 45 of Elvis Presley's "All Shook Up," and a selection of books from *The Happy Hollisters* series, which I at first thought were named *The Happy Halls*. Grandma Hall sent us soft matching pajamas she made out of recycled flannel robes. On Christmas Eve, Nana gave us girls fancy sweaters from the City of Paris in San Francisco where she worked as a salesclerk.

During this time, the four of us kids also got a fancy new mother. Mom now had her hair professionally styled at the beauty parlor once a week. Before then, the only hairstyle I'd known for her was a short bob. I'd seen old photos of her Titian-blond hair styled in a wavy updo studded with purple orchids from the garden. But Dad had done the styling then.

"Oh, your father used to *love* fixing my hair," she said with a gleam in her eye. I guessed at the time she was thrilled to have such a talented husband. I never thought about whether or not other husbands styled their wives' hair or studded them with fresh-picked flowers. As usual, I just thought my father was more artistic than other fathers in the neighborhood.

Fridays during this era were high points. We never knew what our mother's hair would look like when we got home from school. I remember rushing up the front walkway, savoring the anticipation. One week, Mom's hair was teased high on top of her head and down the sides. The bottom flipped up a little. I thought the look was pretty on her—soft, poufy, and stylish. For Sunday Mass that week, she wore a satin turquoise pillbox hat on top of it, the netting circling the base of that spectacular bouffant.

Another week it was a beehive. This time, the top of her head resembled a cone. In the back was a vertical twist. I thought it a severe look—like it might have been painful for her—but my father complimented her on it. I wondered how she slept.

When she disassembled her beehive and twist the next week, a few of us kids gathered around her dressing table. I was hoping for clues as to its mysterious assembly. I would not be disappointed. Buried deep inside that twist were dozens of black bobby pins. It took her a long time to get them all out, which made this particular hairdo even more intriguing to me. I can still hear the *plink, plink, plink* of the metal pins being dropped, one by one, into the dainty, pink glass dish on her ruffled dressing table as the twist slowly unraveled.

Our house got dolled up during this period, too. The new kitchen appliances were all in. We still had the maple colonial furniture from the country cottage—the hutch, rocking chair, and dining room set—but Dad had added contemporary touches, like a mustard-colored floor lamp and a huge hi-fi cabinet with a turntable on one side, a radio on the other, and two large cloth-covered speakers beneath them. He purchased an upright piano for the living room in the hopes his children would learn to play. Caroline took piano lessons for many years, but I was bored after a few months. Tim took guitar lessons when he was eight and has played and sung ever since. Susan never showed any interest in a musical instrument.

Dad painted our living room walls, now freed of their dingy, old-fashioned wallpaper, in a soft, cream color. He arranged prints of Van Gogh's *Irises*, Monet's *Water Lilies*, the *Gettysburg Address*, and my mother's photos of rocky Monterey outcrops and young children at the beach on our freshly painted walls. Mom had studied photography in high school and worked for commercial photo labs during World War II. Toward the end of the war, the US Army Signal Corps hired her to take photos of German prisoners-of-war at Fort Ord, California. When she wasn't doing housework, holding "fussy" babies, or singing in the church choir, she usually had a camera in her hands.

Once the interior remodeling and decorating of our house was complete, Dad spent most weekends out in the garden. I can see him now, out in the pool yard, tanned, muscular, and focused.

I'm sitting by the side of the pool, my feet dangling in the unheated water. Dad is squatting on the bed of river rock gravel next to the pool deck. All he's wearing are his black, blue-and-olive-green, horizontally striped, swim trunks—not baggy shorts but not tight Speedos either—and turquoise flip-flops. His legs and shoulders are a shiny, deep reddish brown, the color resulting, he told me, not from sunburn but from his Native American great-grandmother's heritage. It stayed that color all winter long, so I believed him.

He's in a trance. I don't interrupt him. He creates something from abandoned, rusty iron rims he'd sal- vaged from the oilfield landscape of his childhood, some six inches in diameter, some larger. He has already painted them a pinkish-salmon color—a color popular in the 1950s for swimming pool decor—and has now hung them up by a nail on the pool fence. They're each at a different height, but once they're all up, they look like they're an integral part of a set.

Dad leans back to evaluate the first stage of his project and goes back to adjust one of the tiny rims a little bit higher. Apparently pleased with the arrange- ment, he starts in on the next design phase.

By his side is a tidy pile of twigs, the dead wood plucked from the front yard junipers and the large fig tree next to the back door. Each twig's shape is unique, and their tan-and-brown bark is shiny and smooth. Dad places them, one by one, on the lower part of the rims. He adjusts the little piles this way and that until they are just so. With his slim build, Dad reminds me of a bird arranging twigs and pine needles for its offspring.

Once he has achieved the look he wants—a mix between a nest and an artsy wooden sculpture—he positions half clamshells, sand dollars, and tiny conchs from San Gregorio Beach around the edges. Dried stalks from the tall flax in our front yard and long, leathery seedpods from a mimosa tree down the street he pokes in between the twigs. One or two perfect, plump pinecones, fallen from a neighbor's tree, com- plete the ensemble. Dad had scooped them out of our rain gutters and saved them for this special occasion.

After what feels like a long dream to me, Dad straightens himself up. He backs down slowly over the sloped gravel bed to the swimming pool's beveled

edge. There he squats again and assesses the whole,
taking a long, deep breath as he does. He lets it out as
he turns to look at me with a joyful look in his eyes.
I smile back.

There were many dreamy days like this for me on Birch Avenue after my scary period was over. When it came time to redo the front yard, Dad took a bold approach. He removed half the lawn due to its high water demands, a practice that became popular in California during the drought years of the 1970s, more than twenty years later. He replanted the space with a large bed of low, drought-tolerant evergreens, which he then sculpted, Japanese-style, into what looked to me like a miniature forest.

Around this tiny woodland, he planted desert succulents, arranging them in intricate patterns next to odd-shaped chunks of smooth, graying driftwood he'd collected over at the beach where Pescadero Creek met the Pacific Ocean. Except for the Japanese Tea Garden, I'd never seen a garden so beautiful or interesting. I felt proud of our front yard in contrast to the others with only lawns. I was proud of my talented father, too, though much of the vegetation he chose was ill suited to our environment. The Peninsula was too cool for the desert plants he planted and too dry for the coastal ones. Most struggled to thrive where they were now rooted. Dad never gave up trying, though.

With Susan at the Santa Cruz Boardwalk, 1962

CHAPTER 7: THE BOARDWALK

A sliver of bright morning light shining through the gap in the curtains woke me up. I didn't recognize the curtains. My bed wasn't my own. There were no plinking sounds of Wheat Chex squares dropping into hard plastic cereal bowls. Nor was Mom bellowing out, "Chop, chop, kids," signalizing us to wake up, make our beds, and slip into our school uniforms before breakfast. Instead, she was singing about the cost of a doggie in the window.

I sat up in bed. The pungent smell of salt air and seaweed reminded me that we were in Santa Cruz, that fantastical combination of beach, boardwalk, midway games, fun house, roller coaster, and the ever present scent of suntan lotion. Back then it was all about suntans, not sun blocks. I was ten. Draped over the footboard of my temporary bed were my white denim cutoffs, navy terry swimsuit, and blue checkered shirt. My mother must have put them there after I'd gone to sleep. I slipped into them quickly and rushed out to the main part of the rental house. My siblings were ready to go.

Mom loaded the four of us up with straw-basket totes jammed with striped beach towels, hooded sweatshirts, and green plastic bottles of Sea & Ski. Everything else we'd buy on the boardwalk. She led us down the gently sloped hill to the wharf, holding tightly to Susan's hand. The other three of us followed in single file until we reached the crosswalk.

"Come on now," she said. "Stay close to me."

She'd been hit by a car when she was a little girl, which heightened her vigilance about her children's safety. While we waited for permission to cross, I placed my hand under her white summer purse and lifted it up just a little. It was heavy. I smiled. It meant inside her purse were rolls of dimes for us for boardwalk fare.

"Okay, kids, it's safe now."

We first hit a diner on the wharf for breakfast. Large platters of tiny "silver dollar" pancakes, mounds of whipped butter, and warm syrup in tiny individual pitchers covered our table. A lull settled in while we ate, but once the sugar kicked in, we were fidgety and turned our sights to the boardwalk in full view out the restaurant's bay windows.

One of us would usually plead with our mother to *please* finish her pancakes and leave the payment. On vacations, at least, she smiled at these types of pesky demands. She didn't tell us to wipe the syrup off our chins, or go use the bathroom, or sit still while she finished her coffee, even if her cup was full. Instead, she turned all the way around in her seat to wave the waitress over. Reaching for her straw hat on the coat hook behind her, she seemed as excited for the day's activities as we were. I loved this about her.

The four of us knew the drill because we'd done it before. Mom located a centralized spot on the beach and guided us down the boardwalk's sandy, wooden steps to it. Two of us grabbed the corners of her large beach blanket as she grabbed the other two. Once it hit the sand, someone else anchored it down with flip-flops and suntan lotion and whatever else would keep it down if the wind kicked up.

"Watch everything until I get back," she said.

Mom scurried back up the steps to rent a large striped canvas umbrella. Before long she was sitting in the shade on a low beach chair with a stack of magazines and four sets of outstretched hands at her side. Peeling back the red wrapper on a roll of dimes, she dispensed five dimes apiece. "This is to start with," she said.

Off we scattered, even five-year-old Susan, since at least here Mom didn't have to worry about cars. Plus, we were all good swimmers from years of lessons. From this point on, the four of us, all under the age of ten on this visit, were free to do whatever we wanted until the sun got low on the horizon.

I ran up to the boardwalk where I shot tiny corks at bull-seyes for miniature prizes, threw small rubber balls at towers of milk bottles, and tossed rings over an assortment of toys in the hopes of winning one. I was pretty good at the carnival games but quickly ran out of dimes. By then I was also hot. I skipped down the steps back to Mom and stripped down to my bathing suit.

"Don't burn your feet on the hot sand," she shouted.

I ran to the water's edge as fast as I could and waded out into the cool water until it reached my waist. I dove under water the same way I dove off our diving board at home. But our swimming pool didn't have waves. Suddenly I was in the grip of a powerful one that tossed me in circles. I lost track of which way was up and hit my head on the sandy bottom. Gasping for air, I instead gulped mouthfuls of saltwater. All at once, I shot out of the surf. Nearby, kids were swimming and laughing and tossing colorful beach balls up in the air. None of them, it seemed, had noticed I'd temporarily gone missing. A nervous smile on my face, I swam hard back to shore.

Mom was settled comfortably in her chair with one of her magazines opened on her lap. Under her wide-brimmed hat and dark sunglasses, I could tell she was happy. I wouldn't burden her with the details of my scare. Besides, I was hungry. It was time for another handful of dimes from her, enough to buy a hot dog or a hamburger, fries, and a Shasta soda.

I allowed a moment for my eyes to adjust to the dark in the cave-like diner on the boardwalk before I entered. I ordered a Shasta vanilla cola and a foot-long hot dog with fancy grill marks on it and slid into one side of a metal picnic table.

Warm saltwater from my suit pooled up around me and dripped onto the sandy, concrete floor. The sand in my swimsuit felt gritty underneath me. But I felt proud. I wasn't someone's child as I ate the lunch fare I'd ordered and paid for on my own. I picked out the flavor of cola I wanted, even though I needed the clerk's assistance with the beer can opener. There would be no competition with my siblings over who had the most gold threads in their plastic placemat. I wasn't surveying my parents, hopeful for signs of affection or anxious over signs of disappointment or betrayal. My shoulders were relaxed. Even though I was out of range of my mother, I felt safe all by myself. I took my time eating that gigantic, striped hot dog.

During these summer vacations to Santa Cruz, when my mother had seemed so happy and carefree, she'd already lived through the shock of learning Dad was gay. I don't know how she could have ever been happy again after finding that out. One of Nana's stories gave me a clue, though.

Money was scarce when my mother was growing up during the Great Depression. For Christmas, Nana bought one gift for each of her three children, practical ones like socks or a sweater. According to Nana, after Mom opened up her gift, no matter what it was she'd squeal with delight. To demonstrate, Nana raised her hands high in the air and shook them. Mom would then wrap her gift back up and tape it closed. Moments later, she'd reopen it and squeal with the same level of surprise as the first time. She'd do this half a dozen or so times throughout Christmas Day, Nana said.

"Oh, Laurie, you should have seen her," she said, smiling. "She got the biggest thrill out of it!"

Nana didn't seem sad that her young daughter pretended to receive more presents than she did. I smiled at the cute mental images she painted for me of my mother at six. I wondered how anyone could fool herself like that. I realized how much I resembled my mother, though. Anyone who observed my demeanor the day after Dad came out to me might have thought I was thrilled with the news. Or at the very least that it was of no consequence at all.

I never thought to ask my mother why Dad never joined us on these overnight summer trips to Santa Cruz. Then again, he wasn't a fan of amusement parks, or parks in general. But the wild beaches along the San Mateo County coastline were different.

With our fixer-upper's large indoor remodeling projects and outdoor landscaping nearly complete, Saturdays were freed up for day trips for the whole family. Pescadero State Beach, thirty miles down the coast, was one of our regular destinations.

It was foggy and windy when we arrived one day. This was not unusual for Northern California's beaches. We'd keep our shoes on that day. Dad eyed something in the swash zone and squatted down. He waved us over, warning us to keep one eye on the rough surf.

"Come see the sand crabs, kids! Hurry, before the next wave hits."

And there they were, tiny, gray-shelled creatures burrowing into the sand as a wave retreated back to the sea. From my father's excitement, it seemed he felt that nature was putting on a show just for him, a most appreciative audience of one. I was curious about the crabs and his other finds at the beach but never as excited as he was. His enthusiasm was enough to fill up the space all around us. Soon the soft-shelled crabs scrambled from view. My siblings had dispersed, too.

"But look, Laurie," he said, pointing with a stick. "See those indentations in the sand? They can't completely hide."

I didn't understand how the crabs could survive underground, but Dad assured me they were safe where they were. They'd come out again when they felt safe, perhaps when the next wave hit, cloaking them in foam and making them invisible to predators.

Mom called us over to lunch. She had laid out everything on an old tablecloth she spread out on the sand and weighted down with an assortment of rocks and driftwood. It was windy and we needed to eat quickly.

"We don't want to get *sand* in our *sand*wiches!" Dad chuckled. He always enjoyed a good play on words.

Whatever leftover bit of trunk space was available in our car, Dad filled with chunks of ocean-tumbled wood he collected on our way back to the car.

"See how beautiful and soft this one is," he told me, "Here, touch it."

My siblings were already in the car, but I stayed with him to rub my hand over the smooth, silvery piece of wood. I wondered how it came to be there on the beach. I wondered how long it had been tumbling under a dark sea until it found its way into the light of day and, ultimately, as a prized artifact in my father's garden.

CHAPTER 8: DISNEYLAND
AND THE OILFIELDS

In the summer of 1960, we piled into our brand-new white Dodge Dart station wagon before sunup. I was nine. Our destination was Disneyland, which had opened five years earlier in Southern California.

Along the way, we'd spend a few days with Grandma and Grandpa Hall, who lived on an oilfield. My father grew up in the oilfields. I grew up hearing the language of the oilfields from him. His parents lived on an *oil lease* in Oildale. The house where they lived was owned by the oil company that owned the land. When I was little, I didn't understand the term *lease* and associated it with a place where faraway grandparents lived. This otherworldly landscape was dotted with *pumpjacks*, which we called big grasshoppers, and *oil derricks*, the wooden framework that supported the drilling apparatus.

Oildale was a five-hour drive from San Carlos through California's Central Valley. Our new station wagon had dark-blue seats and no air conditioning. Except for Dad, acclimated from childhood to the summer heat, the rest of us were miserable in the hundred-plus-degree temperatures. We left before sunup to escape as much of the searing heat as we could, but we couldn't escape it all.

Mom spent much of our trip trying to keep her four fidgety, overheated children from whining and tussling with each other, periodically doling out Mr. Peanut bars to us, the one candy bar that didn't melt. Dad distracted us with stories and roadside interests. When we reached Gilroy's garlic fields, he straightened up in the driver's seat, rolled down the window with his left hand, and inhaled deeply. It was a sign we could open ours, too, knowing our mother wouldn't complain too much about the hot wind blowing things around in our car.

"It is the most glorious of all smells, kids!" Dad said.

I was inclined to agree, partly due to my father's enthusiasm. The fragrance was both sweet and pungent. Also, garlic smells and large *Gilroy* signs meant we were nearing Pacheco Pass, the mountain crossing connecting Highway 101 to I-5. Awaiting us at the top of the pass was a restaurant with pancake breakfasts. This wasn't our first trip south.

On one visit, the restaurant's cute individual pitchers of warm maple syrup that came with our plate-size pancakes caught Mom's eye. She picked one up and eyed it from different angles, being careful not to spill any of its contents. I could tell from her focused attention that she hoped to add it to her windowsill collection. But our waitress refused Mom's offer of payment, instead quickly wrapping up one of the sticky empties in a used paper napkin and handing it to her.

"Go ahead," she said. "Just put it in your purse."

Mom, blushing now, tucked it into her straw tote bag and from then on told the story to anyone who complimented this particular find on her sunny window ledge.

"I couldn't believe it," she said. "The waitress was so sweet."

By contrast, my father's tastes leaned toward the expensive, elegant, and artistic. A gift shop inside the restaurant was a favorite of his. It carried pottery from local craftsmen and

colored glass from international artists. On this day, a bud
vase made in Sweden caught his eye. Its solid square base with
rounded edges, the long narrow neck, and a freeform lip at the
top made it more a piece of art than a utilitarian item. Holding
the cobalt-blue vase up to the window, Dad called out to me.
He knew I loved the color blue as much as he did.

"Laurie, look at how *gorgeous* this is," he said.

Catching the bright rays of the early morning light, it really
was beautiful. It came home with us, but not in a sticky, used
paper napkin. This find was wrapped carefully in multiple
layers of magenta-colored tissue inside an embossed gift bag.

Once back on the road, our eyes darted around for the
first sign of a pumpjack. It would be another sign, this one
signaling ever closer proximity to our grandparents. I can't
recall which one of us kids made the first sighting on that day,
but silhouetted against the sky on a distant hill, we saw a single
black pump, rhythmically moving up and down, up and down.
The slow, precise intervals of movement reminded me of the
metronome Dad kept on the top of our piano.

The silence in our car was immediate, as if we were all in a
trance. Soon we spied a few more of them dotting the landscape.
Following these scant early sightings, we'd soon descend into a
flat valley filled with hundreds of them as if the first ones were
merely scouts testing the waters, or, in this case, the oil.

"Quick, kids, look!"

Dad had spotted a tumbleweed. It blew quickly across the
highway and the barren field on the other side. Next came the
black-eyed Susans, which bloomed in a straight line along the
edge of the two-lane highway.

"I used to walk alongside these for miles when I was a
boy," Dad said, his voice trailing off. "They always looked like
they were smiling at me."

I wondered why he was walking for miles alone when he
was little, and why the yellow flowers with the black button-like

centers grew in a straight line. But something about this story made me keep my questions to myself. The important thing was that they made him happy.

"Okay, kids, keep your eyes open now for the mud hens!"

These marsh birds, native to swamps and other low-lying wetlands, also lived here in concrete culverts, the drainage channels edging the road. They blend in with the mud they paddle around in, thus their name. But their camouflage made them hard to spot.

"There, over there!" Dad shouted, slowing the car and waving on the impatient drivers behind us on the two-lane road.

"Just focus your eyes in one spot. Soon they'll come into view."

At first, I couldn't see anything. But soon enough, after I focused for a minute or two, they appeared, looking like small mud balls bobbing up and down in the muck.

"Roll down your window, Irene," Dad said. The hens were on her side of the car. "Let's see if the kids can hear them."

And we did. It was a cacophony of insistently cheery screeches from those funny looking, mud-encrusted hens. After a few minutes Dad sped off, the billowing dust from our fast-moving tires enveloping both our car and our view.

The final leg of our trip was straight, flat, and warmer as we traveled further inland toward the oilfields. Caroline might have told Tim to stop crowding her. Susan was probably attempting to crawl over the front seats. Mom would have been telling us all to "*sit still*," emphasizing each of the two words separately. Our foggy Peninsula town hadn't prepared us for this relentless heat.

At what felt to me like a breaking point, Dad pulled off onto the dirt driveway of a *Big Orange* roadside stand. Clouds of dust again billowed up all around us. The car's tires skidded on the loose gravel until we jerked to a sudden stop. I couldn't tell if Dad was happy for a cold drink or irked at the delay brought on by his increasingly fidgety brood.

"Keep your windows rolled up!" Mom shouted.

Once the light brown dirt particles around us settled, Mom herded us out of the car, one by one, telling us to hurry and get under the shade of the orange-striped awning that stretched out beyond the roadside stand. As a fair-skinned redhead, she knew all too well the damage the Central Valley sun and dry air could do to her four fair-skinned children.

She ordered cups of ice-cold orange juice squeezed fresh by a cheerily dressed vendor right before our eyes. Mom handed each of us one as soon as the sweet, sticky juice reached the top of one of the waxy paper cups. This rare treat, one we'd need to finish before getting back into the car to prevent sticky car seats and door handles, would have to see us to our final destination of the day.

Fine particles of sun-bleached dirt again engulfed our station wagon on the long, unpaved road through the Poso Creek Oil Field to Grandma and Grandpa Hall's house on the oil lease. An abundance of oil derricks, pumpjacks, and the occasional runaway tumbleweed dotted the flat dry riverbed. We only noticed the dirt-colored, tall-eared jackrabbits when they bounced away like coiled springs as we neared them.

Ollie and Grace burst through their screened front door before our car even came to a stop. They must have seen us coming. Grandma Hall was dressed in a short-sleeved, periwinkle-blue dress that had a touch of white lace around the collar, quite a contrast to the dusty monotone landscape of the oilfields. Her face was pink, round, and pretty.

"Well, hello, punkins," she called out, drawing out each word. "Come on over to Grandma *right this minute*." When it was my turn, I fell into her soft embrace. She smelled of talcum powder and lavender.

Grandpa Hall was a stocky man who smelled of oil even in clean clothing. As an oilfield roustabout, his job was to maintain the pumps and oil well heads. When he wasn't wearing his oil-stained work coveralls, he wore high-waisted slacks and white sleeveless, ribbed undershirts that showed off his thick, brown, muscled arms. While Grandma prepared our early dinner, Grandpa bounced me (and probably my siblings, too) on his knee and sang silly songs to us. In one, Davy Crockett became Davy Socket. While he sang, I poked my finger into a deep indentation on the top of his head, the result of an oilfield injury. At age nine, I figured all grandpas were scented with crude oil and came with holes in their heads.

Mom, whose face was now a flushed red from the heat, steered the four of us kids through the front screened door. Dad and Grandpa lingered outside.

"Ollie, Duane, come on in now," Grandma soon called from her kitchen window.

I didn't think it unusual that my father had one name at home—Ralph—but was called Duane by his parents. It had always been that way. I loved the way Grandma stretched out Dad's name, Duuu . . . *ane*. Duuu . . . *ane*.

Grandma set out a platter of fried chicken, a bowl piled high with mashed potatoes speckled with black pepper, two pitchers of light brown gravy, and a serving bowl of mixed peas and carrots. For dessert she served us her homemade boysenberry cobbler.

At sunrise the next morning, when outdoor temps were tolerable, Grandma set up a mud pie station under an awning in her backyard. Caroline carefully sifted handfuls of the dirt beneath our feet with one of Grandma's kitchen strainers and tossed any pebbles off the side of the table. Once the pile of sifted dirt was large enough for a full batch, whatever my talented baker of an older sister deemed the correct quantity to be, Grandpa led us out to his large, metal Quonset hut on the property where he popped off the foil caps from a few of his five-gallon bottles of water. These would do for mud pie molds. I wondered what our next step would be, what

Caroline would want to do with our perfect-looking pies that weren't pies at all. But I decided not to chance any disapproval by asking the question.

After a few days with our delightful grandparents in their delightful oilfield, we were back on the road. Our next destination was a visit to Uncle Seedy. He lived in Alhambra, about ten miles north of Disneyland, our ultimate destination. Red shrubs shaped into box-like shapes framed the front door of his one-story bungalow.

"Hop out of the car now, kids," Dad said. "We're at Uncle Seedy's house!"

Dad had mentioned him before in reference to the classical literature volumes on our bookshelves, or the covered painted jar he kept on his armoire, or a tiny painting of a mother and child above his dresser. Uncle Seedy, he said, had given them to him "a long time ago." Sometimes he called him by another name, Clarence.

"Well, hello," Dad said, putting his hand out to shake Uncle Seedy's hand at the front door.

The warm, rich tone of my father's greeting suggested he was seeing a cherished friend. He didn't sound this way when he greeted the husbands of my Mom's church friends.

Clarence was tall and slim, maybe a few inches taller than Dad's height of five feet eleven inches. He wore creased brown slacks and a white, long-sleeved shirt under a thin, tan-colored knit vest. His gray-flecked black hair was combed to one side, and the black-rimmed glasses he wore were perfectly round, making him look like one of those old-fashioned schoolteachers in movies. He leaned over until he was at eye level with me and shook my hand. He looked much older than Dad.

"Please, come in," he said, walking us past the tall, full bookshelves in his entry to a small but handsomely furnished living room. Mom sat the four of us kids shoulder to shoulder on his dark gray sofa. She and my father took their places in the large, overstuffed chairs to each side of us, with Uncle Seedy's currently empty chair between them, facing us.

"Laurie, may I offer you a glass of lemonade?"

His courtliness triggered a tender sensation in my chest. I sat up straighter.

"Yes, please."

Grandma and Grandpa Hall were plain folks, Missouri farmers who had migrated to California in 1918 for the oilfield jobs in the Central Valley, the year my father was born. They spoke in simple short sentences. Grandpa Hall swore, using words like *dadgummit*, and Grandma called us *sugar*. But my father didn't speak this way. He spoke like Uncle Seedy, enunciating each word as if it were something precious.

Seedy returned with a tray of frosty metal tumblers of lemonade, which he handed to us one by one. Mom was hunched over at the edge of her seat with her legs together and her elbows on her thighs, body language uncharacteristic of her. Dad chatted away. I saw my mother gulp a few times, even grimace, as if she'd tasted something bitter or was having a hard time swallowing something. I'd never seen her look this way before.

Dad settled deep into his big comfortable chair, his shoulders wide and square and his arms gesturing wildly as he spoke. He was like a new version of a father to me, not the version I knew at home, the one who politely but modestly socialized with the families from the church.

While we sipped our lemonades, Dad told Uncle Seedy about our house remodel: the contemporary light fixtures, the *fancy* speckled linoleum in the kitchen, the Degas ballerina wallpaper in the girls' bedrooms, our modern hi-fi cabinet, and, of course, the large rectangular pool, now clear and free of debris. He also boasted of the strikingly tall New Zealand flax plant, the carefully sculpted junipers, and the smooth river rock gravel in the front yard, and the low-water landscape that *Sunset* magazine recommended. The more he boasted, the shinier his face got.

DISNEYLAND, 1960

PUMPJACK IN THE OILFIELDS

He moved on to another favorite topic of his, Mom's "beautiful hair," emphasizing that the color was Titian blond, *not* red. Uncle Seedy nodded sweetly to my mother in appreciation, even though by then her face was blank. I wondered why she wasn't friendlier to him.

CHAPTER 9: THE SPANKING

The smell of chicken-fried steak and the clinking sounds of dinner plates reached me back in my bedroom. Dinner was almost ready. I sat cross-legged on top of my white chenille bedspread pressing one half of the tiny snap on my Muffie doll's plaid raincoat into the other half. The sound of loud organ music grabbed my attention. The ice cream man was nearby. I scooched off my bed, grabbed my piggy bank, and yelled to Tim, "It's the Popsicle Man!"

I heard a thud. Tim must have been on top of his bed, too. The telltale sounds of him jimmying open his slightly stuck dresser drawer came next, followed by the metallic jingle of coins in his piggy bank.

Dad had crafted our banks out of old tomato juice cans. He punched a single slot into the top of the cans with a flat screwdriver, drained the juice into a pitcher to drink later, rinsed the cans well, and dried them out on a towel before giving them to us with instructions to *save, save, save!*

Tim and I leaned over the side of my bed, our piggy banks in hand. It took some serious shaking and one of Tim's tiny pocketknives to slide a dime out of each of the impossibly narrow openings. Dad was sly, but not sly enough for children with dreams of popsicles.

Mom, of course, heard the clanking of the coins.

"No popsicles before dinner!" she yelled from the kitchen.

Tim and I stuffed our dimes into our pockets, tiptoed down the hallway, and slipped out the front door. We caught up with the Popsicle Man at the end of our block, out of sight of the front windows of our house. We handed over our shiny dimes to him for a Big Missile each, those tall, frozen confections made of swirls of sweet cherry and tart pineapple sherbets.

To avoid our mother's prying eyes in case she stepped out onto the front walkway, we carried our prized treats around the block and devoured them there. I remember the sense of pride I felt over how clever we were in our disobedience. Of course, if Mom didn't already know of our misbehavior, our bright yellow-and red-stained lips would betray us as soon as we walked in the front door. Mom in her apron rounded the corner the kitchen. She carried two potholders in one hand and had a severe look on her face.

"Go to your father, both of you," she said, pointing down the hallway. "He's in your room, Laurie. Go on now."

This was something I watched TV mothers do on *Leave it to Beaver* and *Father Knows Best*. June Cleaver and Margaret Anderson turned their children over to their fathers for corporal punishment. But this was the first time it was happening to me. My heart pounded.

Heads bowed down, Tim and I marched slowly toward our father who was sitting on the edge of my bed. We didn't even try to deny our misdeeds. He first put me over his lap, maybe because I was the oldest, and spanked me with his hand. It was my first spanking. I think he hit me only once, maybe twice. Still, I couldn't believe this was something he would do to me. I was too stunned to shed a single tear.

"Now go into dinner, Laurie," he said.

I wriggled off his lap and stood up to go. Before I left the room, I turned around for one final look back at him, this cruel father of mine who now seemed a stranger to me. He averted his eyes. His cheeks were purple. Even at my young age, I knew something was off. He looked to be acting a part. Maybe he was trying to be like the other dads we knew from church who smacked their kids right in front of us at our pool parties. I felt sorry for him and knew without a doubt he'd never do it again.

◇ ◇ ◇

Before my sisters and I entered kindergarten, Dad cut our hair in little-girl bobs with severe bangs. For Susan and me, the two with straight hair, Mom made pin curls on both sides of our cheeks using double-pronged curl clips. I'm not sure what Dad thought of those odd-looking curls, but he never tried to stop her.

By first grade, my hair had grown long enough for a pony-tail, which I loved. By the next summer, it seemed Dad had had enough of it. He'd read an article in a magazine about a fashionable new hairstyle and decided to try it out on me.

"You're going to *love* it, honey!" he said.

I could tell he was excited because the wide smile on his face lingered longer than usual. I didn't want to dampen his spirits, but I wasn't optimistic. I loved my ponytail. I loved watching the girls in my second-grade class at St. Charles walk in single file down the halls at recess, their ponytails all bouncing in unison.

My father's set of professional hair styling tools was impressive. It scared me a little. There were standard shears with long shiny blades, thinning shears with scary-looking sharp teeth on one side, and a small electric clipper Dad held in the palm of his hand when he trimmed the fine hair at the back of our necks.

First came my shampoo. Dad draped a thin, flour-sack dish towel around my neck and fastened it with one of the large safety pins with yellow plastic duck heads Mom kept from our diaper days. After washing and rinsing, he wrung the water out of my hair to squeaky-clean sounds and placed a towel over my head. My eyes were closed tight as he guided me over to the dining chair he'd moved to the middle of the kitchen.

This was well before No More Tangles Crème Rinse for Children came along, though I cried no tears as Dad untangled my hair. He was thorough but gentle, seemingly never in a hurry to finish any part of this long process. Though I was. Before I even understood what was happening, he lopped off my ponytail with the sharp shears. Long strands of hair were spread out all over the newspapers at my feet. *My* hair. Tears stung my eyes.

"Oh, Laurie, honey, it will be okay," he said.

When he pulled out those awful-looking thinning shears, I winced. *Who would intentionally thin hair*, I thought to myself.

"*Stop* it, Daddy," I cried out as soon as I heard the crunch, crunch, crunch of the shears and saw even more hair drop onto the newspapers. "I *hate* it."

"Don't worry, sweetie, soon all the girls will be thinning their hair."

I didn't want to do what all the other girls were *going* to do. I wanted to do what the girls in my class were doing *now*. But it was too late. The remains of my ponytail were scattered beneath me. Dad held up a mirror to show me my thinned hair and short pixie crop. By then I couldn't control my tears.

"I'm sorry, sweetie," he said, "but you have to admit you now look as stylish as Audrey Hepburn."

I didn't know who Audrey Hepburn was, nor did I care. Even though I could see how important it was to my father that his daughters look like her, I was determined he would never again get near me with those thinning shears.

"Take off your shoes, honey," he said. "Come into the living room."

He knew how to bring a smile to my teary face. Soon "Waltz-ing Mathilda" was playing on the hi-fi, and I was standing on his giant shoes, gliding around the living room with him the way he glided around with Mom. His strong, graceful dance moves under my small, bare feet freed me temporarily from thoughts of my hideous haircut. I leaned into his chest and closed my eyes.

No one at school the next day asked me where my ponytail had gone or why my bangs were short and wispy instead of long and combed back like they had been the day before. No one mentioned Audrey Hepburn, either.

FANCY MOM, 1963

MODERN HOUSE ON THE HILL, 1963

CHAPTER 10: BOOMING

I t was my father's time. His income rose steadily as treasurer and office manager of Crowley Company, a thriving plumbing contractor in Mountain View. The city was at the heart of the region later coined Silicon Valley. Defense and high-tech jobs were plentiful, the San Francisco Bay Area's population was exploding. I was ten.

Dad's contacts at Crowley gave him early insights into lucrative real estate opportunities. His daily interactions with contractors, developers, and investors, plus his rising salary, allowed him to take advantage of new investment prospects before unimproved land values soared out of range.

He started small. When he first took us to the shabby four-unit apartment building in an equally shabby neighborhood in nearby Redwood City, I didn't know it was ours, a recurring theme in my family. Paint cans and splotchy canvas material covered the floors of the empty, curtain-less, two-story building. The same buddy of his who helped him with our Birch Avenue remodel helped him with the renovations here, too.

But Dad wouldn't stop here. He soon leveraged the sale of this project into a twelve-unit apartment building he built on a vacant piece of property, also in Redwood City. It was 1962, and the Bay Area real estate boom was in high gear. I was eleven. By the time Mom and the four of us kids piled out of our station wagon onto the muddy construction site one rainy weekend, my father had already skipped up the unfinished wooden staircase leading to the second floor. He pointed to stray pieces of plywood we should use as walking planks to avoid puddles.

"Watch for sharp nails poking out, though," he shouted.

Inside one of the units under construction, Dad showed us a newfangled, built-in contraption on top of the kitchen's Formica counter. He lifted a blender out of a bottom cabinet and fitted it onto the device.

"Look! No cords! And no appliances cluttering countertops until you need them!"

Even though I didn't consider electrical cords or blenders a problem, I could tell by his enthusiasm this slick aesthetic solution pleased my father. He was later heartbroken to learn his renters were not all that interested in his modern contraptions. More often than not, metal breadboxes and cutting boards covered up these wonky connective units when he checked in on them.

"They can't see value in something that isn't traditional," Dad said.

I had to think about that. If I were a tenant in his building, I'd probably prefer my appliances on top of the countertops instead of hidden in dark cabinets until needed. But I never told my father that. He felt deflated enough.

Rental income and larger paychecks now meant that our family was on the move once again. I was in the fourth grade and had already lived in two houses: the three-bedroom country cottage and the four-bedroom fixer-upper in town. My third home would be a custom-built, five-bedroom modern house in the San Carlos hills. During a visit before construction was complete, Dad crowed.

"Look, it's so sleek and modern!"

Waving his arms, he noted the low-slope roof, the long, low horizontal layout, and the floor-to-ceiling windows. Through his eyes, I was impressed by the exterior, which resembled some of the modern art we'd seen in San Francisco museums. But it didn't look like someone's house to me.

Dad guided us up one side of the rough wooden framing for what would soon be three large concrete front steps embedded with large pebbles.

"Be careful of the splinters and nails."

Now that our lives revolved around construction sites, Dad's warnings about lurking dangers was a theme.

He was very excited about the large pond that would go underneath the entry steps. I knew that because he spoke loudly, rapidly, and nonstop about it, not his usual way of speaking.

"I'm going to fill it with koi! You know, those large orange fish at the Japanese Tea Garden! Floating on top will be lily pads like the ones at the Conservatory of Flowers. And there will be a double fountain over here . . . and those gorgeous colored glass balls in it like the ones the crab fishermen at Princeton Pier at Half Moon Bay use to keep their nets afloat. And there will be tiny spotlights."

He was breathless. I felt that way, too. His unique design touches on this particular feature of our new front yard were magical.

Once inside, Dad demonstrated another new gadget for us. This time it wasn't about blenders and mixers; it was a NuTone whole-house intercom/radio.

"We'll be spread out further in this house than we were before. But look! We'll still be able to talk to one another through the intercoms!"

Since my comfort at home was still dependent on close proximity to my parents, my stomach got queasy imagining the distance these intercoms promised to bridge.

Dad had moved to the family room where floor-to-ceiling panels of sliding glass doors framed panoramas of distant hills.

"Look at the views! And come over here!"

The side yard was large enough for a swimming pool. Instead of the traditional rectangular pool on Birch Avenue, Dad would instead install a kidney-shaped pool, he said, like the one featured in *Sunset Magazine*. I was later surprised he wanted a pool up here in the hills when I learned the weather was even colder and foggier in the summer. But as before, he'd enjoy weekends by the pool, shirtless and in his snug swim trunks, skimming leaves off the top of the water, adjusting the chlorine, and somehow managing to get a tan even on foggy days.

The interior of this house Dad would decorate with modern flourishes to match the architecture. He picked out six ultra-modern—and ultra-uncomfortable—Norman Cherner wood veneer chairs to go with our sleek new slate-and-teak dining room table.

Mom was close-lipped while Dad renovated the home. Once we moved in, she seemed more tired than usual, with slumping shoulders and the occasional admission of how "weary" she was of constantly moving, especially to this house in the hills where her four children now needed chauffeuring to school, music lessons, and afterschool sports. Catching herself, she'd quickly add, "But if it makes your father happy . . ."

Most of my schoolmates lived on flat land near school and downtown. Their homes were smaller and cozier, like our country cottage. Interiors tended toward frilly curtains and colonial-style couches, hutches, and dining room sets. Fathers mowed front lawns on weekends. Our stylish new setting couldn't have been more different.

In the four years we lived there, I don't think I invited a single one of my school friends to our house. Even if I had, it would have been difficult for them to accept the invitation. Most of them lived within walking distance of our house on Birch

Avenue. Here, they'd need to be driven up the hill and then picked up later. Most families were large. Even if they could afford two cars, mothers wouldn't have had the time to chauffeur a single child back and forth. Not that I invited them anyway. The distance in miles felt unbridgeable to me. I missed them. I missed our being able to easily walk to each other's houses. I think I was also uncomfortable with the wealth disparity.

My father had always been stylish. But his closet was now filled with expensive, or so I assumed, tight-fitting, custom-made Italian suits, black fedoras, crisp white and pale-blue dress shirts, and silk ties with matching handkerchiefs that he folded neatly and tucked into his jacket pockets. He accented his ensembles with sterling silver cufflinks and tie tacks. Dad was still working for the plumbing contractor, but he must have also been meeting regularly with lenders for his various development projects. He would have been appropriately dressed to impress them.

My mother's wardrobe was increasingly chic, too. On his lunch hour, Dad shopped for new clothes for her at I. Magnin, a high-end department store in Palo Alto. He arrived home with pink-striped gold boxes filled with an assortment of elegant dresses, purses, and high heels. He let Mom choose her favorites and returned the rejects the next day. One of my favorite dresses of hers from that brief period of extravagance was a shiny, chartreuse green sheath. With her fancy new hairdos, tight-fitting fashionable clothes, matching "bags," as she called them, and high heels, my mother looked like a model to me.

However, there was one piece of my mother's clothing that I didn't care for, a short, flared coat jacket. I'd never seen anything like it in a store. It had an unusual (to me) shawl collar and a single large tortoise shell button at the top. The fabric was a flouncy houndstooth of tiny olive-green-and-gray jagged squares. She wore it over pants for trips to foggy beaches, or over a pencil skirt for an evening play or musical.

Other mothers at the time wore those store-bought, camel-colored car coats with the fantastical rope-and-wood toggle fasteners. I wished my mother had one of those. I somehow knew her coat wasn't store-bought and felt this fact made us outsiders of sorts. Today I'd consider it high fashion. Back then, it seemed peculiar because it wasn't like the others. I couldn't understand why she wore it so often.

Dad dressed me up, too. I'm not sure why he set his fashion eyes on me as opposed to his other three children, but I was a grateful recipient most of the time. I appreciated his eye for style and quality and shared it, I think. Though one time he pushed my limits. I was about thirteen and in the eighth grade. He pranced through the back door after work one day holding a shopping bag for me. My geography homework, which consisted of paraphrasing boring paragraphs out of our set of *Golden Home and High School Encyclopedia*, was spread out over one end of the kitchen table. I was grateful for the interruption, though I could tell by the twinkle in Dad's eyes that he was up to something. And I'd be right about that.

Not a single girl I knew was wearing what he pulled out of the bag for me that day. I generally liked what he picked out for me—the brightly colored, flowered windbreaker; the sky-blue nylon ski pants; and, especially, the stylish turquoise, short-sleeved Easter coat with the large, single white button at the top. A short-sleeved coat! However, the pants Dad pulled out of the bag puzzled me.

"Now, honey, these are called *bell bottoms*," he said, slowly. "And soon everybody will be wearing them. Aren't they fantastic?"

I was wary. As with my haircut, I didn't want to wear what everybody else *would* be wearing. I wanted to wear what they were wearing *now*. Then again, I had to admit the sky-blue cotton pants were good-looking. I told Dad I'd try them on.

Pairing them with one of my favorite tops—a white, cropped pullover with three buttons at the top and two ties at the bottom—I viewed myself in the full-length mirror in the hallway, twisting around to see what they looked like in back.

"Hey, Dad," I called out.

He'd already changed his clothes and was in the kitchen rinsing out his thermos. He peered out at me from down the hallway.

"I *like* them!"

He smiled a big smile but didn't say anything. Maybe he wanted the decision to be mine. But he couldn't contain the pleased look covering his face.

"Thanks. I'll keep them!"

Still, I felt self-conscious wearing these newfangled bell-bottoms for the first time. I imagined drivers slowing down to gawk at my curious-looking pants as I walked to a new friend's house a few blocks away. My mixed feelings about them lasted only about a month, though, by which time everyone else—girls *and* boys—were wearing bell-bottoms, too. Dad was usually right about things like this.

CHAPTER 11: BLOOMING

I t was our first day in the new modern house. The four of us
kids had walked to St. Charles school that morning from our
restored traditional home on Birch Avenue in the flats of central
San Carlos. After school, I skipped down the outdoor stairs
as usual when the three o'clock school bell rang. High above
the black asphalt parking lot that served both the school and
the church, I couldn't miss the sight of our large white station
wagon parked there. We'd left one house before school started
that day and would be living in another house after it ended.
I don't recall my mother even mentioning this when we set off
for school that morning.

Mom was quiet on the drive up the hill. Once we piled out
of the car, she told us to go to our new rooms and change out
of our uniforms. Then she'd give us a tour of our new home.
Dad was at work. We started with the master bedroom. It was
located at one end of this oddly long narrow house lined in
floor-to-ceiling plate glass doors and windows. The twin beds
caught my eye, and not because of their shiny new royal-blue-
and-gold bedspreads, either, striking as they were.

The year was 1961. My father was forty-three. Mom was
thirty-seven. They'd always slept in a double bed. Now ten

years old, I didn't know anything about sex, though I'd recently begun noticing how some of the boys I'd ignored for five years were now looking pretty cute. I couldn't stop staring at those twin beds.

Mom turned our focus on other aspects of the room. We entered their impressively long, walk-in closet through a new-fangled accordion door. I'd never seen a closet like this before. Later that year she would assure us that we would all be safe inside it if Soviet leader Nikita Khrushchev dropped an atom bomb on us. I'd push back, noting how radiation could leak in through the one-inch opening under the door. Mom would insist that stuffing newspapers in the gap would save us all. I wanted to believe her.

Mom's call hailing me to the kitchen shook me from my apocalyptic trance. She had already slid open the wooden folding doors of our new pantry by the time I arrived in the kitchen.

"Look at that," she said. "You can see everything all at once now!"

The pantry lined an entire wall of the dining alcove of our new kitchen. It was something she'd long wanted. She pointed out how the shallow shelves would make it easier to see everything at once: cans of tuna, vegetables, and soup; boxes of cereal, flour, and sugar; and bags of rice and dried noodles.

"Nothing is hidden now," Mom chirped. "You kids can hand me things while I'm cooking." I guessed she was happy. She'd at least be getting some help in this strangely long house where everything was so spread out, even her and Dad.

For Christmas that year, our parents bought us shiny new Schwinn bicycles. Mine was a rich royal blue, a color I loved but had never seen on another bike. I knew Mom would have looked long and hard for that color for me.

While the four of us emptied the contents of our stockings onto the floor, I looked up at my parents sitting next to each other on the couch. I think my father even had his arm around Mom. These were rare sightings. I smiled at them but kept my eye on Dad's cigarette pack breaching the top of his shirt pocket. I wanted him to stay where he was and hoped he wouldn't soon reach for his cigarettes and head out to the deck for a smoke. I held no similar concern about my mother. Her eyes were bright and pretty, and it seemed as if her whole body was smiling as she leaned softly into Dad's shoulder. I knew she wouldn't be the one to make the first move to leave.

One of the last extravagances during the four years we lived there was a full-length mink coat my mother rarely wore. Dad brought it home for her one day packaged in an enormous, gold-striped I. Magnin box. He put it down on the sofa and called us all out to see it.

"Oh, Ralph, what have you done now?" Mom said.

She was smiling but seemed jittery. Her eyes were squinty. She pulled back the tissue paper to reveal a full-length mink coat. Dad giddily pointed out her initials that were custom-embroidered on the coat's powder-blue satin lining. She wore this luxurious coat only a few times but never to Sunday Mass. I asked her why.

"Oh, honey, I would *never* do that," she said. "Most of the families in the church are so poor. I wouldn't want them to feel bad."

It was the first time I understood not only the disparity of wealth among church members but also by implication that we were relatively better off than others. During Mass now, I was more aware of sagging wool coats with missing buttons, pilled from excessive wear, that some of the mothers of four, six, and even eight children wore.

One, in particular, I remember well. This mother's unkempt coat was splayed out around her as she herded at least half a dozen children into a long wooden pew. The youngest, a toddler she held in her arms, had a large red birthmark on her cheek. The mother yanked at the sides of her coat, wrapping them around herself while moving her tot from one arm to the other. Her coat was missing all but one button, the one at her neck, which kept the garment on but failed to keep it wrapped around her.

Watching her struggle with her coat made me realize how cold this unheated, cavernous church was. During the winter, Mom bundled up her three daughters for Mass in plush jackets and coats and faux fur hand muffs, which we kept on throughout the service, and Tim in both an undershirt and a long-sleeved shirt under his dressy, little-boy jacket. I hadn't thought of the cold before. I hadn't thought of any of this before my mother told me why she would never, *ever* wear her warm, expensive mink coat to church.

My father was lean and strong but not especially muscular. His bulging biceps, the result of lifting heavy barbells in our garage, were the exception. We begged him often to flex them for us. I couldn't push them down no matter how hard I tried. I was impressed. On the other hand, he couldn't throw a football or hit a baseball. Nor did he watch sports on TV. Our mother was the one who cheered Tim on in Little League. So it came as a big surprise to me when Dad announced the box-seat tickets he had for a San Francisco Giants' game at Candlestick Park. His company had season tickets and doled them out to partners.

Dad guided us to our seats. Down we went from one section to another and then another until he pointed to six seats a few rows behind home plate. This meant that Tim and I, big baseball fans, had close-up views of the hits and plays at home plate. And Dad had a close-up view of the lithe players. When Juan Marichal, the Giants' star pitcher, came to the plate, he sat forward in his seat.

"Okay, kids," he said. "Watch him carefully now."

Dad never mentioned this ballplayer before, nor any ballplayer for that matter. But I guessed he must have been reading about him in the Sporting Green, the sports section of the *San Francisco Chronicle*. All four of us kids followed suit and sat straight up as well, preparing for what, I didn't yet know. We'd soon learn that Marichal, the handsome ballplayer from the Dominican Republic, had an impressive windup. Dad's perennially bronzed face beamed after watching his first pitch.

"See! His kicks are as high as those of the dancers at the San Francisco Ballet!"

In the presence of rowdy baseball fans who had probably never attended a ballet, I didn't wince at his words. It was how he spoke.

Dad next alerted us to the three Alou brothers—Felipe, Matty, and Jesus—also natives of the Dominican Republic. They weren't as rock-star handsome as the stocky Juan Marichal, but the three lean brothers were especially agile.

"See the way Felipe bends around to catch the balls, kids? He's like a rubber band!"

I took Dad's comment literally and couldn't quite make out the connection between an outfielder and a rubber band. Still, it was fun to be on an outing like this where Dad enjoyed himself, unlike vacations to Disneyland or Knott's Berry Farm where Dad seemed bored, distant, or was absent altogether.

If Mom, in her dark sunglasses and wide-brimmed straw hat protecting her fair, freckled skin, was uneasy with Dad's fawning over supple ballplayers, I couldn't say. But I wouldn't have been looking for this reaction from her anyway. Wives wouldn't be concerned about their husbands ogling other men. I was aware of the fact that my father's reaction to the ballplayers' bodies differed from the yelling and swearing of the men and boys seated near us. By comparison, though, I considered my father the more refined man.

The jogging craze of the mid-1960s brought out similarly supple young men to the streets and sidewalks of the San Francisco Bay Area. Only these men dressed in tight shorts and brightly colored tank tops if they wore any tops at all. On a weekend drive over to Half Moon Bay during that time, Dad slowed our car and pointed to one particular jogger as our car crawled past him.

"Look at him, kids!" he said, his voice booming with excitement. "What an Adonis!"

I still can see our four small heads turning in unison toward the shiny, shirtless jogger. I wished I were invisible. To be fair, I squirmed when Dad slowed the car to look at attractive women, too. Now fourteen, I was squeamish about his interest in anyone's body. Conversely, my mother's swoons over Cary Grant or Gregory Peck never bothered me. Maybe it was because she'd usually add how these fine-looking men reminded her of "your father."

On our way to view the Van Gogh exhibit at the de Young Museum in San Francisco, Dad braked gently at a crosswalk. He waved a well-coiffed, gray-haired woman across the street. She wore a classic three-quarter-length, navy-blue dress coat impeccably tailored with a slight flair, two inseam pockets, a flap covering the buttons, and a standup collar, and stylish though sturdy navy-blue-and-white pumps.

"I just love these older San Francisco women," he said, his voice crackling with admiration. "See how confidently she walks, kids. And in her *pumps*!"

Yes, I saw. I'm not sure if any of my siblings were paying attention to Dad's latest praise for something beautiful or stylish, but I admired how this woman, no longer young, walked briskly and confidently in her fashionable pumps just as a younger person in comfortable sneakers would. Dad used this moment as an opportunity to instruct us in big city living.

"You see, kids, these women have probably walked, not driven, all of their lives. I bet she's going to the museum, too, and has just hopped off a streetcar." Then he added for emphasis, "And look how classy she is at the same time."

Even though I assumed all fathers praised stylish city women in front of their wives and children, I reflexively glanced over at Mom. I felt protective, only to be perplexed by the lack of any squirming or obvious reaction on her face. I thought she might have at least glowered toward Dad or averted her eyes. But her face betrayed nothing. Though unsettled, I told myself for the umpteenth time that my father was simply a modern, open-minded man who was well ahead of his time. But it was getting harder for me to convince myself of this.

Dad arrived home yet another time with a large parcel. This one was wrapped in plain brown paper and tied with fat, jute string. He dropped his crumpled lunch bag on top of the washing machine and, with no more than a clipped hello to us, headed toward his den at the other end of the house. He didn't even loosen his tie or remove his hat.

I forgot about the mystery package until a few days later when something bright red caught my eye as I walked the length of our long wooden deck toward the pool. A large terrycloth beach towel shielded me in my new two-piece swimsuit and expanding bustline from the neighbors below. Dad was still at work. I stopped and pressed my face up against the sliding glass door leading to his den. Mounted on the wall was an oil painting the size of the package. On it was a nude man set against a cherry-red background. His genitals were hidden under a crossed leg. I stiffened, tugged my towel tighter to my body, and walked down the stairs to the pool.

I was accustomed to the unique and unusual artwork, furniture, and clothing my father brought home. This painting felt different. But I possessed neither the maturity nor the words to characterize my discomfort, even to myself. I never mentioned my uneasiness to my father. But looking back with new eyes now, I imagine that painting must have been a comfort to him. It must have given him pleasure. He could gaze at a nude man, albeit a painting of one, in his own home with abandon. Because it was art it was okay.

I stayed away from the den after that, preferring the image of my father as someone who taught me calligraphy, crafts, and how to prune shrubs into exotic miniature shapes rather than someone who hung large nude paintings of men in our home.

I was happy when the holidays came around. After I finished clearing the dinner table, Dad approached me with pencils, pastels, and paper in hand.

"Look, honey," he said. "Uncle Seedy sent me this Christmas card during the war, when I was in Alaska."

The simple tan-and-brown sketch of a child angel in a long robe, her head bowed beneath a simple halo, drew me right in. It was a beautiful piece of art, but it was something more, too: simple lines, innocence, the obviously gentle hand of the artist.

"Isn't this the most beautiful angel you've ever seen, honey?"

"I think it is, Dad."

"Then let's make it our Christmas card design this year!" he said. He spread out his art materials on the kitchen table.

I was flattered he'd chosen me for the task rather than one of my siblings. Then again, my father generally chose me when it came to art projects since I was the only one of his four children who expressed much interest in drawing, painting, mosaics, creating string art with Mom's old spools of thread, constructing those impractical but fantastic paper chains out of his cigarette packaging, and more. I enjoyed it all.

I practiced sketching the little angel on the backs of used envelopes until one met with Dad's approval, at which point he handed me a piece of his fancy stationery paper. I added vertical bands of color behind my angel using all the colors of the rainbow. Dad drew a few cards of his own, more subdued than my version but in a finer hand, and together we were able to craft about a dozen cards. Since Mom had a long Christmas card list, which included friends from childhood, she supplemented our dozen handmade cards with her boxed ones from the stationery store downtown.

I could tell that Dad was proud of my work because he kept one of my cards for the family. He showed it off to holiday visitors when they dropped off their homemade divinity puffs, cannoli, and chocolate fudge on colorful paper plates in the days leading up to Christmas. He'd keep this one until the day he died, this sweet little angel standing in front of what decades later would resemble the LGBTQ rainbow flag.

CHAPTER 12: BEFORE THE FALL

Dad's increasingly large real estate projects during the housing boom meant that, at least for four years, he could decorate and outfit the modern house with expensive furniture and other furnishings from the high rents he received. The sapphire-blue globe lamps that he hung over our teak-and-black slate dining room table were favorites of mine. Green-and-blue Art Deco glass vases and heavy ashtrays accented side tables. Two side chairs covered in lime-green fabric bookended a long, shiny Persian-blue sofa heavily embossed with geometric Asian shapes.

The artwork on the walls was all original. Dad created two of them. For one he glued a pair of black wooden doves onto a tall rectangular piece of chartreuse-colored silk and mounted it on a black frame. The doves were so close to each other they almost touched. They looked like a couple to me, though a lonely one set against the vast empty chartreuse background.

Dad's second piece was an oil painting on another tall rectangular background, this one white canvas. It may have been an abstract painting, or the shapes may have represented something specific to him, but what I saw was a huge peacock with its feathers retracted and surrounded by a gathering of tiny nuns in black habits. He never could bring himself to tell us what the shapes were or what they represented to him, even at the end of his life.

My parents would host a few more dinner parties in this museum-like combined living and dining room before our family's fortunes plummeted. I can't say I saw it coming, but I sensed something dark in the whispers in the hallways. Dad no longer suggested art projects for the two of us. He didn't ask about our school day. He worked late, ate dinner silently, and disappeared into his den. I no longer worried about glimpsing the painting of the nude man in there. Dad kept the door closed and the drapes behind the sliding glass door drawn at all times now.

My parents threw one final pool party for Mom's friends from the church, though I didn't know at the time that it was the last one. Dad, as usual, pranced around tan and shirtless in his swim trunks, aviator sunglasses, and flip-flops while periodically lighting up a cigarette or leaning down to pull out the rare weed visible in the gravel planter beds. The other dads roughhoused in the water with their kids, tossing them high into the air and racing them the length of the pool. Dad didn't swim races with us, but had he, I knew he would have let us win the races at least once in a while.

The wives spread out fried chicken, potato salad, lemonade, and chocolate brownies on the kitchen table where the wind wouldn't blow away the neat stacks of paper plates and cups. Late in the afternoon, Mom's head would appear in the tiny opaque bathroom window overlooking the pool, which slid open with a screech.

"Come and get it," she said.

LAURA, AGE THIRTEEN, 1964

MOM AT THE APARTMENTS, 1965

CHAPTER 13: BUST

The next few years were grinding for my parents. It was the mid-1960s, and housing starts in the Bay Area had finally outpaced need. Property values plummeted. Inexperienced investors like my father found themselves in over their heads. His personal real estate bubble burst.

The lavish dinner parties were no more. I wish I'd paid attention to the last one and fixed the details permanently in my mind, when life felt so indulgent. If I had, I'd probably recall the fresh, piney smell of gin; the perfectly spaced arrangement of bite-sized cheese tarts on a sterling silver platter; an expensive cut of beef; an array of fresh steamed asparagus, all cut to the exact same size; a large loaf of crusty bread from Tasty Bakery where Mom worked before she got pregnant with Caroline; and perfectly round globes of vanilla bean ice cream drizzled in amber-colored Grand Marnier for dessert. Dad would carry his modern pewter coffee set out to the dining room on a matching platter without spilling a drop.

My father and his business partners at Crowley Company had responded to the postwar housing needs of returning soldiers and their large families by overextending themselves in large apartment investments in Mountain View and Redwood City. In ten years, the area would be the heart of the burgeoning Silicon Valley with its increasing demands for more dwellings to house those flocking to high-tech jobs from other parts of the state and country. But by then my father would no longer own any properties there.

My parents went silent and dour. Their hushed communications took place in dark hallways. All talk about fetching baseball players, must-see musicals, golden koi, and "stunning" sapphire-blue hanging lamps ended. In fact, most talk ended. At the dinner table, Dad no longer asked me about my school day or offered to help me with my homework. Mom whisked away my dinner plate while my fork holding the last bite was still in mid-air. Once Dad finished his meal, he slid his chair back, rose slowly, lumbered over to the sink to rinse off his plate, and slipped out the other side of the kitchen to the back rooms without passing by us. I wouldn't see him until dinner the next evening.

My night terrors returned. In a recurring one, I was suffocating under a pillow. In another, electrical wires hovered over me. In both versions, I expected to die. As I'd done as a little girl, I screamed myself awake. But my parents no longer came running to me. They may not have even heard me back in their bedroom at the far end of our large house. Frozen in fear and more than a little embarrassed, I didn't run to them, either.

Mom surely knew her sensitive second-born was struggling. At some point, without a word from her, the desk lamp outside the bedroom I shared with Susan remained on all night. I was comforted by the light when awakened by my nightmares, but I still didn't know how to make the horror stop.

I had a recurring fantasy. In it, I was adopted by Sister Michela, my strict eighth-grade teacher. It started when I ran out into the street at recess one day to retrieve an errant kickball. Sister gave me a stern warning. If I did it again, she said,

I'd have to sit out the game. I could tell by her lack of even the faintest of smiles that she wasn't fooling around. She was tough on me in class, too. She made me read aloud, even when my voice cracked, standing there at her well-worn wooden desk until my nerves settled down. I think I saw slight nods of approval afterward. This is when I began to fantasize about spending all of my time in her tough, protective presence.

In my fantasy, I was a forlorn orphan. I had no lunchbox and no parents to sign my homework. Scuffmarks covered my old, white oxford shoes. This imaginary world even came with its own dialogue.

"Laura Hall! Your homework isn't signed?"

Sister Michela's voice boomed. All eyes in the class turned toward me. I slumped down into my chair.

"Uh, no, Sister, it isn't."

She marched toward me in military fashion, her eyes red and glaring. Tears ran down my cheeks. It was only when she got close to me that she realized something was wrong. Her voice softened.

"Why didn't your parents sign your homework, Laura?"

"I don't have any parents."

It was how I felt at home. I was on my own. At this point, Sister would offer to take me home with her. Of course, home was the convent, which I hadn't reconciled in my make-believe saga. But inside my fantasy, I felt safe and protected. I couldn't wait to get to school each day to play the part of the frightened, sad little orphan in my mind, one whom this tough, attentive nun would protect.

At home, Dad now exploded over the slightest thing. He might have added salt to the spaghetti sauce Mom was simmering on the stove.

"Oh, Ralph, please don't do that," she'd say. "I've already salted it."

"Your sauce never has enough salt, Irene!" he'd roar.

Another day Mom might question one of his purchases, perhaps a crystal bud vase he insisted would make him happy. My mother rarely questioned his purchases before our financial reversal, at least not in front of her children. But now she didn't even try to muffle it in a whisper.

As Dad's voice rose, I scurried from the kitchen to my bedroom, shutting the door behind me and sitting on the edge of my bed. I could hear Mom trying to quiet him down. Though I couldn't make out her words, I made out his.

"I work hard, Irene," he yelled. "I have a right to buy whatever I damned well please!"

After some mumbling, presumably Mom's, he'd start in again.

"And I am tired of hearing you say that, Irene. Why would you even question me like that?"

Next would come the words I dreaded most.

"I'm sick of this," Dad said. "I'm sick and tired of it all!"

Hunched over the edge of my bed now, I cradled my knees to my chest, awaiting the inevitable. I couldn't finish my book report or work on my paint-by-number mill scene or go outside and play handball with the neighborhood kids. I could barely breathe.

"Oh, Ralph, please stop," Mom said. "The kids will hear you."

Her voice was sweet, but it must have irked Dad even more. He shot back, "Now you think I'm frightening the children?"

His voice was at a feverish pitch. Then everything went silent. A chill racked my body, knowing what was to come. The walls of the house shuddered as Dad slammed the back door. His tires squealed as he zoomed out of the driveway and down the hill.

Each time this happened, I wondered if we'd ever see him again. I believed he really was sick and tired of us all. Increasingly frightened and alone in my bedroom, I'd creep out toward the kitchen, toward my mother. Some of my siblings appeared, too, from where I'm not sure. It seemed to me we were all cocooned in separate worlds in those years.

"Go sit at your places now, kids," Mom chirped. "And put your napkins on your laps."

Her voice was surprisingly pleasant. We did as we were told. None of us asked the whereabouts of our father. No one said a word.

After Mom served us our dinner, she seated herself and asked about our school day. Caroline might have shared what was going on in her freshman homemaking class, perhaps how proud she was of the lemon squares she'd learned to bake that day. Tim had recently joined the Major League's baseball team, a league more advanced than Little League. He might have wanted to know if Mom would drive him to his game and bring a cooler of ice-cold Shasta sodas for his team. She would have said yes. Susan might have asked Mom to iron her cowgirl outfit for another parade somewhere on the Peninsula, though as funds dried up, her extracurricular activities would come to an end.

Under the tablecloth, I would have picked at my nails. Mom would have redirected our attention to the frosted, chocolate walnut brownies or to another one of her homemade desserts awaiting us if we cleaned our plates.

Dad never stayed away for long after these outbursts, at most maybe an hour. He'd walk into the kitchen, his cheeks flushed and his chin dipped low. He'd sit down to his dinner, which Mom had already pulled out of a warm oven when she heard his car pull into the garage. Even though I couldn't bring myself to look him in the eye and was still picking at my nails, I exhaled.

HANDMADE DRESS

CHAPTER 14: BANKRUPTCY

There never was a *For Sale* sign in front of my father's modern dream house. I can't explain that. But one day we were driving down the Peninsula to Palo Alto to look at apartments. Neither of my parents had announced the purpose ahead of time.

The six of us squeezed into an elevator and got off on the fourth floor of a building that smelled of new carpets and fresh paint. Dad raved about the modern appliances, naturally, and the fact that there were *four* bedrooms, something the local rental market in San Carlos did not yet offer.

If I assumed anything that day, it would have been that Dad wanted something fancier for us than San Carlos had to offer, even fancier than our modern house. I'd already lived in three houses and had come to expect these regular moves to some place better.

"Oh, Ralph, I couldn't bear to leave San Carlos," Mom said. I looked up at her, startled by the looming reality. But she'd already turned her face the other way and was now fussing with her purse. I wondered if she was searching for a tissue. I didn't look at Dad. The elevator trip back down to the ground floor and the ride home were both silent.

Mom won out. We'd remain in San Carlos, near St. Charles Church and school, our friends, and Nana. But our family would be living in two separate apartments now. My parents and Tim had the two-bedroom townhouse. The three of us girls shared a one-bedroom unit directly across the hall in the multi-story apartment building. As the eldest, my older sister got the bedroom to herself. Susan and I slept in a corner sofa sleeper in the tiny living room.

The family ate dinner together in the townhouse every night. More often than not it was only the five of us. Mom's eyes were downcast during this period. I didn't dare ask her where Dad was. I didn't ask her any questions at all.

We no longer used the pretty Wedgwood china because we wouldn't have company over here. The fragile china, packed in labeled moving boxes and stacked in one corner of the small living room, remained wrapped in their spongy sleeves for the duration. I wished I could have wrapped Mom in protective padding to cushion her from all the jutting corners in these small quarters.

Every night when she came to say goodnight to the three of us girls, she warned us not to open our front door after dark to anyone but her. She reminded us that *a nice policeman* and his wife lived next door to our unit, *just in case*. Although I was entering high school in the fall, I was once again anxious at night, this time in a unit without my parents. Caroline and Susan slept soundly, though, and if they were bothered by the light I left on all night in our tiny, unused kitchen, they didn't say anything to me about it.

My parents were tightlipped. For all I knew, we'd be living like this from that point on. Mom's normally light-blue eyes were now a dark gray, as if she'd just come indoors out of the bright sunlight. Dad left for work early. When he did join us for dinner, he'd disappear in the townhouse's bedroom upstairs as soon as he finished eating. The only words I recall hearing from him at the table were requests for the bread or salt to be passed to him. Inexplicably to me still, four months later, in the fall of 1965, we moved to another new modern house in the San Carlos hills.

At the start of the school year, Mom enrolled Caroline as a sophomore and me as a freshman at Notre Dame High School, an expensive all-girls' Catholic school in the adjoining city of Belmont. From our kitchen window, we had a view of Carlmont High School, the free public high school, which was well within walking distance. Nonetheless, it was important to Mom that we stay in the Catholic school system, even if it meant someone had to taxi us there and back.

Dad worked long hours at Crowley Company now, often arriving home after we were all asleep. Once in a while I'd catch him eating dinner alone under a single light in the kitchen. If I was still awake when he got home, I'd watch him from the top of the stairwell as he walked up from the garage, his shoulders now drooped. The paper bags he carried were worn and wrinkled. I'd return to my bedroom and close the door before he reached the top of the stairs. I didn't want him to feel any worse than he did.

I don't know what was in those paper bags; perhaps his thermos and plastic containers from lunch, or aluminum cans he collected on the streets for recycling, a lifelong hobby but now perhaps for spare change. But I did know that the bags didn't contain fancy dresses from Saks Fifth Avenue for his three daughters, or an enameled Asian platter for himself from Gump's, or matching satin-covered pumps and handbags from I. Magnin for Mom. Though there was one exception.

The day of my first dance at Notre Dame was coming up. The boys from Bellarmine, the all-boys' high school from further down the Peninsula, would join us. I had already finished dinner and was in my room pounding coils of brass into jewelry when I heard a soft knock.

I opened the door to see that familiar look of pleasure on my father's face, a look I hadn't seen in a long time. His eyes sparkled and his smile was tender and gentle. He held two packages in his hands, both in the familiar shiny gold wrap with pink stripes and printed with the name, I. Magnin, in elegant cursive letters on top. Over the years he'd bought fancy clothes for Mom at this store but never anything for me.

I pulled back the pleated tissue in the first box. Inside was a sleeveless top and matching A-line skirt. Dainty, see-through white lace overlay the powder-blue layer of material underneath it. The dress in the second box had a scooped neck and light pink bodice; its attached skirt looked like one of those fancy wedding cakes I'd seen at the Tasty Bakery. Rows of white lacy ruffles encircled the skirt, the soft pink peeking through just as the blue material showed through on the first outfit. Assuming our family still had lingering financial problems, coupled with Dad's lowered voice, I felt guilty loving them as much as I did.

"Oh, Dad."

"Try them both on, honey, and pick the one you like best," he said.

He closed my bedroom door gently on his way out. I changed into the skirt and top and rushed out to the full-length mirror in the hallway. Dad padded out of the kitchen in his moccasins to take a look.

"Oh, Dad, I love this!"

I also loved seeing him happy again. I next tried on the dress and again raced out to the mirror. It was beautiful. I was beautiful. How would I choose, I wondered. I ran out to the kitchen where Dad was now eating his late dinner in the near-dark.

"Oh, no, Dad, I love them both! I can't decide. . . ."

His big blue eyes twinkled.

"It's okay, honey," he said. "You can go ahead and keep them both."

He dropped his eyes and looked away. I wish I'd honored what I saw in his face and selected only one. I knew without either of my parents telling me that we couldn't afford both. We probably couldn't even afford one.

Even though fashion, and my own preferences, would soon evolve to the bohemian, hippie look of the late sixties, I wore my lacy pink dress and blue skirt-and-top duo as often as I could until I outgrew them. This time I wasn't concerned that no other girls wore similar dresses. They remain in my mind the prettiest dresses I have ever owned, the last dresses my father ever bought for me.

◇   ◇   ◇

The school bell at Notre Dame rang. It was an obnoxious mechanical sound. The girls in final period history class leaned over in unison to pick up the textbooks at our feet. We walked out the door in single file toward the school's main entry/exit. Shielding my eyes from the bright afternoon sun, I searched for Mom's white station wagon in the parking lot, but I didn't see it. Mom was never late to pick us up.

"Laurie! Laurie!"

The mother of one of my classmates was waving me over.

When her daughter and I reached her pink station wagon, she informed me that Mom asked her to drive me home. My chest tightened. Something was obviously wrong.

Her daughter got into the front seat, and I slid in the back. The three of us remained silent during the drive up the hill to our house. Mom was at the front door before I got to it.

"Your father is in the hospital, Laurie," she said. Her tone was hushed.

"But why?"

"Shhhh! Tim and Susie are in the kitchen."

"*Tell* me, Mom," I whispered.

It was the spring of 1966. Dad was forty-eight, Mom, forty-two. At fifteen, I was four months' shy of completing my freshman year at Notre Dame. Mom shook her head from side to side.

"It's his insides, honey. It's from all the stress."

I squinted my eyes, imagining the horrific battle brewing inside my father.

"Come along now," she said. "When your dad gets home from the hospital, we'll have to be real quiet until he gets better."

She escorted me inside with her arm gently on my shoulder.

Dad spent ten days in the hospital and was then off work for five additional weeks. The only time I remembered seeing him sick before was during the Asian flu pandemic of 1957, nine years earlier, a flu that had flattened all six of us. There seemed a still darkness inside our house now, even in the daylight, one interrupted only by Dad's shrieks of pain.

I sat in my usual position between my parents' chairs for dinner, though Dad's chair would remain empty for another month. One evening, before we even finished cleaning our plates, Mom sprung an announcement on us.

"I got a job at Brittan Acres," she said, referring to the public elementary school located across the street from St. Charles School. She hadn't worked outside the home since before Caroline was born. "I'll be working in the cafeteria. I start tomorrow." Her no-nonsense tone, and the way she began wiping the dirty table afterward, reminded me of the curt receptionist at our dentist's office. Neither invited further discussion.

"Okay, kids, it's time for dessert!"

After a few weeks, Dad's disturbing cries had leveled off to a once-a-day occurrence. But it wasn't the end of our bad times. I opened my bedroom door one night before bedtime after hearing my mother's fingernails lightly tapping on it. She stood in the dim light of the hallway.

"We have to pull you and Caroline out of Notre Dame."

As usual, there'd be no room for questions. I wouldn't have tried anyway. I could see how miserable my mother was, how unhappy both of my parents were. Their pallid faces and expressionless eyes unnerved me. At times, I could hear heated whispers in their bedroom adjacent to mine. At the dinner table, no one spoke. After dinner, my parents retreated to their own domains, Mom remaining to clean the kitchen, Dad out in the garden until dark. He no longer invited me outside to pull weeds or prune junipers or make paper chains with him. I was older now anyway, and more interested in boys and girls my age. But I missed his engaging presence in my life.

Walking up the hill after school one day, I spied my uncle smoking a cigar in his Studebaker. He was parked in front of our house. Nana, who didn't drive, greeted me when I reached the front door.

"Your mother is in the hospital," she said. Her voice was stern. "She's having back surgery. We're all going to have to help out."

Nana didn't mince words. Now Mom would be the one in agony in the back room, but her recovery would last longer than Dad's. She rang a brass claw bell she'd scavenged from one of our bedrooms to call us to her bedside while she healed. I can remember the soft chimes it made. She'd lift her head slightly off the bed, wince, dole out a few orders, and then allow her head to drop back down. She sighed during this time but never once complained. I wanted to stroke her formerly red hair that had turned soft and snowy white in recent years. But I didn't want to hurt her. Despite her discomfort, she issued strict orders to all four of us on a regular basis. Nana did the grocery shopping. Caroline cooked. Susan and I cleaned the kitchen. I ironed sheets and pillowcases. Tim vacuumed two floors of thick carpeting.

I can't say what my father did during this time because I rarely saw him. We passed each other in the hallway late at night. His thick terry cloth robe hung heavy on his bony shoulders. He was pale, almost ghostlike. He glided slowly past me through a thick fog, the kind that billowed through the Golden Gate Bridge in summertime.

During this period of my mother's recovery, the four of us moved separately from room to room in quiet slow motion, our ears attuned to Mom's soft-chiming bell. Our heads were down, too, our minds focused on chores once we finished our homework. We brought bulging sacks of groceries into the house for Nana and bags of garbage down to the garage. And we all dusted, a lot. This one task was of paramount importance to Mom; she could sense when it got to the point where visitors would notice it, though there were few visitors now.

Then, unbelievably, things got worse. Two months after Mom's back surgery, Dad left his job at the now-failing Crowley Company where he'd worked for nineteen years. The classified section of the *San Francisco Chronicle* was now laid out on the kitchen table every morning. Job prospects were circled in red.

Five months after Dad left his job, Macy's Union Square in San Francisco offered him a part-time job in the men's clothing department. Mom made a point of telling us this low-paying, low-skilled sales job was only temporary, that he'd soon find something better.

"And I also have a new job," she said. "I start work on Monday." She'd be working full-time now developing photographs, the type of work she'd done during World War II when Dad was stationed in the Aleutian Islands. Whether these two announcements were positive for our family or not, I couldn't tell. But it was my mother who kept our household going now. She made sure we'd hold onto our house. No more moves. No more separate apartments for us. She kept us clean, well fed, and well educated, although she'd no longer be there when we got home after school.

Dad had been working at Macy's for about two months when the Veterans Administration Hospital in San Francisco offered him a full-time clerical position in the doctors' billing section. He would start immediately. I could tell that it was a big deal and that he was proud because he was the one to announce it this time.

Mornings took on a reassuring familiarity. While we got ready for school, Dad was hustling around, packing his lunch. His shoulders were straight again. There was a jauntiness to his step as he walked down the stairs to the garage wearing a black sports coats, pressed slacks, and ties with stylish tie tacks. The sweet smell of Old Spice once again lingered in the air after he was gone.

The VA Hospital staff took well to Dad. He told us he was able to produce far beyond their expectations. He was such a competent worker, in fact, that some of his coworkers accused him of being "one of those efficiency experts" sent in to assess employers' work procedures at that time. Dad laughed when he told us this story, and he told it more than once. Things were looking up. The hospital's filing system was such a mess when he got there, he said, he didn't have to do much to please them.

Six months later, he was fired.

Mom didn't use the word *fired*, though, when she whispered the news to me in a darkened hallway that evening. She was jittery. Her blue eyes were so dark they were almost black. I never understood how her eyes could change color when she was upset.

"Your father doesn't have that job anymore, Laurie."

She didn't explain why he was fired, and I knew from the way she looked not to ask. I also knew there had to be more to the story. Dad had been a valued partner at Crowley Company. He only left his job there when the housing bubble burst and paychecks stopped. But the real estate market didn't affect the Veterans Administration. Dad had been an adept bookkeeper in the Army, at Crowley Company, and at the VA Hospital, too.

I knew this, but it would be four decades before I discovered what was behind his firing. The US Civil Service Commission found out from a 1940 arrest that he was gay. Eight years after he was fired, on July 3, 1975, the summer Dad came out to me, the commission stopped discriminating against gays and lesbians. But by then, more than five thousand federal employees had been fired for being gay. My father was one of them.

With this latest blow, all six of us moved around our big house like wooden puppets on fixed parallel tracks again, our paths rarely crossing. Mom worked and shopped for basics. The four of us kids attended school and completed our homework and housework without discussion. Caroline cooked dinner and sewed clothes for Susan and me. The rest of us washed dishes, vacuumed, dusted, and ironed. We kept our heads down. Dad was at best a dark shadow in the house again, invisible at worst. Romantic reminiscences stopped during this time. My parents didn't have to say a word. I knew we were in survival mode.

The year was 1967. I was almost sixteen. After finishing dinner and my chores, I'd retreat to my bedroom to make jewelry, some of which I sold at a consignment store downtown. I hammered away at coils of copper and brass on a steel anvil. The deafening *plink, plink, plink* of metal on metal quieted my mind. Only when Mom knocked on my door saying she was going to bed did I put my hammer away for the night.

On late-night phone conversations, I could hear Mom whispering words like *Chapter 13* and *bankruptcy*. Susan innocently opened the front door one day to a bill collector. Since my bedroom was near the front door, I heard the man ask her a series of questions. *Were our parents working? Did we have a new phone number?* When she later reported it to our parents, Mom lined the four of us up in the kitchen and told us to stop answering the phone and the front door until further notice. *No matter how long the ringing goes on.*

Dad returned our two first-off-the-assembly-line 1964 Ford Mustangs to the dealer. He returned home with a basic 1966 Volkswagen Beetle for the six of us. It was in this tiny stick-shift car I first learned to drive.

I alone for some reason accompanied Mom when she drove down to I. Magnin in Palo Alto to return her full-length mink coat. A prim salesclerk ushered us into a large changing room in the back with cheery, light pink walls and carpet, and a soft, padded white settee. The saleslady closed the white, louvered double door behind us. I am almost certain I heard her latch the doors together.

At first, Mom described our troubles to her in a low tone of voice. I picked up some phrases.

My husband lost his job.

We can't afford the monthly payments. . . .

I didn't know clothes could be purchased "on time" like homes and cars. Mom's fur coat must have been very expensive, I thought to myself.

It was the first time I heard my mother speak bluntly about family troubles. She seemed to have forgotten I was there, or maybe secrecy no longer mattered. She was desperate.

The saleslady told her she could not accept the return because of Mom's monogrammed initials in the lining. I sat frozen in the plush settee, not knowing what we would do now. Would my father go to jail?

Mom stood her ground. She was fierce. I was shocked. She might have even stomped her foot once or twice. She would protect our family from ruin, I thought.

"My husband has been shopping at this store for more than ten years," she said indignantly. Her voice was guttural and uncharacteristically loud.

"You *must* take it back."

She leaned in and said something to the clerk, hoping I wouldn't hear, I'm sure. But I did. I am pretty sure I heard the word *bankruptcy*. I am certain I heard her say, "I am not taking it home."

Miraculously, the clerk relented, though from what I understood, the store would only issue a partial credit. I guessed they would use some of what we owed them to replace the fancy initials in the lining.

"Come along now, Laurie," Mom said.

She grabbed my hand and off we marched, all the way through the store to the parking lot in the back. I could feel the other salesclerks' eyes on us. Or maybe it was my imagination. But my mother held her head high, giving me a comforting sense of security.

My father's place setting at the table was missing one evening, and it wasn't because he hadn't arrived home yet. He wouldn't be coming home, Mom said. I looked over at her in horror. She stood at the kitchen sink, scrubbing, rinsing, running the garbage disposal, and roughly clanking the dishes. When I asked where Dad was, she said he now worked as a night clerk at a sleazy motel near the San Francisco Airport. Maybe she didn't use the word sleazy, but that's what I heard in her voice.

By day, Dad would now be sleeping in a residential hotel in San Francisco's Tenderloin District, a neighborhood inhabited, I gathered, by prostitutes and violent drug addicts. By night, he dealt with the same type of clientele renting rooms by the hour at the motel. We didn't see much of him now, even on weekends. The four of us kids kept quiet at home. We had already learned not to answer the door or the phone. Mom dragged herself around the house. I pounded even harder on the coils of metal, later and later into the night. Mom no longer told me to stop.

Five months into his job, Dad called us into the living room to make yet another announcement. He'd landed a job at Standard Oil's corporate headquarters in San Francisco's tony Financial District. The position was junior clerk typist, the bottom of the pay scale, but it had still taken a lot of convincing on his part, he said, to persuade the human resources manager to let him have the job.

"She told me I was overqualified," he said. "She said it wouldn't be right to give me this job given my decades of book-keeping experience and the size of our family."

I didn't know someone would be refused a job because they were too good at what they did, or because they had a large family.

"I told her I was confident I'd quickly work my way up the ladder," he said. "And she must have believed me."

I believed him, too.

Dad began his new job in San Francisco in the summer of 1967, coinciding with the Summer of Love, the defining cultural movement of the Sixties. The gay liberation movement—later coined the gay rights movement—got into high gear two years later, in 1969, with the Stonewall Uprising in Greenwich Village where patrons of the Stonewall Inn spontaneously rose up against regular police raids on the gay bar. San Francisco saw its first semblance of a gay pride parade the following year. And Dad's new workplace was in the middle of it all.

CHAPTER 15: MY FIRST KISS

A high school junior shouted *Hey* to me from his lunch-time perch in the school's breezeway. I'll call him Jim. It was the Fall of 1966. Despite the warm weather, Jim and his fellow gawkers on the concrete ledge wore their bulky wool and leather varsity jackets.

I was fifteen, a sophomore, and new to this mating game. I blushed but slowed my stride. At lunchtime the next day, I slowed down a little more. Jim hopped off the high ledge, took my hand, and walked with me. His hand was clammy. I didn't yet know his name, but he somehow knew mine. He walked me to my next class, Spanish II, while shouting *Hey* to friends passing by in the opposite direction.

This was nothing like my parents' romantic fairytale begin-ning. Jim's eyes were dark and beady, unlike the big blue eyes my mother first spied on my dad. His face was pockmarked with acne scars, and his teeth were caged in metal braces. Jim's nod to the styles of the time was a chunky silver identification bracelet that jingled when he lifted up his arm to show me his engraved initials on it. It had taken him a long time to save up for the bracelet, he said, and extra to have it engraved. The old-style lettering was handsome. "Cool," I said.

I felt little physical attraction to Jim, but I liked the idea of having a boyfriend. I'd become a member of an enviable group. Though I wasn't an outgoing, popular girl, I now joined those considered popular who stood between the legs of their boyfriends on the noontime perch. Walking hand in hand with Jim after the bell rang, I could tell by the nods of his buddies that they considered me at least a modest trophy.

The second week of our relationship, if you could even call it that, Jim showed up outside the door of my final period geometry class. He took my hand and walked me the few blocks up the hill to my house. I can't remember if we talked about anything, or if we talked at all. But I do remember the tears that burned my eyes when he kissed me good-bye at the front door, his braces digging deep into my lips.

The following week, Jim followed me inside the house after school. I shot a look down the hallway. Mom wouldn't be home until dinnertime. Caroline's bedroom door was closed. Tim was probably at baseball practice. Susan, a strong runner by then, was likely running around the high school track down the hill from our house. I guided Jim downstairs to the den and tuned the TV to *Never Too Young*, the first soap opera geared toward teenagers. It was one of my favorite shows.

I'd barely seated myself on our green Naugahyde couch when Jim began French kissing me and fondling my breasts after a rough start unhooking my bra. This routine went on for a few weeks. My body, if not my heart, was aroused. I waited anxiously for his calls in the evening, hurrying others off the phone in the kitchen that the six of us shared during our bankruptcy years. Not that Jim and I had much to say on those calls, but I felt reassured by the attention. Then one night he didn't call.

I imagined him with another girl, kissing her, unlatching *her* bra. My sleep was fitful that night. When I pushed him the next day to explain, he let out a grunt and shrugged his shoulders. Now I was the one grabbing *his* hand in the breezeway. When this didn't quell my growing panic, I demanded proof of his allegiance. His ID bracelet would do, I told him. I'd already played with unfastening it from his wrist once before, but he'd quickly snapped the clasp back together and thrust his hand in his jacket pocket. Our back and forth went something like this:

No, you can't have it.
If you really cared about me, you'd let me wear it.
I saved up for a long time to get it.
But other boys let their girlfriends wear their ID bracelets.
I don't care. It's mine. I wanna wear it.
If you don't let me wear it, I won't be your girlfriend anymore.

The threat worked. Jim unlatched his bracelet and handed it over to me like someone handing over ransom. As I struggled to close the clasp, he turned and faced away from me, offering no assistance of any kind. When I finally got it on, I was surprised by how anxious I still felt. It had made no difference. The bell rang. We went our separate ways without saying good-bye. I knew I'd behaved badly, but I lacked the self-reflection then to ask myself why.

The next day at school, Jim asked for his beloved bracelet back. I fished it out of my purse—I couldn't even bear to put it on that morning—and surrendered it over. It marked the end of our relationship, one that had lasted no more than a month, one with a boy I was not even attracted to.

◇　◇　◇

My friend Vickie had been seeing a handsome, dark-haired boy from school for about six months by then.

"Aren't you worried about him cheating on you?" I asked.

She shot me a quizzical look as if I were speaking a foreign language. "I'm really not," she replied.

There was something about the perplexed look on her face that has remained with me. She considered me ridiculous for even asking the question. But I told myself I was the shrewder girl, the one who knew the truth about boys and men. They were all unfaithful. You could never *ever* trust them. I held fast to my belief, and it held fast to me. Never questioning the root cause of my instinctive distrust of the opposite sex, I was ever on the lookout for signs of betrayal. When I was unsuccessful at turning up even a shred of evidence, my anxiety didn't dissipate; it got worse. I didn't ask myself why. I just kept digging.

LAURA, AGE SEVENTEEN, 1968

CHAPTER 16: THE SUMMER OF LOVE

The social and cultural revolution that was the Summer of Love kicked off in June 1967, the month I turned sixteen. Tens of thousands of young people from all over the country flocked to San Francisco. Coined *hippies* and *flower children*, droves of them congregated in Golden Gate Park and the adjoining Haight Ashbury District.

Young women with dangling earrings and long flowing hair and skirts, and young men in fringed jackets, woven headbands, and shaggy hair chanted and kissed and danced to live rock, blues, and folk music in the park's glades and fern gardens. Many if not most were on their own for the first time without a means of support. Lines of hippies sat against the glass storefronts of head shops and food co-ops on Haight Street and panhandled curious tourists. A steady chant of *Spare change?* was matched by the rhythmic beats emanating from the drumming circles in the park a few blocks away. Protests against the Vietnam War, nuclear war, consumerism, and government in general snaked down the Panhandle toward Golden Gate Park. It wasn't just a party; it was a party with a conscience.

By late summer, my father had left his night manager job at the cheap motel south of San Francisco and was firmly settled into his junior clerk's job at Standard Oil's corporate offices in the Financial District. This conservative district's location a few miles from Golden Gate Park ensured that its culture would soon display the effects of the changing mores.

During Dad's first year at Standard Oil, he dressed the part of the clean-shaven corporate worker in his black and gray Brooks Brothers suits, neatly pressed white or pale-blue shirts, silk ties, and sterling silver tie tacks with matching cufflinks. But by the following year, he looked more like the hippies who remained in the city after the Summer of Love. His thick, salt-and-pepper mustache was the first sign. I thought it made him look like the Beat poets who read passages I didn't understand from tall wooden stools in the basement of the City Lights Bookstore in North Beach. Next came his beard, almost white, which over the course of about a year grew long and wild. He let his wavy hair grow long down his back now, sometimes pulling it into a ponytail. I didn't think it a flattering look, especially given that the top of his head was bald, but I felt proud that I had a father who evolved with the times. Mom was wary, though.

"Maybe you should trim your hair up a little, honey," she said.

Dad smiled at her suggestions and then ignored her advice. If she caught us hearing her criticize him, she'd follow up with a compliment.

"But you know, kids, *from the front* your father looks just like Sean Connery." Despite Dad's long beard, she must have relished the fact that she still had a slim husband with the looks, albeit qualified, of a movie star. Many of the other fiftyish husbands were by then jowly and pot-bellied and still wearing checkered or horizontally striped shirts and polyester pants, typical 1950s fashion.

◇ ◇ ◇

Dad came home one evening with a huge silver ring on his right hand. It surprised me, as I'd never seen him wear a ring. As a little girl, I'd asked him repeatedly why he didn't wear a wedding ring to match Mom's. He'd either change the subject or give me a different answer each time.

I don't like how they catch on things.
I'm afraid of scratching it when I'm working in the garden.
I'm not someone who wears rings.

I wondered what had brought on the change. Giddy in the telling, he relayed how a talented street artist on Market Street made this large ring by heating the thick handle of a sterling silver spoon. When pliable, he bent it to form a band. Dad didn't take this artistic ring off while he was gardening. It looked so good on him that I decided not to remind him of his long-ago excuses.

The following week he showed up wearing a second ring on his ring finger, this one studded with a thick slab of abalone shell. When he walked into the kitchen, I looked over at Mom at the stove. She was stirring a large pot with a large wooden spoon. When she adjusted the heat with her left hand, I saw the wide, simple gold wedding band on her ring finger. It was shiny as ever. As my father breathlessly described how another talented street artist crafted this second ring, I told myself that maybe he just didn't like *conventional* wedding rings. When he and Mom married, during World War II, wedding ring design must not have met his high standards. I was constantly bending the truth to prove to myself that he loved Mom, though I was unaware at the time that I was even doing so.

The rings were not the last of Dad's new collection of body adornments. Next came a wide, hand-stamped leather wrist-band and a necklace made of disks of turquoise interspersed with white puka shells, things he also purchased from street vendors in San Francisco.

In place of his standard corporate uniform of expensive Italian slacks and thin black leather belts he at first wore to work, Dad now dressed in skintight, stovepipe blue jeans or purple corduroy bell-bottoms with braided leather belts he'd made himself. Out went his Italian loafers, too, replaced by those square-toed Frye leather boots with the blocky heels and heavy brass buckles.

Expensive, well-tailored dress shirts that required dry cleaning were replaced by open-collared, white muslin shirts that he hand-sewed and blue denim work shirts. On their pockets and collars, he embroidered colorful daisies, doves, and peace signs. He topped off his look with a handcrafted leather cowboy hat.

Dad's new ensembles resembled what many young men and women wore in the Haight Ashbury and *outside* the heavy brass and glass doors of Standard Oil's corporate headquarters, but not inside them like he did. As well, my girlfriends' aging fathers didn't embroider flowers on their shirts, or wear knotted macramé belts made by their daughters, or enjoy the folksy protest music of Joan Baez and Crosby, Stills, Nash, and Young. It was as if Dad and I were both coming of age at the same time in history.

With the exception of his long ponytail and that time he came home with a tattoo he got on his lunch hour, I appreciated having a father who was part of the changing times. The petite red rose new to his left wrist, he told us at dinner one evening, was similar to the one he'd seen on the bare buttocks of a "gorgeous man over at that nude beach" in San Gregorio the prior weekend. After seeing it on this gorgeous man, he said, he just *had* to get one like it for himself, though he could only afford a smaller version.

He actually said those words out loud, in front of me, in front of Mom, and probably in front of one or two of my siblings, too. I felt sick to my stomach. All I could think of was my mother's feelings and how creepy and disrespectful the story must have been for her. I craned my neck, looking back over the kitchen island toward the sink. I caught her just as she turned back to the dishes.

◇ ◇ ◇

As Dad predicted, he rose quickly through the ranks at his job, from the lowest-level clerk–typist position to payroll accountant. But with promotions and pay raises came increased scrutiny about his rebellious appearance. It seems his boss had been eyeing his cowboy hat and blue jeans and open-necked muslin shirt, and maybe his turquoise beads as well. Dad mimicked his words.

This isn't a construction company, Ralph.

Dad howled in laughter when he related this to us, but I didn't think it was so funny. Though I admired the way he dressed, I remembered Mom's phone whispers about bankruptcy. I didn't want to be told to stop answering phone calls and doorbells again.

"Da-ad!"

My tone was one of horror. He immediately took a more serious stance.

"Don't worry, honey. I told him I understood and then I walked out of his office."

"But won't you get fired?"

"Oh, honey," he said, now in a more lighthearted tone. "They won't fire me. They think I'm a pretty smart guy."

Well, I thought he was a pretty smart guy, too. But I assumed there were plenty of other smart guys who could do his job who would be more than happy to wear corporate-appropriate attire. But Dad went right on dressing in his new style, paying no heed to his supervisor. Perhaps Standard Oil didn't have a formal dress code. Or maybe they couldn't force him to conform. But his supervisor eventually dropped the matter altogether.

◇ ◇ ◇

For holidays, employee birthdays, and retirement parties, Dad booked banquet rooms at Trader Vic's, Perry's, and other trendy San Francisco restaurants for Standard Oil's seventh-floor employees. The parties, he said, were popular not only with his fellow clerks but increasingly with the supervisors, too. No one at Standard Oil ever again told him to stop dressing like a cowboy or a fashionable construction worker.

Dad would prove my fears even more baseless the following year by getting a $3,000 award and a formal commendation, personally signed by Standard Oil's chairman of the board, for "employees who make outstanding contributions to the success of the company." Still smarting over his prior dismissal, I wondered why the VA hadn't recognized the stellar employee they had in my father.

Dad, now in his fifties, appeared to be getting younger. Once he'd recovered from his surgery, he became a health and fitness buff as did so many others at the time. Inspired by the national jogging craze, he rose at four in the morning to run laps in the dark around my high school track before work. He'd return to the house to prepare a tall thermos of Tiger's Milk for the day, a bitter brew developed by Adele Davis, a popular nutritionist of the time. His four children turned up their noses to the pungent smell of brewer's yeast and blackstrap molasses, but Mom cheered him on.

"You ran how many laps this morning, Ralph?"

Naturally, he kept meticulous records of his running stats, the highlights of which he posted on the refrigerator door for all of us to see.

"You're getting almost as fast as Tim," she said.

If she was suspicious of Dad's tattoo and the story behind it, his skintight jeans, his burgeoning collection of street artist jewelry, or his regular weekend jaunts to the nude beach matched by his increasingly dark tan when he returned home, she didn't let on. We lived in one house again instead of two separate apartments. Gone were the worries about bill collectors at the front door, phone calls to dodge, and expensive items to return. Her family of six was intact.

CHAPTER 17: A BOY AND A MAN

Bill reminded me of a young Bob Dylan. His hair was light brown and shaggy, and he wore faded blue jeans, a white T-shirt, and black leather motorcycle boots. We met at a party in Moss Beach out on the San Mateo County coast. When the incense sticks had turned to ash and the pot had all been smoked, Bill shuffled toward the front door. He turned to me.

"Wanna ride?"

He opened the passenger door to his parents' 1966 cream-colored Mercury Monterey Breezeway. I ducked my head and slid into the front seat. The boxy, four-door sedan came with power steering, new at the time and not a feature in our budget Volkswagen Beetle.

Bill sped out of the gravel driveway, flicking cigarette ashes out his open window. With his other hand, he spun the steering wheel one way and then the other. The *tick tick ticking* sound of the power steering reminded me of the sound the nail-studded wheels made when the carnival workers at St. Charles spun them for prizes.

It was the summer of 1967. I was sixteen and a junior at the public school. Bill, a nineteen-year-old high school dropout, lived with his parents in San Mateo a few miles north of San Carlos. They both had fulltime jobs, so we had the house to ourselves during the day.

Bill's bedroom was impressive, the type of room I imagined many young people at the time inhabited. The walls and ceilings were papered with psychedelic rock posters advertising live shows at the Fillmore Auditorium and Avalon Ballroom in San Francisco. The artwork with its twisted lettering featured popular rock bands of the time: The Grateful Dead, Big Brother and The Holding Company, Jefferson Airplane, and more. Bill played his 45s, stacked ten-high on his tiny record player, while we made out on his bed. He hummed Rolling Stones songs in my ear, off-key, while we slow danced in his bedroom.

Though Bill sported counterculture looks and slept in a psychedelic wonderland of a bedroom, his political views leaned conservative. He supported the Vietnam War, even though a physical condition prevented him from serving. He voted for Nixon for president the following year. John Wayne movies were a favorite.

We couldn't have been further apart on the cultural and political issues of the day. But on the one thing that mattered most to me, we were a good match. I didn't worry about him spending time with other girls after he dropped me off at my house. He called when he said he would call. He was on time for our dates and picked me up at school every day in his parents' car. We nuzzled at drive-in movies and cuddled on the beach at sunset. Unlike Jim, who had rightly fought me on his ID bracelet, Bill was more accommodating. If I wanted one of his beloved rock posters that was tacked to his bedroom wall, he'd take it down and help me mount it on my own bedroom wall.

On Saturday nights, Bill and I drove up to the Haight Ashbury where pot dealers in heavy pea coats strolled up one side of Haight Street and down the other while chanting, *Lids for sale, lids for sale,* under their breath. Bill would slide a ten-dollar bill into the dealer's hand in return for a lid of grass rolled up tight inside a sandwich baggie. Beat cops patrolled the streets, which worried me, though they seemed to turn a blind eye to pot sales. Their focus may have been on the harder drugs that were beginning to flood the area.

In this hippie wonderland, Bill dressed the part. He introduced me to the psychedelic art and music of the times and had easy access to a steady supply of marijuana. Though I was never a fan of pot or of the much stronger, mind-altering LSD and mescaline increasingly in circulation in the city, which I never even tried, I fancied myself a flower child in the costume of the time: tie-dyed T-shirts, bell bottoms, ponchos, long dangly earrings, beaded headbands, sandals with thick leather straps, and peasant blouses Caroline made for me out of paisley-print Indian bedspreads.

I was a sheltered teenager from the suburbs playing a part. I picked and chose only the artistic and crafty aspects of the revolution. Even though Bill and I were not a match politically, I think the intoxicating effect of the Summer of Love softened the edges of any potential discord, at least temporarily. There was an ease about us.

Then I met Jay.

A few girlfriends and I were out at the coast at that same house in Moss Beach where I met Bill. I don't know where Bill was that evening. I walked in the door to see Jay holding court with half a dozen attractive, giddy, teenage girls seated around him at a large rectangular wooden table. His hair was thick and blond. He bemoaned the atrocities of the "senseless" Vietnam War, issued a warning about the near certainty of nuclear weapons annihilating humanity, and expressed sympathy for the millions of children starving in Biafra. I didn't know about the civil war in Biafra, or even where Biafra was, but I was riveted by his seeming compassion and breadth of knowledge about world affairs. He was the stark opposite of Bill.

The girls seated at the table shot me a quick glance then turned back to Jay, whose blue eyes caught mine. I turned away, seating myself at the far end of the table, as starstruck as the others but tongue-tied. I was intimidated by Jay's seeming intellectual rigor about dire situations I knew little about. The other girls peppered him with questions about the war.

What is it even about?

"The ridiculous fear of communism," he said.

I imagined him saying *Next?* in his mind.

Should my parents build a bomb shelter?

"No one will survive a nuclear war," Jay said, his tone grounded in certainty.

The questions continued unabated. I didn't ask one, but each time I got up my nerve to look directly at Jay, he wasn't looking at the girls asking the questions. He was looking at me. As the hour grew late, and the patchouli-scented candles on discarded coffee can lids burned down into runny puddles of melted wax, Jay stood up and stretched. He was quite tall. He grabbed his tan-colored newsboy cap off the table and walked by me, placing his hand on my left shoulder.

"Would you like to take a walk with me?"

I froze in shock. I couldn't even look up at him. I guessed the other girls, those with the adoring gazes and ridiculous questions, were surprised, too. My cheeks burned. I hoped Jay couldn't see how red they were. I slipped into the quilted parka I'd draped over the back of my chair and followed Jay into the cramped living room. When I saw him grab a sleeping bag off the floor in the corner of the room, I hesitated, though only for a moment. Of course, he had a sleeping bag. He was hitchhiking down the California coast to Monterey and back to San Francisco. Like most hippies at the time, I told myself, he either wouldn't have had hotel fare or fancied the bohemian style of "crashing" in the homes of people he met along the way.

I gulped in the damp, pungent night air that hit me the minute Jay held open the front door and waved me through. It smelled of briny seaweed. Without the harsh glow of city streetlights on the coast, the stars lit up the night sky and the path ahead of us. It snaked around the top of the sand dunes. Jay put out his hand to me and I took it. It was much larger than mine and felt strong and purposeful. I guessed he was only a year older than Bill, but I detected something different right away. Jay was a man.

My bellbottoms brushed up against the sage on either side of the path, scenting the air with its thick herbal fragrance. When we reached a small clearing, Jay unrolled his sleeping bag without fanfare. I stared at it.

"Let's sit," he said.

I lowered myself down without saying a word. Jay sat down with his legs crossed yoga-style. Our bodies touched. He draped one of his long arms around me so gently I barely felt its weight. When he leaned over and kissed me, it was as if it were the most natural thing in the world to kiss someone you'd only just met. His kisses were at the same time gentle and passionate. I accepted them graciously. The breaking waves below us sparkled with the reflections of the stars.

Not once that evening did I see myself as a cheater.

Jay eventually broke the silence with a mention of an anti-war protest in San Francisco planned for the following weekend. He would be attending it once he returned from Monterey.

"Would you like to join me?"

I spit out, "Yes!" without hesitation. It may have been my first word to him that evening.

"Take the 5-Fulton toward Golden Gate Park," he said. "It stops right in front of my house, one block from the Panhandle. Look for the purple Victorian. A friend and I share the top flat."

He didn't give me their flat number—I didn't even know what a flat was—but I knew I would find him. Though I wondered how I'd be able to keep up with this handsome, intelligent, progressive man. He wasn't a boy. But I was still a girl.

◇ ◇ ◇

I told only one friend of my plans to meet Jay at his home the following Saturday. When the day arrived, the two of us boarded a Greyhound bus for San Francisco, then took a local bus over to the Panhandle. We walked the block until we spied a tall, narrow purple building on Page Street. I still don't know how we happened to find it. We climbed the two flights of stairs up to Jay's flat. He opened the door and may have said hello or welcome to us, but I don't remember. What I do remember is that he greeted me not with a kiss but with a polite, outstretched hand which he then extended to my girlfriend as well.

The sweet smell of burning incense drifting onto the landing drew us into what could only be described as a bohemian Disneyland, with one dazzling display after the other. Instead of interior doors, strands of colored glass beads hung from tops of door frames. I wondered what they had done with the doors. Indian print bedspreads covered the ceilings and, as I'd soon find out, the beds, too. Filigreed metal roach clips leaned up against what looked like hand-crafted ceramic ashtrays. Colorful batik prints hung on the walls near the ceiling of this nineteenth-century flat.

Jay made me a cup of hot herbal tea of some sort and offered me a snack of cool, crunchy carrots and raw cashews after which he led me to his bed. He asked me if I had ever had sex as he unzipped his blue jeans. I shook my head no.

"I'm too scared," I said.

With that, he zipped up his jeans. I let out a relieved sigh and sunk into one of his pillows. I couldn't believe he wasn't angry. He didn't seem to mind at all. Instead, he enfolded me in his arms and kissed me for what seemed like forever.

"Let's go downstairs and march," he said.

I was so giddy I kicked off my shoes and marched barefoot, not feeling the blistering pain on the soles of my feet until we got back to his flat. I felt as if I'd been floating the whole time.

As Jay and his roommate saw my friend and me off to the bus, he asked if I could come back the following weekend.

Yes. Definitely yes.

On the long bus ride home, I realized for the first time I had betrayed Bill. Still, I tried to convince myself that there was nothing wrong with seeing Bill *and* Jay. After all, husbands openly shared stories with their wives of the nude beaches they visited. I was just cool like my dad.

The following weekend, my girlfriend picked me up in her Datsun. We planned to repeat our journey to the bus station and to Jay's flat. On our drive to the station, I asked her to stop by Bill's house. I skipped up the concrete steps to the front door wearing a soft, doe-colored suede skirt, a white blouse with ruffled lace down the front, and an unbuttoned, chestnut-brown velvet vest. I'd tied my long hair up into a ponytail using one of my father's silk handkerchiefs, the olive-green-and-aqua one with geometric shapes on it. I was ready for Jay. But in case things did not go well, I wanted to make sure Bill would still be there for me.

I knocked on the door. When no one arrived, I opened it. Bill was vacuuming the carpet and didn't hear me above the noise. When he saw me, he turned off the vacuum cleaner.

"We're headed up to the city for the afternoon to see these two guys we met," I said. "I'll call you when I get back."

I was so naïve. Bill was such an uncomplicated and devoted boyfriend I think I expected him to send me on my way with a smile. Of course, that didn't happen. His blue eyes pierced mine.

"If you go, you will never see me again," he said.

Shocked by how bold he was in drawing a clear line in the sand with me, I stood immobile at the threshold of the door. The choice before me was stark. One was a boy who was true but didn't light me up. The other was a man who frightened me because he *did* light me up.

I turned and looked out the open door toward my girl-friend's car idling at the curb, aimed toward the bus and another exotic adventure in the city. I looked back at Bill, my sure thing. In a moment, I went from imagining the agony of never seeing Jay again to, *How could I ever keep this sophis-ticated San Francisco intellectual from cheating on me?* I'd be all alone then.

Waving my friend off, I stepped into Bill's house. I can still remember the finality of the click of the front door closing behind me. I would never see Jay again. To this day, I wonder if he ever thinks of me. I wonder if he even remembers me, this young teenager from the Peninsula suburbs who never showed up that day or ever again.

CHAPTER 18: IN THE BACK SEAT

I t happened at the drive-in. I was seventeen. Bill took me to see the movie *Bullitt*. He attached the speaker to his car window and the two of us climbed into the back seat where we had unprotected sex to the sound of cars on the screen screeching down steep, winding streets of San Francisco.

The year was 1968, one year after the Summer of Love broke open sexual norms for unmarried couples. And though the FDA had approved birth control pills eight years earlier, in 1960, I didn't know how or where to get them. I didn't even try. Halfway through my senior year of high school, I was pregnant.

Bill's family doctor, whom I saw to avoid having my family doctor tell my parents the news, confirmed the pregnancy. I nodded to Bill, who sat hunched over in the waiting room.

"Well, what do you wanna do?"

"We need to get married," I said.

"Uh, okay."

◇ ◇ ◇

Despite the emotional and academic toll that switching from a private to a public school halfway through my freshman year took on me, and the turmoil the bankruptcy caused the family,

I'd done well in school and had already received my college acceptance letter. My intention was to join my older sister in the fall at UC Santa Barbara, in the same city where our parents had honeymooned three decades earlier.

I put off announcing my pregnancy to my parents until a bout with the German measles forced the issue. Susan, then fifteen, arrived home from school one day with a rash on her face. She didn't appear sick otherwise. At dinner a few days later, Mom brushed off the appearance of red spots on my face.

"Oh, look, Ralph," she said. "Laurie now has the German measles!"

Her voice was gleeful. I didn't understand. Mom got up to clear the dinner table.

"It's good the girls get this before they're married," she said, not even bothering to look at any of us. It wasn't even a serious issue.

I had my back to her. My eyes surveyed those at the table. Tim, sixteen, stared blankly out the large window he faced. Dad took another bite of his dinner and turned his neatly folded newspaper over to the next section. Susan was still eating, and Caroline was away at college.

"Uh, why is that, Mom?" I tried to feign nonchalance in my voice.

"The baby could be seriously deformed," she said.

Mom's voice and manner were still lighthearted when she delivered bowls of bright green mint chip ice cream to Tim and me.

"Finish up, Susan," she said.

She knew there was no use hurrying Dad. Besides, he preferred to scoop out his own ice cream in perfect spheres, adding milk to the bowl afterward, something that made no sense to any of us. If Mom noticed anything unusual about my facial expression, which must have betrayed my horror, she didn't let on.

I stared down at my bowl, eating my ice cream as slowly as I could. We were still down to one phone for all six of us, a wall phone in the kitchen. I wanted to be the last one in the room. Mimicking my father, I took a long pause between each tiny spoonful. When Dad finally finished his dessert, I told my mother not to worry about the dishes, that I'd put my bowl in the dishwasher and turn it on when I was done.

As soon as I was alone, I dialed Bill's number and sank down on the floor, facing into the corner to keep my voice from traveling.

"I have the German measles," I whispered.

"Yeah?" he said.

"My mother says it's dangerous for unborn babies."

"Yeah?"

"Especially when their brains are forming, like now."

"Oh."

◇　◇　◇

I peeked out the door of my bedroom. Through the dark hallway, I could see the back of my mother's head. She was sitting in one of the overstuffed chairs in the living room drinking her after-dinner cup of coffee. A magazine, *McCall's* or the *Ladies' Home Journal,* was opened up on her lap. Daisy, our jumpy terrier, had wedged herself in between Mom and the armrest. It looked like no one else was around. I crept down the tiled entry hallway and sat down in Dad's favorite chair, stiff, high-backed, and covered in chartreuse-colored silk fabric. I angled it in her direction and took a deep breath.

"Mom, I'm pregnant."

She looked up from her magazine and gasped. Her faced was ashen. She yelled for Dad.

"The German measles! Ralph!"

I was somewhat relieved that the topic was again the German measles.

Dad emerged from the back room in his long blue velour robe. Tim hopped up the stairs, taking two or three steps at a time with his long legs. Susan wasn't anywhere around. Maybe she was taking a bath.

Tim sat cross-legged on the carpet, his shaggy, sixties-era curls hanging down past his collar.

"What's going on?"

Mom bit down on one side of her lip.

"Tim, your sister's pregnant," she said, her voice strained and serious. The sound of it reminded me of the voices actors playing doctors on TV used when notifying a family member of a loved one's dire affliction. Mom's daughter was afflicted with a pregnancy, and a doomed one at that. I moved over to the sapphire-blue sofa, lay down, and pulled our old afghan over my legs. The pink, blue, and gray crocheted afghan had been in our family for as long as I could remember. I couldn't even look at my mother.

Tim grimaced and looked down at his folded legs. After about ten minutes, he walked back down to his bedroom without saying a word. Dad walked over to me and dropped to his knees. Our eyes were at the same level.

"Are you okay, honey?" he said.

My throat tightened at the love and concern in his voice. I knew he wouldn't judge me. I choked back tears. I wanted to turn away, but his piercing eyes held mine in check.

"Yeah," I said. "It's okay. Don't worry. Bill and I are gonna get married."

I wondered if he'd yet again correct my use of the word, *gonna*. He hated slang. But this time he didn't bother.

◇ ◇ ◇

That weekend, I opened my bedroom door to Dad's quiet knock. He invited me to join him outside. I was still in the early stages of pregnancy. I followed him down the hallway, reflexively on my tiptoes to keep anyone from noticing. He opened the heavy front door for me and led me down the front walkway, past his succulents, gravel, driftwood, rusted farm implements, and all the open windows. As we neared the front sidewalk, Dad stopped and reached for the pack of cigarettes in his shirt pocket. He turned it upside down and tapped it a few times on the palm of his left hand, *smack, smack,* before edging out one of the cigarettes and raising it to his lips. It was the ritual I'd witnessed all my life. I picked at my nails and tugged at my jeans, which were already uncomfortably tight at the waist. This was taking forever.

Dad reached deep down into one of his pants pockets for his heavy, sterling silver lighter, and flipped open the top with his thumb. The sound of the metal top sliding against the metal base made a kind of whirring sound. The day was windy, so he had to spin the wheel more than once. When the flint successfully ignited the flame, he held it up to his cigarette and took a long draw. The tip turned a bright orange-red and, as it burned, it crackled like crumpled tissue paper disintegrating in a fireplace.

He turned his head away from me to exhale, blowing the smoke out slowly and evenly. Only then did he turn to look at me. I gulped. Was he finally going to let me know how disappointed in me he was?

"You know, honey," he said. He paused to look out into the distance, above my head, before focusing his eyes back on me. "You do not have to get married."

This was unexpected. I don't know what I expected, especially with all the buildup. But it wasn't this.

"You can stay here," he said. "Your mother and I will help you with the baby."

I knew at the time that his message was important. I knew I should pay attention to it. But I couldn't admit, even to myself, that I'd made a horrible mistake. Dad's words had barely left his mouth before I jumped in.

"It's okay, Dad," I said. "I *want* to get married."

I noticed a momentary flicker of disappointment in his downturned eyes before I turned away. I could tell he held out no hope for the marriage's success. I knew he wanted me to go to college. I knew he wasn't able to finish college many years ago, though he never told me why he dropped out.

The month before I turned eighteen, Bill and I married in a hasty wedding in Carson City, Nevada. I'd already earned enough class credits to graduate halfway through my senior year. In the honeymoon suite of a musty Victorian inn, I stared at the tired old light fixture in the dark-blue ceiling while we had sex. It was then, at four months' pregnant, on my honeymoon, staring at an antique light fixture, that I admitted to myself that I didn't love Bill but that I'd do my best to soldier on.

We rented a tiny apartment in downtown San Carlos not far from my grandmother's house. Bill worked steadily at a machinist job, and I took a clerical job in Burlingame until I could no longer camouflage my pregnancy from my employers and coworkers. I never even told them I was married. My father never wore a wedding ring. I never wore my wedding ring to work.

PREGNANT AT SEVENTEEN

A MOTHER AT EIGHTEEN

CHAPTER 19: THE ARRIVAL

My mother called me early on a Saturday morning with a directive.

"You need a rocking chair," she said. "Every new mother needs one."

She sounded breathless, perhaps because I was in my third trimester and would be needing one soon. The family rocking chair I'd grown up with would now be mine. I first needed to pick out some new fabric for the pillows. My mother didn't say why, but this particular point seemed important to her. Maybe she wanted her soon-to-be grandchild to have something pretty and new.

"Can you be ready in an hour?"

I selected earthy green corduroy at the yardage store in the Hillsdale Mall. It was still the sixties, after all, and nubby fabric was in vogue. The corduroy wasn't what Mom would have chosen. But she didn't say anything, keeping her focus on the finish line. She purchased the fabric and said she'd deliver it and the pillows to a local upholsterer. "No problem," she said. I sensed her urgency.

I made room for the rocking chair in our one-bedroom apartment's tiny living room by jamming the coffee table we'd repurposed from a large discarded wooden spool into one corner. I angled Bill's suitcase-sized stereo speakers against the wooden apple crates that held our boxy stereo and combined collections of vinyl records.

Mom's focus the following weekend was on a *layette*, a word I'd never heard of before it came out of her mouth. Off she and I headed to Sears to pick up soft "receiving" blankets, burp cloths, cloth diapers and safety pins, creepers, and warm knitted booties. I wasn't even sure what all these things were, but I didn't ask questions. Mom was all business. She hurried me and my growing up along, assuring me I would understand everything once the baby was born. Onesies for the baby, maternity clothes for me, and Corning Ware casserole dishes for our under-furnished kitchen were her next priorities. That, and Lamaze classes. But I put my foot down on that. I didn't want to think about giving birth.

Early on Saturday, December 6, 1969, a warm liquid cascaded down my legs. I might have known what this meant if I'd taken the Lamaze classes or read books about childbirth. I woke Bill up from a deep sleep. He was as bewildered as I was. I called the doctor's answering service, even though I felt no pain or cramps, and was told to get to the hospital right away.

By mid-afternoon, Jody Lynn entered the world free of birth defects, though the delivery was complicated. My doctor had allowed my pregnancy to go ten months. Jody weighed almost nine pounds. He told me I should have had a caesarean but that it had been too late for that. I spent the next four days recovering in the hospital, seeing Jody only at "feedings." I was in too much pain to even think about breastfeeding, something I hadn't been amenable to anyway, and fed her formula from a bottle. Despite my immaturity, the difficult birth, and my decision not to nurse her, Jody was an active, happy baby.

Bill worked all day and drank and smoked pot in the evenings. My few girlfriends were away at college. When the boys

I knew turned eighteen, many were drafted and shipped off to Vietnam. I was on my own with a newborn. Though I was just as conscientious in caring for Jody and running a household as my mother had been with the four of us, I was lonely, exhausted, and despondent about my interrupted education. Things only got worse when Bill started night classes.

CHAPTER 20: CHEATERS

The doorbell rang late one evening. Bill was in class. Jody was asleep in her crib. After asking who was there, I unlatched the door chain and opened the door to a boy I knew from high school. As one of the lucky ones with a college deferment, he had avoided Vietnam. I'll call him Kevin.

I stood to one side as he walked in. He dropped his motorcycle helmet and leather jacket on top of our apple-crate bookcases which wobbled under the weight. He smoothed his sweaty mop of dark brown hair with one hand before making himself comfortable on our couch. I turned off *The Mod Squad*, or some other TV show of the time, and joined him. Kevin had just applied to graduate school. Bill, a high school dropout, was at night school preparing for his GED exam.

My social circle at the time consisted almost entirely of my parents, grandmother, aunts and uncles, and Tim and Susan, who were still in high school. I knew only one other young mother. We lived in the same apartment building, and she had a little boy a year older than Jody. Other than that, she and I had little in common. I itched to join students protesting at nearby UC Berkeley. They were marching for civil rights, against the war, and against nuclear power plants, the same hot issues Jay and I had talked about before I chose Bill, before I got pregnant.

Now it was Kevin who was sounding like Jay. I was impressed. When I stood up to get us something from the kitchen, he leaned over and pulled me onto his lap and kissed me hard. His beard reeked of marijuana, which I didn't care for, but the sweet smell of motorcycle grease on his fingers was intoxicating. I kept one ear cocked for the *putt-putt* of our Volkswagen bus though. But by the time Bill got home, Kevin was long gone and I was in bed. I feigned sleep when Bill slid in next to me hoping for some action.

◇   ◇   ◇

My affair, which now included sex, was in its fourth week. Kevin's intellectual banter had jolted me. I wanted out of my marriage. I was now twenty. Jody wasn't yet two. Bill was shocked.

"You're leaving me?"

I rushed to reassure him that he'd done nothing wrong.

"I'm just going crazy here, Bill."

He got up and poured himself a second and then a third glass of Almaden jug wine.

"But you're the one who wanted to get married," he said.

He ran his fingers through his long, soft hair, suspending them there for a moment.

"I know I did. I'm so sorry."

The next weekend I moved back in with my parents, Jody in tow, the scenario my father had envisioned for me before she was born. My teen marriage had lasted just under two years. My parents welcomed me home, neither one questioning me or judging me for my decision. They weren't surprised. I had hoped to continue my relationship with Kevin, only to discover that he didn't consider ours a serious relationship. He was involved with a few other girls. *Cheater*, I thought, oblivious to my own status of infidelity.

I was eager to date boys and continue living my irresponsible pre-pregnancy teenage years. But my mother, working fulltime herself due to the bankruptcy, would have none of it.

"Money's still tight," she said. "You need to get a job."

She'd heard that Fairchild Semiconductor, one of the pioneer firms in what soon would be known as Silicon Valley, was hiring clerical staff. Mom handed me a phone number. I did as I was told. It was a booming time, and I easily landed a fulltime clerical job. I dropped Jody off at a nearby nursery school every day and retrieved her ten hours later. Mom made sure there would be no freewheeling adolescent life for me. I was a mother now, albeit an absent one most of the time.

I performed well in my job, which didn't require much beyond good typing and filing skills. But Jody cried every day when I dropped her off, and I cried all the way to work.

My hormones raged on. One Saturday I spied a handsome young man out the front window of my yellow VW bug as I pulled up to the curb at the family home. I'll call him Greg. He was perched on the low step of the family's front walkway, his long and slim blue-jeaned legs stretched out before him. His movie star looks included dark brown hair, light brown skin, square shoulders, square jaw, and a cleft chin. As I rounded the car to retrieve Jody and a bag of diapers out of the back seat, I noticed that he noticed me, too. I looked away. My arms now full, I flipped my long sun-bleached hair back and sauntered breezily past him toward the front door.

Greg was the older brother of Susan's buff surfer boyfriend. She told me later he wanted to ask me out. "Would that be okay?" I assured her it was.

After a quick dinner, Greg took me to his friend's apartment and seduced me. As with Kevin a year earlier, I didn't resist and became clingy afterward. When his calls stopped a few weeks later, I began looking for a boy I could trust. Like Bill, the one I'd recently discarded. By the second year of living with my parents, I would meet him and repeat my pattern.

I'll call him John. He called when he said would. He invited Jody to join us on our excursions to local beaches and on camping trips in the Sierras. Three months later, we moved to Sonoma County, a two-hour drive north. We both worked in high-tech jobs during the week and tended to our vegetable garden on weekends.

Six months later, I pressured him into marriage. We were both twenty-three. John and I picked up a marriage license at the county courthouse and found a local judge to marry us in one of the corridors. No wedding dress. No honeymoon. No friends or family members except for Jody, now four. These should have all been warning signs to me, but I told myself it was the freewheeling seventies, and everyone else was getting married in the same casual way. No, everyone wasn't. I informed my mother about the marriage two days later on the phone.

"You did *what*?" she said, her voice rising.

"It's no big deal, Mom," I said. "Marriage isn't the same as when you and Dad got married."

I didn't want to discuss it with her or my father. I wanted to be married. I didn't want to even think about the fact that it was my second marriage. I didn't want to be a single mother. I didn't want to be alone. I didn't want any man to hurt me again. Still lacking any self-reflection, I skipped over the part about my own infidelities.

Quickly moving into high gear, Mom planned a wedding reception for us the following weekend. It was just for the family. She ordered a traditional, two-tiered wedding cake from Tasty Bakery for the reception. Dad shopped for new dishes and stemware after asking us to select patterns. I'd now have my second full set of dishes in less than four years' time.

After a brief period of ease in this second marriage of mine, I began suffering from migraine headaches for the first time. I had been fretting over my second husband's friendships with other women, which were many, as well as his whereabouts whenever he left the house. Hypervigilant in order to justify my anxiety, I searched for unfamiliar phone numbers and girls'

names in his pockets. I'd scan his face to see if he was looking at other girls at parties. When I spotted him glancing in a
girl's direction, I badgered him, even as I experienced a sense
of relief. *I'm not crazy*, I told myself. I'd been right all along.
Men were not to be trusted, even the two trustworthy young
men I'd married.

When my hunts for hanky-panky came up empty, instead
of being reassured, I tightened my efforts to uncover evidence.
In two short years, I'd squeezed all the intimacy out of my
second marriage.

Around this time, my supervisor at work called me into his
office to look at a drawing of an integrated circuit board on his
computer. He pulled a chair over to his desk and summoned me
to it. One hand pointed at the screen, the other landed on my
thigh. This led to my second extramarital affair and subsequent
plans to leave my second husband. This affair took but a few
months to run its course, just as the first one did.

By age twenty-four, I was twice married, twice unfaithful,
and twice divorced. I was ashamed of myself. I was hoping to
pin the blame for my weak character on anyone but me. All
bets were on my father.

CHAPTER 21: THE VIEW FROM BOTH SIDES

"You remember Uncle Seedy, Laurie?"

Dad wasn't done telling me his story that fateful day on the hill. Of course, I remembered Uncle Seedy. We'd visited him on our way to Disneyland. And Dad had spoken often of him in reference to a piece of pottery or a painting or the vintage classical books of literature in the family bookcase. Those were all gifts from this person the four of us kids referred to as our uncle.

I nodded.

"Well, he wasn't your uncle."

"Yeah, Dad, I figured that out."

I can't pinpoint the moment I knew. But at some point, I realized he wasn't related to anyone in our family.

"His name was Clarence," Dad said. "And he was a very good friend to me back in the day."

Clarence was the organist for The Little Church of the Flowers in Glendale in Southern California. He also taught private piano and organ lessons. Dad seemed impressed relating all of this to me. I now wonder if his admiration for Clarence was why he wanted the four of us kids to learn to play the piano.

Dad had already covered a lot of ground with me that day. He'd always been gay. Mom found out in 1957 when I was six. He didn't love Mom in a romantic way.

"Laurie, there's something else," he said.

He cleared his throat. My stomach clutched. Did it get worse, I wondered. He paused longer than usual.

"*What*, Dad?"

"Well, honey," he said, "of all the kids . . . Well, I thought you might be—"

I assumed then that he thought I was gay. I didn't wait for him to finish his sentence.

"But I like *boys*, Dad."

I turned my shoulder to him and gazed out into the distance, away from the afternoon sun. Smog clouded the long view. Images of my tomboy childhood came to me. My slicked back bangs in the first grade resembled a boy's haircut. I loved baseball. Most girls at the time did not. I snuck Tim's high-top sneakers out of his closet.

Dad appeared to be stifling a laugh, which was odd. He was never one to laugh at me.

"No, no, no, honey," he said.

This time he let out a silly-sounding chuckle, again out of character for him.

"That's not what I'm talking about."

I must have had a blank stare on my face. It was like taking one of those tests in school where none of the questions make sense even though you've prepared hard for it.

"Huh?"

"It's just that, well, you've always seen things from both sides," he said.

At twenty-four, I knew this about myself. I think I always knew, though I had no words or context for it. But I didn't know how it related to the topic at hand. I knew I wasn't gay. I must have looked bewildered or maybe stunned because Dad stopped there. I never did get him to clarify. I wish I had. If we were having the conversation today, we would have a wealth of resources about gender identity upon which to draw.

There's a photo of me at six where I'm wearing Tim's blue jeans and pointy cowboy boots. The jeans are held up by a wide leather belt with a big silver buckle. A studded holster carries a cap gun with a white enameled grip. A knotted kerchief around my neck is tucked into Tim's plaid flannel shirt. My hands are on my hips, and I have a pleased look on my face. I *was* pleased with myself. I knew I looked tough and strong. Like a boy. However, I didn't want to *be* a boy. I loved being exactly who I was, someone who loved dresses and sports uniforms, art and baseball, patent leather flats and high tops, just like many girls of today. But not like most girls then, at least none than I knew of.

Fortunately, my gay father and straight mother not only allowed me to be myself, but they encouraged me to be exactly who I was, someone who was drawn to traditional interests of both boys and girls. It was my mother who attended my baseball games. She bought my baseball mitt, bat, softballs, and hardballs. She found me the same kind of short-sleeved sweatshirt the neighborhood boys wore in the streets after school while we played pickup games of baseball. But my father was the one who bought me my first pair of blue jeans. Only they weren't called jeans then.

"They're called *ranch pants*," he announced when he unveiled them.

I was ten and enchanted. No other girls I knew of—except for those out in the country riding horses—wore such pants. Only boys did. When I pulled on the tight denim blue jeans, pulled up the zipper in front, and buttoned the sturdy metal fastener, I felt both cute and powerful. Years later, in the mid-1960s, many girls had begun dressing in T-shirts and blue jeans. Like boys. It seemed like most people wore blue jeans. Dad had again been ahead of his time.

Not only did I identify with both genders from a young age, but I also empathized with anyone who was hurting. My older sister struggled with my crying over someone's bad fortune.

"Laurie's head must be filled with straw. She cries over everything."

I read this note of hers the morning after she babysat the three of us. I was confused. I knew I cried a lot. But I didn't know what straw had to do with it. Maybe she was comparing me to the scarecrow in *The Wizard of Oz*. He didn't have a brain. I didn't feel stupid, though, just sad when anyone got hurt.

To be fair to Caroline, I did take longer than most to start speaking in complete sentences. Mom listed a few of my favorite sayings in my baby book—*Daddy boy*, *down the creek*, *baby doll*, and *I don't know*—but no complete sentences until I was three. Grandma Hall had what my father later told me were "grave concerns." She may have been comparing me to Caroline, who spoke in complete sentences at twelve months. Thinking I might be "retarded," the term used at the time, Grandma encouraged my parents to take me to a doctor "just to see about it." Dad said that he told his mother, "Laurie is fine." I loved that he knew that about me.

He may have assumed that about me the day on the hill, too, that I was fine. Perhaps he thought I was more than fine because I could see things from different sides, not just the feminine or masculine, gay or straight. I'll never know. But I empathized with him as a bullied child and cultural minority. I also felt empathy for my mother. By the time I found out, she had known for decades that her husband was gay. Even after Dad came out to me, it would take me decades to see things from my side, a third side.

IN MY BROTHER'S COWBOY OUTFIT

CHAPTER 22: PRETENSE

D aisy had long since ceased frolicking in the scrubby vegetation. Dad leaned down and clipped the leash to her collar.
He gestured for me to go ahead of him. Today I would have
preferred to be walking behind him. I didn't want him to talk
to me on our way back to the house. And he didn't. He may
have been in as much shock as I was.

The late afternoon air was thick and heavy. I maneuvered
my way around large rocks and small pointed ones, sharp star
thistles, and scarlet red poison oak on the path home, toward
Mom. I worried about how to act when I saw her.

It was the mid-1970s, almost a decade since the freewheeling Summer of Love in San Francisco. Images of muscular,
leather-clad men, and dolled-up drag queens from Gay Pride
parades showed up every year in the *San Francisco Chronicle*.
I wasn't sure at the time what leather or men dressed up as
women had to do with being gay, or even if they did. However, I knew even then that these exuberant displays of one's
sexuality must have been intoxicating for those who'd long
been in hiding.

Openly gay Harvey Milk was running for San Francisco
supervisor for the third and ultimately successful time that fall

of 1975. He used his platform to urge gay people in hiding to come out of the closet as a political act—for themselves, for other gay people, and for the larger LGBT movement. Working in San Francisco and reading the *Chronicle* every day, my father would have known this. With that supportive, energetic wind at his back, coupled with my question about his certain infidelity, I may just have given my father the opportunity to come out to me at a perfect time in history.

When he and I reached the street, with the family house now in full view below us, I thought of my mother. Would I look different to her? Would I look older, or more serious? Would I look like I was hiding something? I wasn't the same daughter who'd left for a hike just a few short hours ago. Who was I, then? My father's confidante, someone who knew he didn't love his wife, my mother? I didn't want to know this much about my parents' relationship. However, I didn't want to go back to not knowing either.

I wish I could have opened up to my mother that day. I wish we could have had a heartfelt conversation about our feelings and our fears. But that was not her way. She shied away from topics that were too personal or intimate, like my first period. In the seventh grade, I heard whispered bits of conversation from classmates about blood and belts and something called "panty pads." Suspecting something might soon be happening to my own body, I brought up the conversation awkwardly over dinner one evening.

"What're panty pads, Mom?"

She jumped out of her chair, not an easy feat. Dad had recently redecorated our house with modern furniture created more for its look than for support and comfort. The narrow metal back of Mom's chair tipped at an angle when she tried to scoot her chair back. Catching it just in time, she set it straight and headed for the kitchen sink with her dinner plate. After rinsing it off, she turned to me and said, "We won't be discussing that, Laurie." She didn't say, "We won't be discussing that *right now*." I knew it meant wouldn't be discussing it at all.

I've thought about my poor timing then and at other critical moments in my life. Why would I ask something so intimate during dinner and in front of the whole family? I may have figured my chances for getting a straight answer from my mother were higher in the presence of witnesses. I was wrong.

I arrived home from school a few days later to discover a thin pamphlet on my bed with a mint green cover titled "Sally and Mary and Kate Wondered." It was published by Modess, maker of sanitary napkins. Because of its silent, mysterious appearance, I sensed I might discover the secret code about my body in there. I settled on the edge of my bed and flipped through it before I even changed out of my itchy wool uniform.

The information was vague. Page after page of stick-figure drawings contained sing-song-like refrains like, "I can't go into the pool today. The other girls don't understand why." However, even with the information in the booklet, I still didn't know why some girls couldn't swim or go horseback riding on certain days. On the last page of the book was the advice, "Any other questions? Ask Mother."

I didn't dare.

Another day, I arrived home from school to find a pink paper bag on my bed with the name *Pam Jo's* on it. I was in the seventh grade. Peeking inside I saw a small, white quilted bra. I pulled it out with my thumb and forefinger as if it were a forbidden item and dropped it on my bed. As I stood staring at it, Mom walked by my door.

"Oh, honey, Violet and I went shopping for you and Bonnie today," she said.

Her voice was chirpy. Bonnie was my classmate at St. Charles School. Mom kept right on walking.

Even though my question about "panty pads" appalled my mother, and we didn't discuss my first period or my first bra, I tried one more time with her. I'd begun to hear kids at school murmur new words in the outdoor corridors. I was thirteen.

Mom stood at the stove, stirring something in a small saucepan. Dad had already seated himself at the end of the dinner table and was reading the evening newspaper. The four of us hungry kids milled around the table.

"Mom, what does the word *fuck* mean?"

I said it just like that, without any warning. My siblings slinked toward their places at the table, seating themselves without making a sound. They kept their heads low as if they expected Mom might hit someone, even though hitting was near nonexistent in our household.

Mom dropped her wooden spoon hard on the Formica counter, *clunk*, and walked over and stood above me. She seemed so much taller than usual. I felt as small as Alice in Wonderland after she drank the magic potion. Her eyes widened, showing a lot of white in them. Her normal restraint was gone. For the first and only time in my life, my mother raised her hand to me. As it neared my face, I crouched in horror. She pulled back and put her hand over her mouth.

"Go to the bathroom and wash your mouth out," she ordered.

Huh? I'd heard about this bizarre method of discipline in TV shows like *Leave It to Beaver* and *Dennis the Menace*. However, it had never happened in our house. I'd never seen anyone perform this act on themselves. *How can you even get a bar of soap into your mouth anyway?* I turned around and looked aghast at my father, the only one whose head wasn't down-turned. He looked straight at me, not blinking or saying a word.

"I just wanted to know what the word meant," I whined.

I shuffled to the bathroom, ran the water, dampened the bar of soap, and waited a few seconds before coming out.

Dinner was on the table when I returned so I seated myself in my usual position between Mom and Dad. I couldn't tell if my siblings were shocked by my impudence, impressed by my courage, or afraid of further reprise from our mother. Whatever the reason, they ate in silence.

As we ate, Dad asked me how I was coming along with my memorization of "The Children's Hour," Henry Wadsworth Longfellow's poem about a father's love for his three daughters. My assignment was to write it all out on a sheet of binder paper and recite it from memory in front of my class the following Monday. Still smarting with humiliation, I didn't immediately respond.

"Honey, I can teach you my fancy handwriting if you would like," he said.

I'd seen displays of Dad's dramatic handwriting on some of his old envelopes. He knew how impressed I was with it.

"I'll show you how to write out your poem after dinner."

"Okay."

As soon as I cleared the dinner table, Dad brought out two fountain pens and a small stack of fancy paper. The paper's texture was soft but also nubby. It wasn't lined binder paper with three holes in it, the type assigned for class. It was much finer. I chose Dad's marbled blue fountain pen for myself.

Sitting side by side with my father at the table that evening, I practiced the elegant handwriting of his that I'd only glimpsed before. He wrote out a stanza and then handed it to me to copy. I got good at the fantastical upward dashes, the large round O's, and the T's with vertical lines on just *one* side of the horizontal lines. Looking back, I wonder if my father was demonstrating for me how he was one who often broke the rules, too.

"You're doing really well, honey," he said.

He seemed so pleased with me, this impertinent second child of his. Once I finished the entire poem, he told me to stand at the far end of the table and recite it to him.

Between the dark and the daylight.
When the night is beginning to flower.
Comes a pause in the day's occupation
That is known as the children's hour.

"That's good, honey," he said. "Now, why don't you try it this way?"

Between . . . the dark . . . and the daylight.
When the night . . . is beginning . . . to flower.

I can still hear his deep baritone voice, the way his tone changed from high to low, and his dramatic pauses. Each evening that week, I practiced with him and was ready on time to recite it from memory before class. I not only learned to write and speak like my father, but I was in his good graces, too. He must not have thought I was a delinquent daughter for asking what *fuck* meant. He never offered to explain it to me, though, and for that I was relieved.

By the time Dad came out to me, I had learned to keep conversations with my mother at a polite but superficial level. If she wasn't comfortable talking to me about my period, or four-letter words, or bras, there was no way I'd bring up Dad's homosexuality or even homosexuality at all. I'd never even heard the word *gay* mentioned in our house.

Dad and I had reached the front of the house now, our only words on the walk being his commands to Daisy. He touched my arm and moved ahead of me on the narrow walkway to the house. He held open the heavy front door and ushered Daisy and me inside, staying outside to smoke his premeal cigarette while plucking weeds and removing dead leaves from the entry garden. He told me that was how you can spot a real gardener.

"They can't walk by a weed without pulling it out," he said while chuckling.

Weeds were the least of my worries that day. Walking in the front door with a forced smile on my face, I found myself relieved to chat with Mom about casual topics. She told me Jody had been playing with my old Barbie dolls and Tim's old Lincoln Logs.

"She sure entertains herself well," Mom said.

Jody had been playing and Mom had been making our dinner of beef stroganoff, green salad, and garlic bread while Dad was saying the words I never expected to hear from him: *Honey, I'm gay.*

The dining room was set with the *nice* dishes, the pale-blue-and-white, shell-edged, Wedgwood china my parents purchased early in their marriage. When Mom slipped the dinner plates, salad plates, and delicate sugar bowl and creamer out of their protective felt sleeves, she reminded me that they would be mine after she and Dad died.

"There's your china, Laurie!" she said.

She knew how much I loved the pale-blue color and those beautiful dishes. I stood by my place at the table and eyed the tall, chocolate-frosted angel food cake—Jody's and Mom's favorite—on the kitchen counter just around the corner. It sat high on its own glass pedestal. Jody stood on a stool at the kitchen sink, her grandmother's pink rubber gloves covering her arms up to her tiny shoulders. Mom called to Tim downstairs and Susan in her back bedroom to come to dinner.

"Laurie, please go tell your father dinner is almost ready."

I lumbered to the front door, opened it just a crack, and yelled the two-minute warning. I wouldn't be taking any chances of further secret conversations today.

Mom lifted portions of drained flat noodles out of the colander sitting next to the sink and placed them on our dinner plates. She covered each with a ladle-full of the stewed beef in thick sour cream mixture from the large pot on the stove. A tray of sliced French bread, blue goblets of ice water, and my father's newly created centerpiece of driftwood, dried flowers, and a candle completed the dinner setting.

The front door squeaked. I heard the sound of Dad kicking off his hiking shoes and shuffling around for his moccasins followed by his quiet footsteps on the tiled hallway. Tim and Susan started in on their meal right away. Dad sat down, but I didn't look at him. After Mom served him, she and Jody chatted away as if it were any other day. It was any other day for them.

"Mam let me use her gloves, Mommy," Jody said.

Mam was the name Jody used for her grandmother when she was little and couldn't pronounce *Grandma*. Mom relished her unique moniker.

"And Jody did a great job with the frosting, Laurie," Mom said. "She measured out the powdered sugar and Hershey's cocoa all by herself."

Jody beamed.

Meanwhile, I was thinking about the fact that Mom had known about Dad being gay since 1957, nearly twenty years ago. I had been six, a little older than Jody was now. That summer at the Boardwalk, Mom had seemed carefree and happy. I wondered how she soothed herself after she found out Dad was gay. It may have been her ability to pretend, something she honed as a little girl in a struggling family.

CHAPTER 23: THE BAPTIST MINISTER

My escape fantasy in grade school centered around a protective nun. Dad's escape fantasy was to live on a farm. His aunt and uncle lived in Dinuba, a farming community a hundred miles from Fellows, the unincorporated town set in the middle of the flat, dusty Midway–Sunset Oilfield where my grandfather worked and my father grew up.

"Their farm was this peaceful, green oasis, honey," Dad said.

He told me he believed that if they moved there, his problems would go away. He begged his parents to move or to at least let him go live there. But they dismissed the idea, perhaps not knowing of the emotional tolls their eldest son faced at school.

My grandparents had fled their Missouri farm life for higher paid "black gold" jobs in California's Central Valley a decade earlier. Farming held no allure for them. Besides, their son's grades were excellent, and his teachers had already skipped him two grade levels.

Fortunately, high school was a better experience for him. The students were more mature, he said. Boys no longer stoned him after school, and he was popular with the girls. One day in study hall, a girl wearing high heels caught his attention. It was the first time he'd seen a girl wearing them. Her name was Dorothy. Though he was a sophomore and she a freshman, they were the same age.

"I really loved her, Laurie."

They went together for four years, through Dad's first semester of community college. Once Dorothy graduated from high school, they became engaged. I'd heard about Dorothy throughout my childhood. More than once, I asked Dad why they didn't get married. He did the same thing he did when I asked him why he changed his name. His eyes averted mine. His normally articulate words were vague and rambling.

After he died, I found the following note Dorothy wrote in his 1935 yearbook:

> *We have been going together pretty near four years now, and I have enjoyed every minute with you. Everything I had hoped for is coming true, and I hope it will end up the way we have planned.*

But it wouldn't go as Dorothy had hoped. Dad was anxious.

"I just wanted to talk to someone," he said. "Anyone. To see if maybe I was crazy. I thought I was the only person in the world afflicted with my condition."

He'd found this person in his recently widowed paternal grandmother who went by the name of Fanny. Despite her conservative Midwestern roots, she was generous in her acceptance of everyone. To escape the scorching heat of the Central Valley summers, Fanny stayed in a trailer out at Pismo Beach on the coast. One day in 1936, when my father was eighteen, he drove out to visit her. When he told her about his "orientation," he said she was calm and "not at all shocked or horrified. She said something like, 'God understands everything.' She thought I was a good person."

Fanny encouraged him to go back to church. He'd stopped going, I assume due to the fire-and-brimstone tone in Southern Baptist churches. She told him about a young charismatic minister named Jack Yancey. He was new in town, and she wanted Dad to meet him.

"And so I did, Laurie, and I liked Jack immediately," Dad said.

His mother also liked Jack and invited him over to have dinner with the family. Afterwards, Dad offered to drive him home.

"When we got to the front of his house, Jack told me to turn off the motor so we could talk for a while. And that's when I thought, I'm going to talk to Jack about my condition. He's a man of God. Maybe I can find out what I should do—should I kill myself, should I jump off one of these oil derricks? Then he reached over and put his arm around my shoulder."

I girded myself for the next part of Dad's story.

"And then he told me that I wasn't alone, that he was the same way. It blew me away because I was convinced for so long that it was dirty, wrong, and a sin. And here was a man of God who was just like me."

He knew he had to break up with Dorothy. He told her that his sexual orientation was such that they couldn't get married.

"There was no word for it then. She was upset and so was I. She returned my ring and the next week she left town."

The following week Jack invited Dad to join him on a trip to Los Angeles. En route from Oklahoma to Fellows earlier that year, Jack had made a stopover in Los Angeles and met members of the local gay community. He told Dad he wanted to introduce him to someone. That person was Clarence, the man whom my siblings and I grew up calling Uncle Seedy.

The year was 1937. My father was nineteen at the time. Clarence, fifty-three, told him he had someone he wanted him to meet, one of his piano students. I'd never heard this story before, nor any of the other stories that were now pouring out of my father on a regular basis.

"I'll never forget it, honey," Dad said. "As soon I got out of the car, I looked at him, he looked at me, and it just clicked. Oh, God, I told myself. If love at first sight is possible, it happened to me then. His name was Stanley."

Though I didn't want him to hide any of these stories from the past, I didn't know what to do with them. My parents were still married to each other. My mother didn't know I knew that Dad was gay, although he'd eventually tell her. Her romantic, love-at-first-sight story was all about my father. My father's love-at-first-sight story wasn't about her. It was about Stanley.

From that point on, Dad said, he and Stanley got together as often as they could. During a one-week vacation, they stayed with Fanny out at the coast. They began thinking about how they could spend their lives together. Stan was starting college. The 125 miles between Fellows and Los Angeles seemed insurmountable, especially because neither of them had a car.

"I realized that this was what I wanted," Dad said. "I decided to go back to school. Clarence told me that I could live with him and go to Pasadena City College, which I did."

His goal was to become an English teacher.

The two maintained their relationship during that time. Dad started college, lived in Alhambra, and took the trolley out to Pasadena on school days.

"I was very excited about being back in school," he said.

For a time, my father was in a loving relationship with another man, the result of his talk with my great-grandmother, Fanny, who died two years before I was born. I wish I had somebody like her when I was struggling. I was now the one asking if there was anyone else in the world like me, someone with a gay father and a straight mother. In the past, Dad had been my version of Fanny, someone who was always available to me, willing to listen to my stories and problems for as long as it took. But now his stories, not mine, dominated our conversations. They poured out of him. I closeted my anxiety over his secret, which was now my secret. Neither of my parents knew my struggles during this time. Migraines and nightmares of being in a small space with the walls closing in were a constant now. Dad's "affliction" had become mine.

CHAPTER 24: THE MENTOR

"Clarence was your father's mentor, Laura," Jim said. "Arthur was mine. He taught me how to be gay."

Jim was an elderly gay man in San Francisco whom I met after my father died. I didn't understand what he was saying.

"Weren't you already gay?"

Jim explained. When a young gay man is in the closet, he said, he assumes the mannerisms and interests of the majority around him, those boys and men who are considered normal. Often these are not the best fit. Before the gay rights movement, older gay men played a crucial role in assimilating young, uncultured, closeted gay men into big-city gay culture. They often played matchmaker, too, Jim said. It was often the only way two men in hiding could find one another.

The idea of a gay mentoring network made sense to me. I wonder if my father would have read Walt Whitman and Ernest Hemingway, or taken us to operas and Picasso exhibits in San Francisco, if it weren't for Clarence. California's Central Valley oilfield culture wouldn't have cultivated those interests in my father.

Clarence also introduced him to the culture of Hollywood, which in the end didn't bode well for Dad. In the summer of 1940, he attended a party in the Hollywood Hills. He was twenty-two. I know my father would have been enamored of the lush, exuberant hillside gardens and movie industry culture, especially as someone who hailed as he did from Depression-era poverty, conservative mores, and the flat, dry, monochromatic oilfields of Fellows. I imagine creative, talented gay men, inspiring modern architecture, dramatic views of palm trees and the Pacific, and contemporary music greeting him that evening.

I pictured the gay Hollywood elite as they might have been in an old black-and-white movie, mingling in their white dinner jackets, smoking L&Ms, sipping gin fizzes, and listening to the swing music of Count Basie and the Dorsey Brothers or the bebop jazz of Dizzy Gillespie on a boxy hi-fi.

I could even see the connection between Hollywood and the modern architecture, interior design, sweeping views, kidney-shaped swimming pool, and lush plantings around our long horizontal modern house in the San Carlos hills that Dad custom designed for us in the mid-1960s, though Dad never discussed that connection with me.

"Then, all of a sudden, it came to an end, honey," Dad said.

(Left) Duane, age nineteen, 1937. Photo by Stanley
(Right) Stanley, 1937. Photo by Duane

THE WEATHER

Los Angeles Times

IN THREE PARTS — 42 PAGES
Part II - LOCAL NEWS — 25 Pages

TIMES OFFICE
202 West First Street

VOL. LX   C   THURSDAY MORNING, FEBRUARY 6, 1941   CITY NEWS—EDITORIAL—SOCIETY

BY THE WAY

With BILL HENRY

Police Shake-up and Arrest Scandal Rock Pasadena

SEE DAUGHTERS—Senator and Mrs. Patrick A. McCarran of Nevada as they appeared on visit here yesterday.

Senator McCarran Visits Here on Brief Western Tour

Nevadan Interested in Cattle and Air Industries; Plane Production Delays Laid to Nature of Task

Bowron Files Race Papers

Mayor Acts as Host When Campaign Workers Who Laud His Regime

Police Department Declared Demoralized

BLOSSOMS—Jacqueline White, standing, and Ann Connelly enjoy blossoms at midwinter flower show, which has display of rare plants valued at $150,000.

Midwinter Flower Show Opens With Display Worth $150,000

'Garden of Gardens' Declared Most Spectacular Horticultural Exhibit of Show in Biltmore

Vice Squad Abolished

'Doctor' Who Treated Suspected Violators Jailed on Plot Charge

Crime Bureaus to Be Reopened

Divisional Detective Offices Again Will Operate Within Month

Mayor Sees New Argentine Consul

Emilio Lascano-Tegui Calls on Bowron

Luis Alberni Files Suit for Divorce

Granddaughter of Judge and Fiance Apply to Marry

WEDDING DAY NEAR—Mary Morgan Veil, 16-year-old granddaughter of Judge Georgia Bullock, shown with fiance, Emery S. Hamren, as they applied for wedding license.

Jerry Colonna Burned In Studio Accident

LAPD ARREST, *LOS ANGELES TIMES*, FEBRUARY 2, 1941

CHAPTER 25: ARRESTS

"There was a loud pounding at the front door," Dad said. "And then someone yelled, *Police!*"

Oh no. I hoped they were only there to ask the partygoers to turn down the music.

Dad and I were sitting out on the family deck that overlooked the YMCA and high school, away from open windows. I was now in my thirties.

"It was just chaos afterward," Dad said. "We were handcuffed and herded into a paddy wagon."

It was a raid.

"They drove us to the Pasadena Police Station for booking," he said. "I was so frightened, Laurie."

With my father's flair for long pauses and the dramatic, he seemed to relish the telling of this horrible story. I felt frightened by the details of what might be coming and wanted it to end quickly, though. I hurried him up.

"What happened then, Dad?"

He took a long drag off his cigarette.

"I was booked into a cell overnight," he said. "None of us were allowed to make any phone calls."

"Isn't that against the law?"

Dad, ignoring my question, told me that the guards escorted him into the courtroom the next morning to receive his sentence.

"The judge asked the arresting officer to confirm that I was touching the man I was dancing with," he said. "You see, honey, that's the only way they could legally charge me."

I struggled to understand.

"I was shocked by what the officer said."

Dad's eyes grew moist, but they also twinkled. I suspected things had turned out okay for him.

"He said he couldn't be absolutely sure I was touching the man," he said, emphasizing the word, *absolutely*. "But I *was* touching him. For some reason, the officer took pity on me." Then, after another drag off his cigarette, he added, "Why, I'll never know."

I knew why. The officer must have seen what a sweet young man my father was, that he didn't belong in jail with drug dealers and murderers. That is what I thought then. Now I wonder if the officer himself might have been gay.

The judge informed him that he was free to go. I couldn't believe how lucky he was. Dad lit another cigarette and walked me to the back of the deck. Unfortunately, his story wasn't yet over.

Before his college courses began in Pasadena, Dad had continued to live a closeted life in Fellows. He worked as a men's clothing salesperson at A. Asher and Company in nearby Taft. Come fall, he moved to Los Angeles to begin his new, openly gay life with Stanley.

By December, semester's end was just days away. Dad boasted to me about the A he received in geometry, a class not even offered at Taft Union High School.

"I was so proud of that," he said. "I worked really hard to catch up with the other college students."

"Congratulations, Dad!"

"But then something terrible happened, honey," he said.

I steadied myself in my deck chair for what was coming. I expected another dreadful story but hopefully one with another positive outcome.

After class one day, he said, he headed to the intersection of California Boulevard and South Lake Avenue. There he would catch the Pacific Electric streetcar back to his room at Clarence's house. But on this day, he just missed the streetcar. He decided to make a quick trip to the below-street public restroom on the corner before the next car arrived. He ran down the flight of stairs and threw open the door. There a man stood staring straight at him.

"I wasn't interested, honey," he said. "I wanted to get home to Clarence's and my schoolwork. This poor man was crippled and on crutches. He pleaded with me. I felt sorry for him."

I grimaced, knowing what the man must have been pleading for.

"Against my better judgment, I agreed," Dad said. "I suggested we do it right there, isolated, downstairs."

Imagining my father having sex in a public restroom repulsed me, whether with a man or a woman. But I didn't stop him from telling me more.

"He said he wanted to go do it somewhere else," Dad said. "When I told him I had to catch the trolley, he told me not to worry, that he'd drive me home afterward."

Dad took another drag off his cigarette, flicked the ashes into the pea gravel around one of his potted succulents, and looked far into the distance. The silence went on for some time. My anxiety rose.

"You know, honey," he said. "Frequently in my life, there has been this little voice on my left shoulder, whispering advice into my ear."

"Yeah?"

"This time it said, 'Don't do this. Just go home.' Why I didn't listen to that voice that day, I will never know."

If I'd been able to hear my own inner voice, it would have said, *Tell Dad to stop.*

The crippled man struggled up the stairs and limped to his car. Dad, just twenty-two, followed. After driving for a few miles, the man stopped at a gas station, saying he had to call his sister.

"The voice on my left shoulder got louder," Dad said. "It told me, 'Get out of this car and go home.' I knew I didn't want to do this."

But he didn't get out of the car. And I didn't stop him from telling me the rest of this appalling story. The man finished his call, hobbled back to the car, and drove miles of winding roads up to Lover's Lane in the Pasadena Hills. He turned off the ignition and suggested the two of them move to the back seat.

"All of a sudden, there were loud raps on the windows," he said. "I looked up and saw two uniformed police officers staring at me. I was absolutely terrified."

They demanded he get out of the car and into their patrol vehicle. They didn't demand this of the man who drove him there. It was quickly apparent what had occurred.

"It was a setup," Dad said.

As I tried to make sense of the scenario, Dad said the officers drove him to the police station where they jailed him. The crippled man followed in his own car.

A sting operation run by the Pasadena Police Department's vice squad had nabbed my father. The man in the public restroom was an undercover decoy. He'd stopped on the way to Lover's Lane not to call his sister but to call the police. My father's intuition would have saved him.

"I couldn't believe it, honey," Dad said. "This nice man. I went all to pieces. I was crying at the police station, saying, 'Why, why did you do this to me?' He had the saddest look on his face. I think he knew it would ruin my life."

I was having a hard enough time comprehending what had happened. But now my father was telling me that he could see the humanity on the face of someone who had entrapped him?

Dad spent the night alone in jail. He was prohibited from making a phone call. When he didn't return home that night, he said Clarence was beside himself with worry.

The next day he again stood before a judge. This time he wouldn't be let off. The judge charged him. It was only after my father died that I found out what the charge was, an "abnormal sex act," a felony in the State of California.

"The legal process was quick," Dad said. "The judge didn't ask me any questions. I had no opportunity to rebut."

My father was now a felon sentenced to a jail term. But the judge offered him another option. If he attended weekly sessions with a court-appointed psychologist for treatment of his homosexuality, he wouldn't have to go to jail.

"Though I would have to pay the psychologist five dollars a week."

It was a hefty sum at the time. The country was just climbing out of the Depression. Five dollars in 1940 is equivalent in purchasing power to about ninety dollars in 2020.

"Naturally, I agreed," Dad said. It was the week before final exams.

"I gave up, honey. I knew I couldn't go back to school. And I didn't. With this on my record, I knew I could never be a teacher."

It was during that year, 1940, when California enacted the nation's first law revoking the teaching license of anyone convicted of sodomy. My father would spend the majority of his adult working life not as an English teacher but as a desk clerk because of the man in the restroom, the LAPD's entrapment scheme, and the fact that he didn't listen to his inner voice telling him to go home.

When I was growing up, my father spoke often of how much he'd wanted to be an English teacher. I pushed him to explain his reasons for not becoming one. His reply was never satisfactory. He gaze was again off into the distance, not on me.

"After the war, well, we had you four kids and all. . . ."

I knew he could have gone to college long before that. His explanations, which varied, never made sense to me. The war ended in 1945. My older sister, Caroline, wasn't born until 1949. Mom had a job in a photography studio. They were living rent-free in The Little House behind Nana's main house. The GI Bill, which had just been created, provided tuition assistance to World War II veterans attending college or trade schools. It would have been the perfect time for Dad to earn his teaching credentials. I didn't want to believe that my siblings and I had been the reason he never lived out his dream. But, of course, he wouldn't have told me the truth when I was little, that as a man convicted for an abnormal sex act in 1940 in California, he'd never teach in a public school.

After his second arrest, Dad said, he left Stanley. He gave up his room at Clarence's house, dropped out of Pasadena City College before completing his first semester, and returned to the family home in Fellows.

"I wrote to Stanley and Clarence. I told them I could no longer accept the horrors of being queer."

He told my grandparents he dropped out of school due to illness. They didn't question him. I imagine he probably looked grim enough at the time to pass for sick. Once a week he boarded a bus to Los Angeles to see—and pay—the psychologist.

"The whole setup was obviously a fake," he said. "His office was in a scroungy little walkup. I could tell he wasn't a degreed person. He held up a string with a crystal tied to the end of it. He said to keep looking at it and I would be cured."

When Dad told me this, even I knew homosexuality wasn't something to be cured.

"I pretended I was cured. The appointments lasted five minutes. It was ridiculous."

Dad's trips to the psychologist continued for two months, until February 6, 1941. That was the day he stepped out onto his front porch to find a shocking headline in that morning's *Los Angeles Times*.

"I couldn't believe it, honey," he said. "On the top of the front page was a big story about the Pasadena Police Department scandal and how they knocked down hundreds of other men like me."

The term *knocked down* seemed a perfect way to describe it.

"The judge was in on it, the police were in on it, and the fake psychologist was in on it. They were all in this scam together, sharing the enormous fees. Someone finally had the courage to resist and expose it."

After the extortion was exposed, Dad was free of the psychologist and the fees, but not of his record. He took a fulltime job at Sanitex Cleaners in Taft.

He soon made the decision to join the US Navy, as his brother and many of his uncles had, but was turned away when they found out from his arrest record that he was gay. Two months later, in April 1941, he received a letter from the US Army.

"They were calling people up according to some kind of numbers," Dad said. "But I didn't wait to be called up. I volunteered for the draft and went to Fort Ord for my basic training. So, honey, that was the beginning of my new life."

There were times after my father first told me the story of his second arrest and the strange characters—the crippled man, the fake psychiatrist, the extortion—when I wondered if it really happened at all, if an article about it in the *Los Angeles Times* even existed. I was unable to find a record of the article while my father was still alive. But in 2014, six years after he died, I typed just the right combination of key words into a search. The three words I typed were, "abnormal sex acts," which I came across in a book on gay history.

Up popped the article on my computer screen. Above the fold, in the February 6, 1941 issue of the *Los Angeles Times*, was the headline, Police Shake-up and Arrest Scandal Rock Pasadena. My father had seen this exact article on his front porch more than seven decades earlier.

The following week, on February 15, 1941, the *Los Angeles Times* published a follow-up article titled, Vice Squad Officer Demoted after Inquiry in Pasadena. The reporter described the punishment meted out to the sergeant in charge of the sting operation.

"Demotion of Sergeant Samuel Bailey of the Pasadena Police vice detail to a patrolman's rating and suspension from duty for three months without pay was announced yesterday by Pasadena City Manager C. W. Kolner as punishment for asserted questionable practices.

The action was taken, Kolner said, as a result of an extensive investigation into charges that the police officer while in charge of the vice squad ordered numerous defendants arrested on morals charges to take treatments from Dr. Paul Wheeless."

This swindle forever changed my father's life and probably the lives of many other gay men. Some of them may have fared worse than he did. The officer who ordered this illegal extortion received but a temporary demotion and a three-month suspension of duty.

RALPH, NEWLY ENLISTED IN THE ARMY
WITH NEW NAME, 1941

WARTIME WEDDING, 1942

CHAPTER 26: A WORLD AT WAR

The date was December 7, 1941. A photo shows my father sitting close to the stage of a USO concert at Fort Ord. Judy Garland was singing. An announcement came over the loudspeaker, interrupting her song, "Zing! Went the Strings of My Heart." The announcer ordered the soldiers back to their barracks where they'd learn the news that Japanese forces had bombed the US Naval Base at Pearl Harbor. Panic ensued, especially on the West Coast, which was considered vulnerable to future attacks from Japan.

"It all seemed like some grand theatrical act in which I was now playing an important role," Dad said.

I chuckled inside at my father's optimism and dramatic flair despite what I knew about the horrific attack and the years of bloody wartime that followed. He said he took well at first to Army life. Given his humiliating arrests and past disappointments, he may have appreciated how orderly and predictable his days as company clerk at Fort Ord were. He kept tidy payroll records and met deadlines. After the attack, though, the routine wasn't as predictable. The federal government began laying the groundwork for a new war effort based in California. Defense work in the aircraft and shipbuilding industries ramped up. The mining of California's vast mineral and oil resources kicked into full production. Trainloads of migrants from other states flocked to California to snap up defense jobs while soldiers dispersed.

On December 8, 1941, the day after the attack, Company G traveled by jeep caravan to the Sierra Nevada foothills. Their mission was to protect key railway bridges, including the architecturally stunning Keddie Wye railroad junction in Plumas County, from potential attacks from Japan. Dad said he considered it a silly strategy.

"I couldn't imagine the Japanese bothering to bomb this bridge out in the middle of nowhere," he said.

The soldiers rotated turns patrolling the bridge twenty-four hours a day, though, just in case. Dad described the time as one of quiet solitude, clean mountain air, brilliant starry nights, and the occasional howl of a lone coyote or the silhouette of a fox in the distance while he was on night duty. Snow-dusted sugar pines and white firs, shown in his photos from that time, glistened on moonlit nights, he said. In a letter to my mother, he said they reminded him of Christmas trees during that cold December of 1941. When he described this time, his apparent resilience surprised me. Telling the story, he didn't sound as if he had been defeated by his arrests and college dropout.

Four months later, in April 1942, his unit deployed to an even colder and more remote locale, Cold Bay, in Alaska's Aleutian Islands. A few months before they set sail, he first laid eyes on my mother's red hair. After that evening, the new couple spent two months dating before Dad's next assignment. They attended art shows at the Stanford University Museum, watched movies at the Carlos Theater a few blocks from where Mom lived, and sipped chocolate malts at the Borden Creamery in downtown San Carlos. They must have looked like any other young couple on the precipice of a war, grabbing every moment they could before an inevitably long separation.

"We decided that if I did get back from the war, we'd talk about getting married," Dad said. That was the only time I heard him use *if* when discussing the war. Even though he spoke of the grand drama of wartime and the glorious natural sites he had seen, he was not as naïve about the potential realities facing him as I'd originally thought.

A few weeks later, just two months after my parents first met, Dad's unit sailed on the *SS Mormac Sea* under the Golden Gate Bridge toward the Aleutian Islands. Company G arrived at their destination, Fort Randall, on June 26, 1942. There were no trees, Dad said, and no buildings, roads, or any other people there but themselves. Their orders were to complete construction of an airstrip for the Eleventh Air Force to provide protection for the small port, Dutch Harbor.

Most of the soldiers in Fort Randall worked in freezing temperatures on the construction of new roads and an airstrip. As he had at Fort Ord, though, Dad held the indoor job of company clerk. Because he was valued in that job, he was never required to work outdoors. But he appreciated some aspects of the natural Arctic tundra.

Though trees couldn't survive there, one flowering plant burst through the top layer of the permafrost for a few short weeks every summer. The way he described it, flower-like bunches of its leaves sprang out of the thick, tangled mat of soggy bogs of the seasonally exposed streams and small lakes. When the temperatures dropped back below freezing, those frilly leaves turned scarlet red for a single day before they shriveled up and died. It sounded dreamlike to me, that single day every year when a bog plant burst out into the monochromatic world in color.

One dark winter, before the leaves blackened, Dad said he plucked a few of the scarlet plants out of the tundra and pressed them between the pages of a book. A few weeks before Christmas 1943, he pulled out the dry flattened plants, still bright red, and used them to make a Christmas card for my mother. On it he printed in all caps, "MERRY CHRISTMAS, BELOVED." Though both of my parents had spoken of this card, I saw it for the first time when I went through my father's wartime letters after he died. I could see the same careful thought he put into the design as he did with the Christmas cards he and I made when I was a child. The lettering has an Art Deco flair to it, perhaps something he picked up during his brief time in Los Angeles.

If someone had asked me when I was little, at the time Dad first described his crafty talent to me, if I considered it unusual for a man, a soldier no less, to fashion a Christmas card for his wife out of flowers he pressed himself, I would have been surprised by the question. As my father, he was my model for what being a man meant.

Four months after he arrived in Cold Bay, his unit awarded him one of three coveted two-week furloughs. He said he considered it a sign. History shows that most soldiers at the time wanted a wife back home, a symbol of the American Dream for which they were fighting. My father made a decision that day. He wouldn't wait until the war was over. He composed and sent a telegram to my mother asking for her hand in marriage. As a little girl, and even as an adult, I never tired of this story.

"Tell us what the telegram said, Mom!"

"Unexpected furlough," she said. "Arrive Frisco tomorrow. Marry me, dearest."

Sometimes she'd get the wording slightly wrong and Dad would jump in to correct her. Each word seemed to take on a preciousness to both of them. Because of that it became precious to me. Before I learned how unlikely their pairing had been, I thought their romantic and dramatic love story would make a fabulous movie.

My mother, who was eighteen when she received Dad's telegram, said she was stunned. She had just graduated from high school. They'd only known each other for five months and were separated by war for three of them. She was afraid to tell Nana, knowing she wouldn't approve of her youngest daughter marrying an older man she'd just met, especially a twenty-four-year-old soldier stationed nearly a thousand miles away.

Not only did Nana disapprove, so did my Aunt Helen, my mother's older sister. Her best friend, Enid, did, too. They tried to discourage Mom by telling her that her soldier probably wouldn't survive the war. *What a horrible thing to say to a young woman in love*, I thought. Enid described this time to me a few years after my mother's death.

"There was nothing we could do to dissuade her, no matter how hard we tried," she said. "After she met your father, there were stars in her eyes. They blocked out everything else."

Dad was on his way to her from Alaska before he even knew her answer. He phoned her the following day from Fort Lewis, Washington, en route to California.

She said yes.

He arrived at her house on the San Francisco Peninsula the following evening. They were married in a small, no-frills ceremony at St. Charles Church in San Carlos. Dad wore his formal US Army dress uniform. Mom wore a brown skirt and jacket, a white-collared blouse, a brown wide-brimmed wool hat, and basic pumps. A gardenia corsage Dad purchased for her from a local florist was her only embellishment.

"After all, it *was* wartime, Laurie," Mom said of her modest choices.

After a reception at home with her family, the newlyweds drove down the coast to the quaint coastal town of Santa Barbara. All along the Pacific Coast, blackout drills were in effect. The week before, a Japanese plane had dropped bombs on a forest on the Oregon coast. California was on high alert.

When they arrived, Santa Barbara was nearly deserted. As one of only two couples staying at the elegant Hotel Mar

Monte, they ate dinner in a near-empty dining room. Later they strolled through Santa Barbara's darkened downtown.

"It was as if time had stopped," Mom said.

A few days later, Dad introduced her to his family, now living in Oildale, about 150 miles inland. Soon he was hopping a bus to Seattle to catch a ship back to Alaska. Mom went back home to Nana. They wouldn't see each other again for another year and a half.

"It seemed like the war would go on forever," Mom said. "I didn't know if I would ever see your father again. But he wrote me the sweetest letters. He had the most beautiful handwriting I'd ever seen."

After my father came out to me, I had to remind myself that when Mom told us these stories, she already knew he was gay. But she continued to happily relive the time before she knew, just as she'd done with her rewrapped Christmas presents when she was little. I sometimes wished I could do that, too. She kept a box of Dad's wartime letters, dozens of them, on the top shelf of her closet. Occasionally she pulled the box down, placed it at the edge of her bed, and began re-reading them. I wonder what she was thinking at those times.

Dad spent his final year in the Army back at Fort Ord on the Monterey Peninsula, where four years prior he'd taken his basic training. When Mom heard he'd be stationed just a hundred miles south of San Carlos, the town where she still lived with Nana, she readied herself for a move. But, she said, Dad tried to discourage her by telling her they needed the money from her photography job on the Peninsula to purchase a house after the war was over. Besides, he said, there was no housing available near Fort Ord since all of the other soldiers' families had already moved there. He was fine living in the barracks and assured her that the war would be over soon.

Before I knew my father was gay, his reticence to move in with my mother confounded me. Now I wonder if he was anxious about starting their new life together. A long-distance romance with a woman would have been easier for him to maintain. But Mom took the matter into her own hands and applied for a job on the base.

"Oh, I missed your father terribly," she said.

She was able to get a job with the US Signal Corps where she took and developed photos of German prisoners-of-war. Fort Ord had taken approximately a thousand of the four hundred thousand World War II prisoners in the United States. Mom was busy and well paid. She found them a tiny, inexpensive flat by the beach in nearby Pacific Grove. They moved in together in October of 1944 and lived there until Dad was discharged a year later.

Although they suffered a miscarriage while living in Pacific Grove, my mother said it was one of the happiest periods of her marriage. On warm evenings, they picked up takeout at the local delicatessen and walked a few blocks down to the beach at Lover's Point where they ate dinner and watched the sunset.

Later in the evening, she said, she did something that Nana never would have allowed. She ate crackers in bed. This seemed to be one of my mother's favorite stories from that time. She giggled each time she repeated it. She was now a married woman and a grownup, one who at age twenty-one could spill cracker crumbs in her bed if she felt like it.

Dad dolls up Mom

Four babies in five years

CHAPTER 27: BABY BOOM

The Japanese surrendered on September 2, 1945. World War II was over. On October 6, 1945, my father was honorably discharged from the Army. He had served for more than four years, most of it during wartime. Mom wanted to move back to San Carlos, her home. The blistering heat and ultraconservative Southern Baptist culture of the Central Valley of his childhood made San Carlos an easy choice for my father. But they weren't alone in seeking a permanent home in the area.

San Francisco had been a major port of embarkation for those fighting the war in the Pacific. Many soldiers who came from the hot, humid climates of the Eastern Seaboard and Southern states, or who knew the challenges of the freezing winters of the Midwest, or were discriminated against, were eager to relocate to the mild and culturally open-minded Bay Area. The military sent others to Stanford University, ten miles south of San Carlos, to study in the defense-related fields of nuclear physics and aerospace engineering. The result was a glut of former military personnel in the region and a severe housing shortage.

My parents couldn't find a place of their own. While they searched for housing, Nana invited them to stay with her and my great-grandmother, Grandma Mary, in the same small, wood-framed house in San Carlos where Mom had served the handsome soldier her homemade banana cake on the first night they met a long four years earlier. They searched for an apartment as far north as Burlingame and as far south as Palo Alto, but their search came up empty.

It was during this time that they experienced their second miscarriage. Mom was twenty-one and Dad was twenty-seven. They wondered if they would ever have children, Mom told me. She found another photography job, this time at Foreman's Camera Shop in nearby San Mateo. Dad worked as a salesclerk for Roos Brothers, an upscale men's clothing store in downtown Palo Alto. Photos of him at the time show him in stylish fitted suits, wing-tipped shoes, and a fedora.

Their bedroom in Nana's small house was located behind Grandma Mary's bedroom. To get to their sleeping quarters, they had to pass through hers. I was ten when Grandma Mary died, old enough to be well acquainted with her deep, gruff voice and her bedroom heavily furnished with religious icons. The bedroom light was low and tinged a yellowish orange. On her vanity, sitting atop white doilies she crocheted for that purpose, were small statues of Jesus, the Virgin Mary, and St. Joseph. In front of the statues stood small racks of tiny prayer candles she lit for people she knew who were suffering.

Grandma Mary usually had a set of rosary beads in her hands. Some were made of smooth, bare wood about the size of large marbles. Others were made of cubes of ivory that looked like tiny dice, or round, purple glass beads. She made sure each of her great-grandchildren never left the house without a set of their own. Wooden and metal crucifixes hung on each of her bedroom walls. One was even affixed to her headboard, which meant I was often staring wide-eyed at the bloodied, dying Jesus while, nudged by Nana, I reluctantly paid a visit to my bedridden great-grandmother.

This was also the view my father would have had on the day she had a talk with him, the one he described to me after our momentous day on the hill. She grabbed his hand one day as he walked by, stopping him in his tracks.

"She said, 'I know all about you, Ralph.' I couldn't believe it, Laurie. She just glared at me."

I glared at Dad when he told me this even though he was laughing as if it were a big joke. Maybe he admired her audacity. I knew he appreciated that in people even when he disagreed with them. It sounded to me as if she'd fired the first shot, though. She may have figured out that he was gay and was concerned for her granddaughter, though I'll never know.

Then again, how could she not know? The photos of my mother at the time have her in fancy French twists and wavy updos studded with lavender blossoms from the back garden. Mom had long ago told me that Dad was the one who styled her hair that way, sounding as if she were bragging about having such a talented husband. She even enlarged the photos years later.

Grandma Mary lived to be 101 years old. According to my father, she never spoke like that to him again. Maybe his disciplined work ethic and good manners, and being a good father to her four great-grandchildren, got him on her good side. I suspect she also said more than a few prayers for her inexperienced granddaughter.

Fortunately, Nana came up with a solution to the housing problem that would get my parents into a house of their own. Although she was reserved and someone who shied away from public speaking, Nana made a public request at a meeting of the San Carlos City Council. She pleaded for permission to build a tiny, second unit for the young couple at the rear of her large lot.

"My son-in-law served our country honorably for four years during wartime," she told the elected officials at the hearing. "Now there's no place here for him and my daughter to live."

There was the familiar refrain again, for someone who from the beginning felt as if he didn't belong. There was no room in his uncle's Colorado farmhouse for his mother to deliver him en route to the California oilfields. My grandmother gave birth to him in a corncrib. The Presidio was full after the Pearl Harbor attacks, so he and his fellow soldiers of Company G encamped first in tents at the San Francisco Zoo and later at a defunct country club. Now, after the war, there was no housing for him and his wife.

Fortunately, the city council acquiesced. For the first time in San Carlos history, in 1947, they allowed two houses on a lot zoned for one. This practice would become trendy and legal toward the end of the twentieth century as the region continued to grow and prosper, and property values soared. However, then it was illegal and unimaginable by all except my determined grandmother.

After five years of marriage, three of it during wartime, my parents had a home of their own. The tiny one-bedroom house was narrow, no more than twelve feet wide, with full-length windows along its front. A Dutch-style front door opened at the top to let in light and air. My mother said it looked like a dollhouse. They coined it The Little House, just like the one in Virginia Lee Burton's children's book that bears the same name. The book was published in 1942, the year my parents met.

Nana divided the large yard between the back of her house and the front of The Little House into two. The two halves couldn't have looked more different. Nana's lawn with trimmed hedges, beds of small pink and red begonias, narrow brick footpaths, and a classically styled bird bath resembled the modest but stately gardens she left behind in Minneapolis when my grandfather gambled away their home.

Dad designed the other half. Part of it harkened back to the practical and edible Midwestern-style front yards of his Central Valley childhood. He staked young apricot and plum trees in rows, creating a miniature orchard at the center of the yard. In a sunny corner, he grew zucchini, tomatoes, and bell peppers. In the remaining area, he planted ornamental succulents, birds-of-paradise and other exotic plants. Well-suited to the warmer climate of Hollywood and Los Angeles, they struggled to thrive in the foggy Bay Area summers.

My parents suffered yet another miscarriage after they moved into The Little House. It was 1947 and this time it was twins. But two years later, after seven years of marriage and four miscarried children, my mother finally carried a pregnancy to full term. Caroline was born in November 1949.

"It was the happiest day of my life," Dad said.

Perhaps most parents say this about the births of their children. Nevertheless, more than once, I saw my mother roll her eyes when he said it. She might have wanted to hear that the day he met her was the happiest day of his life. On the other hand, she raved about his parenting skills, especially when we were babies.

"Your father was *so* good with you kids, honey."

From the moment he got home from work, she said, he'd take over. He shampooed our hair, gave us our baths, read to us, helped us with our homework, and kept us out of the kitchen until dinner was on the table. Mom said she never had to ask him to do it.

"My friends were impressed," she said. "They told me your father was *so* different from their husbands." After I knew Dad's sexual orientation, I couldn't imagine her saying that line with a straight face.

Dad also talked about how special my mother was, repeating the story of their chance meeting at the USO dance, his face always lighting up when he described the early exit he and his Army buddy almost took.

"Then I heard this sweet voice say, '*I'll* dance with you.'"

Invariably, one of us kids would ask, "What happened after that?"

"Then we were blessed with all of you," he said.

My father was generous with his kisses and hugs for the four of us kids. Nowhere in my own memory, though, are romantic kisses or passionate embraces between my parents that matched the passionate telling and retelling of their initial love story. When my parents recalled the night they first met, I felt I'd been born into one of the world's greatest love stories. The ground beneath my feet felt solid in those moments.

CHAPTER 28: INCRIMINATING PHOTOS

M om showered Jody with hugs and kisses at the front door. Her eyes twinkled.

"I've been waiting for you, Jody."

I could smell the Gravenstein apple pie baking in the oven. It had that distinctively tart smell. The mound of leftover pie-crust on the kitchen counter got Jody's attention. She knew the drill. Mom pulled the butter dish and cinnamon sugar shaker out of the cupboard and handed Jody the rolling pin. For a moment, I was tempted to stay in the kitchen. The flaky, crispy strips they were about to make tasted best right out of the oven.

It had been a few weeks since my conversation with Dad on the hill. He was stooping near a flowerpot at the far corner of the back deck, so focused that he didn't at first notice me. With his gloved hands, he nudged flat smooth rocks around the thick trunk of a jade plant. He took care not to accidentally knock off any of the plant's thick, oval-shaped leaves or disturb the small clumps of yellow-green moss matted around the plant. After moving the rocks around, at most an inch or so in any direction, he stood up to view the results.

A thick layer of cold fog drifted over from Half Moon Bay. I tightened the hood of my sweatshirt around my face but otherwise remained motionless until Dad's satisfied sigh signaled an opening for me. I glanced back over at the sliding glass door to make sure I'd closed it all the way.

"Hey, Dad, can I ask you another question?"

He turned his head toward me. "Sure, honey, anything."

"Um, what happened the day Mom found out?"

Dad pursed his lips. I thought he looked either embarrassed or ashamed, but he may have just been nervous. Then his expression changed. He relaxed. His face glistened. He pulled a pack of cigarettes out of his shirt pocket, tapped it on the bottom to release one, and lit it. After taking a long draw, he guided me over to the two patio chairs that faced the cypress trees on the bank of the back hill. We sat there in silence until he stubbed out his cigarette in a flowerpot at his feet.

"Well, honey," he said. "She called me at work. She was hysterical."

I grimaced.

"She said I should come home immediately," he said. "I could tell it was bad. I thought something had happened to one of you kids. I raced home."

Dad described his every movement while I tapped my feet on the graying slats of the deck. He described how he sped down the freeway, pulled in the driveway, bolted out of the car, ran into the house, and shouted, "Irene! Irene!" But the house was quiet. The kitchen and dining room were empty. He rounded the corner of the living room to the hallway leading to their bedroom.

"Your mother was lying on the bed crying, the evidence—the photos—spread out all around her," he said.

He fanned his arms out as he spoke.

"There were razor blades by her side. . . ." he said, trailing off.

I turned away from him, taking myself to task for asking yet another question I wasn't sure I wanted answered. I tried not to think of my mother just twenty feet away from me on the other side of the glass door.

"What photos, Dad?"

I couldn't even think about the razor blades, let alone ask him about them. I never would, either.

"Well, uh . . . well, some of the neighborhood men and I . . ."

He hesitated.

"What, Dad?"

Now I just wanted him to get it over with.

"Well, we'd get together in one of the fellows' garages. One of the men was a photographer. Your mother broke the lock on the box. . . ."

I ran my hands through my hair and wondered why I was doing this to myself again. Images of my father cavorting, possibly naked, with other men in a neighbor's garage while I was a six-year-old playing tetherball in the back yard horrified me. I couldn't even imagine what seeing the revealing photos had done to Mom.

"Well, honey, I went all to pieces," he said. "I acted like an idiot. I blamed her for invading my privacy."

"You blamed *her*?"

"I yelled at her. I said, 'Why? Why would you do this to me, Irene?'" he said.

I wanted to say, "But she wasn't doing anything to you, Dad." But I didn't. I was afraid he'd stop talking. I wanted to know everything.

"I told her I'd come back after you kids were in bed. I'd pack up my things and be out of her life for good. I would send her every penny I ever earned, for her and you kids, for the rest of my life. I promised her she would never have to see me again. I told her I was very sorry. And I left."

I guessed that meant he didn't plan to see us kids again either. I remembered my night terrors and stabbing stomachaches that first year we lived in the old house in town. It was that year.

He came home that night, he said, and packed up his things. I imagined myself at the time, asleep in my room as he backed out of the driveway. He was on the verge of leaving us, maybe for good. It was dark, he said, and as he backed out of the driveway, he saw my mother. She was running toward him, tears streaming down her face. He stopped the car, leaving the ignition on, and got out.

"Your mother threw her arms around me and said, 'Please, Ralph. Please don't leave. I still love you.'"

Dad leaned over to remove a flat weed with sharp spikes on it from a small planter between our chairs. He dropped it on the warm redwood deck so it wouldn't reseed somewhere else. After taking one last draw from the now-short stub of his second cigarette, he leaned over again, extinguished the burning butt in the planter, and left it there to decompose. He stood up slowly and faced me, leaning his head to one side. His shoulders were soft.

"So, I turned off the ignition. I got my things out of the trunk and went back into the house," he said. "We agreed never to speak of it again."

I stared at him without saying a word. This was a lot to process.

"And here we are," he said.

"Yes, here we are, Dad."

I may have only said that to myself. I never asked him about the razor blades.

DAD (MIDDLE, BACK ROW), SAN SIMEON, 1941

DAD BEFORE SUSAN GOT SICK

CHAPTER 29: CALM BEFORE THE STORM

None of my siblings gave me any indication they knew about Dad. Then again, I didn't give them any indication I knew, either. It was now September 1975, four months since Dad had come out to me. My questions had only increased in number.

Dad and I walked slowly down the front walkway of the family house. I chose the side sheltered from the hot autumn sun by a deep overhang.

"Does anyone else in the family know, Dad?"

He turned to the blanket of blue sedum, a creeping succulent draped over the side of the retaining wall on his side. Leaning over, he pointed out the petite but showy pink flowers on it.

"Yeah, they're pretty, Dad," I said.

I sounded curt even to myself.

"Yes," he said. "Caroline knows."

It seems she'd figured it out on her own. Tim and Susan were now the only members of the family who didn't know Dad was gay. Though the four of us kids were born into the same family, our paths rarely crossed, especially after our money troubles in the mid-1960s put an end to family vacations. We behaved as our parents behaved, living in the same house but leading separate lives.

The bathroom window slid open.

"Ralph! Laurie! Lunch is ready."

"Okay, Mom."

When I got to the front door, I looked back at my father. He was twenty or thirty feet behind me, moving slowly, fingering stray vines of ivy around the wire lattice on the wall.

"Tell your mother I will be right in," he said.

Mom was still dressed in the breezy print dress she'd worn to Mass that morning. Her hair, now platinum, looked striking set against the dress's mauve background. It had been ten years since I stopped going to Mass with her. Dad's defection around the time I entered high school had emboldened me to do the same. Maybe the Catholic Church's opposition to homosexuality drove him away, though he never said that.

My own reasons for defecting were simpler. I attended Catholic school from the first to the ninth grades, but the dogma never stuck. Mom never spoke to us about religion, sin, or the Bible. It seems odd, given the fact that having her four children in Catholic school was so important to her. Instead, she talked about how much she enjoyed singing in the choir and how much she loved the nuns and priests when she was little.

"Oh, Laurie, they were so kind to me," she said.

This would have been important to her. From the time she was three, she was without a father. Her brother and sister were years older. Nana worked outside the home as a store clerk six days a week. Catholic school and church were her second home.

Mom was cheery after Mass that day. Even though I was an unmarried teen when I got pregnant, at least she now had a granddaughter she cherished. And she enjoyed her photography job. Bills were again paid on time.

Even Dad had a new hobby, one he could do at home. Handy with a sewing needle since childhood—patching worn-out knees in dungarees and darning holes in socks—he now turned to handcrafted items. Counterculture types popularized this practice in the sixties and seventies as an act of rebellion against commercial mass-production. Dad had seen it in the street artists outside his office. He joined in the fun by purchasing large pieces of thick, cowhide leather from a local tannery and making purses and belts out of them. He stamped yellow flowers on a purse for Mom and the outline of a butterfly on one for Susan. He hand-braided the leather shoulder straps. For himself, he made braided belts with large brass buckles. He taught Tim how to make them, too.

Soon our friends wanted what we had. Dad kept up with the orders from Mom's friends in the choir and from some of my girlfriends. He also ran cases of soft drinks and snacks up to the office on weekends, the profits going to company parties that he organized. He jogged in the early mornings, and from the looks of his tanned skin, probably visited the nude beach at San Gregorio on weekends.

Caroline enjoyed living in sunny, coastal Santa Barbara. Tim, still living at home, attended classes at San Francisco State University. His goal, just as Dad's had been three decades earlier, was to be a teacher.

Susan, twenty-one, also living at home but not interested in college, was in her third year working at Pacific Telephone. She and her sweet surfer boyfriend, Matt, made lists of people to invite to their wedding. They registered for dishes and glassware at the Emporium.

For her birthday earlier that year, our parents gave her a carved wooden hope chest. Susan had already filled it with colorful kitchen towels, place settings of sterling silverware, and heavy ceramic bowl sets. She and Matt were preparing for a future together.

Susan and Daisy

CHAPTER 30: A LUMP

I heard the ringing of the phone from the garage. It was the evening of Wednesday, October 15, 1975. I'd just arrived home from work. I picked up the receiver. It was Mom. She was breathless and her voice uncharacteristically loud and high-pitched.

"Mom, I can't understand you!"

"Your sister is very sick, honey."

"What?"

"They found a lump, Laurie," she said. "Susan has cancer."

"What do you mean, Mom?"

I heard my own voice rising now.

"The doctors are removing her spleen tomorrow," she said. "After that, she'll need extensive treatment."

"What are you talking about?"

She didn't answer.

"Is she going to be okay, Mom?"

"We don't know, honey," she said.

I was taken aback, her words displaying none of her usual optimism or reassurance.

"Jody and I will come down this weekend, Mom," I said.

"Oh, honey," she said. "Do you think you could you come down now? Your father and I are beside ourselves."

She'd never made such a request of me before. I told her we'd be right down.

"Oh, thank you, Laurie. We need you here."

Since we hadn't eaten dinner, I'm sure I put together some snacks for Jody to eat on the ninety-minute drive down from Sonoma County. I must have thrown our nightgowns and toothbrushes into a bag, too. But I don't remember anything that happened after my mother's call. Off we went. Jody was five.

I walked in without ringing the doorbell. Mom was walking down the dark hall toward us. She must have been watching for us out the bathroom window. Her eyes were dark. She hugged Jody and me at the same time.

"Thank you for coming, honey," she said.

She looked toward Jody.

"Come to Mam, honey," she said.

Mom fought back tears as she led Jody to the large jigsaw puzzle on the kitchen table. She then walked me back to Susan's room in a solemn, procession-like manner. Susan's eyes were wide, like someone awakened from a nightmare. Tim sat on one side of Susan's bed. I knelt down on the other. Dad stood staring at her from the foot of her bed. Mom must have been behind me. I placed my hand on Susan's arm.

"I love you, Sue," I said. She looked at me with those big, doe-like eyes of hers and didn't say a word.

For ten years of our childhood, Susan and I shared a bedroom. We swapped trading cards, jewelry, clothes, even our furniture. She was tall, athletic, and slender, and the prettiest of all three of us girls. Her having a serious illness made no sense.

Four months to the day after my father came out to me would mark the beginning of four years of experimental radiation, crude chemotherapy treatments, X-rays, biopsies, and surgeries that Susan would endure at nearby Stanford Hospital. My private and awkward conversations with my father came to a sudden end. Susan's health now eclipsed everything else in our lives.

CHAPTER 31: CANCER'S
LONG SHADOW

A coworker of mine at the high-tech company where I worked in Marin County told me Susan would not survive. He said his wife was a nurse and that she'd seen this scenario play out with many young adults afflicted with Hodgkin's disease.

Then there was the story my mother spun for us over the next four years. She repeated the story so many times I can still hear it verbatim. The son of her dental hygienist, she said, had survived his initial diagnosis of Hodgkin's disease for going on *seven* years now, she said.

"Your sister has *many* years ahead of her, Laurie," Mom said. "Don't make yourself sick over this."

She wanted me to focus on Jody and my job and a hopeful future for Susan. But it was impossible to ignore the evidence. Susan's long, thick hair fell out in big clumps. Radiation treatments triggered early menopause and its side effects three decades prematurely. Her throat, raw from radiation, made eating and talking difficult. By the second year of her illness, she weighed less than one hundred pounds.

I did my best to heed my mother's advice and to focus on Jody, now in second grade, and on my clerical job. Jody's teachers told me she was well behaved. Her grades were good, especially in reading. I read her *The Little House* and other bedtime stories my father had read to me. Her Mam mailed her Valentines and chocolates and made sure she had the appropriate dresses for each and every holiday, plus warm pajamas and coats during the winter. Mom and I both kept ourselves busy during this time. But I couldn't outrun my returning night terrors and now, for the first time, migraine headaches.

Dad didn't run from the truth, though, taking the opposite approach. His flashy, exuberant appearance that was on high display the year he came out to me was no more. First, it was his long hippie beard, which he shaved off completely. Then he lopped off that unsightly ponytail.

He stored his bold, colorful rings in the Italian, leather-tooled valet box on his armoire during Susan's illness. His long-sleeved muslin and denim shirts, the ones he had hand-embroidered with colorful butterflies, daisies, and doves, were replaced by plain gray and tan ones. I'd never seen my father's clothing look anything but well-tailored. But during those years, he allowed his shirts to grow tattered and threadbare. The rose tattoo on his wrist was the only outward evidence I could see of his life before Susan got ill, though he now kept it hidden under long-sleeved shirts most of the time.

From the outside, Mom looked well dressed, well coifed, perky, and fierce, as did I. Nevertheless, her blood pressure spiked. By the third year of Susan's illness, she experienced fainting spells. Her doctor put her on "some kind of medication," she said, that kept her symptoms at bay. Still, my mother worked long hours at the photo lab and rarely if ever said no to holiday overtime duty.

When Jody and I visited, Mom busied herself serving us spreads of ham sandwiches, potato or macaroni salad, and fresh-squeezed lemonade while Dad lurked around the house like a ghost. I'd glimpse him in the corner of a room, but when I turned away and then back again, he would have already vanished. Our conversations in the garden ceased being about his sexual orientation or the "smart young people" he'd seen at an antiwar protest in San Francisco, or the "talented" street artists, or the "elegant" office parties he planned.

What he did do was point out unlikely plants thriving in the garden, though not the showiest and prettiest ones as before. One time it was a stunted succulent that was growing in the least likely of places, a crack in the retaining wall. In retrospect I wonder if his focus on the struggling plants in his garden may have mirrored his hopes for Susan, that she might survive and one day thrive despite the terrible odds.

Dad now stamped out his cigarettes in a worn, sand-filled plastic bucket or an empty tuna fish can he kept out on the deck. Gone were the exotic, sculptural ashtrays and fancy planters topped with tiny gravel. Sticky spider webs now crisscrossed the driftwood wall hanging he'd made with soda can pop-tops salvaged over at Coyote Point. His skin was now pallid and a little yellowish. I guessed he wasn't visiting the nude beach and ogling tattoo-covered bodies anymore.

When I brought up Susan's declining health, he'd gaze up at the clouds or fog coming in over the hills and say, "Yes. Our poor little Susie."

He grasped my hand and shook his head from side to side. I'd sit with him in silence. I don't think he even noticed when I got up and walked back into the house. Mom tried to perk up her four children. I tried to perk up my father. He didn't try to perk up any of us. In a 1993 interview of him I listened to after his death, I found out what else was on his mind.

"When Susan got sick," he said. "I realized I couldn't play the game any longer. Irene accepted it."

Dad dug out his Tiger's Milk recipe, the same bitter brew he consumed to rebuild his body after his own illnesses, job losses, and bankruptcy in the 1960s. To entice Susan to down a small amount of the healthy drink each day, he served it to her in her favorite glass, a miniature A&W Root Beer mug. When she was little, she begged Mom and Dad to buy it for her on the rare day they treated us to diner burgers, fries, and floats.

Before we could say anything more, Mom peeked in the room and told us lunch was ready.

"Please don't wake up your sister," she whispered.

When Jody and I returned home that evening, I received a call from a former college professor. We'd been friendly correspondents for many years. Recently divorced and fifteen years older than me, he asked me if I was available for dating. My father was distant now, but this professor wasn't. I said yes. He was kind and fatherly to me throughout my sister's illness.

Susan was down to eighty-five pounds and bedridden by the fourth year of her illness. I'd found a sure way to connect with her on my visits. All I had to do was bring up Jody, who was now eight years old, and she'd brighten up. I shared Jody's drawings of houses and families on my last visit, told her about the day Jody rode a two-wheel bike for the first time, and showed her a photo of Jody in a witch costume for Halloween.

That is what I planned to do that day in late spring, 1979. I sat down on the padded stool next to Susan's bed.

"How are you doing, Sue?"

I heard my mother's childlike and hopeful voice in mine.

Susan opened her eyes and swallowed hard. A slight, forced smile came over her face. Her lips were cracked and dry. I placed my hand on top of her bony hand and launched into a story. I looked forward to her eyes lighting up.

"You should see how fast Jody can skate now," I said. "She hardly falls at all any—"

Susan put her hand up. I stopped. She licked her dry lips and looked me straight in the eyes.

"I can't talk about Jody anymore," she said.

Her voice was strong and clear. There was no light in her eyes.

"Uh . . . okay," I said.

A lump in my throat stung. Susan and Jody had been so close. Only fifteen years apart in age, they'd been more like sisters than aunt and niece. They played cards, skipped, bicycled, and swam together before Susan's illness put an end to it all. I would no longer believe, or try to believe, Mom's hopeful prognosis. My little sister was dying.

I wish now that I'd had the courage to talk to Susan about death, about any fears she might have had, any last thoughts of hers. However, I didn't. I sat frozen in place until she dropped off to sleep. I slipped out to join the rest of the family and told Mom what had just happened.

"Susan doesn't want to hear about Jody anymore," I said.

I hoped it would trigger a conversation, that it would stop the pain in my throat. It did neither. Mom obviously already knew what I'd just figured out for myself. Moreover, we wouldn't be discussing it.

In Susan's final months, Mom and Dad alternated leaves of absences from their jobs, taking turns nursing her. Mom kept up her attempts to buoy the spirits of her three other children. The son of her dental hygienist was now in his *eighth* year, she said.

"Don't worry, Laurie," she said. "Susan has at least another two more years, maybe three."

The last time I saw Susan alive was on Sunday, June 10, 1979. We had all gathered to celebrate my twenty-eighth birthday a day early. Mom had even bought Susan a new outfit for my party that she'd laid out on Susan's bed. I tiptoed back to Susan's room. I couldn't imagine her dressing herself.

"Can I help you get dressed?"

Her alert gaze and a curt *no* told me to back off. When I repeated this to Mom in the kitchen, she told me that Susan didn't want any of us to see her body. It was scarred from multiple surgeries and radiation burns and was now emaciated as well. I reeled at the image, especially in contrast to the birthday presents to open, new clothes for a dying child, and the fancy Wedgwood china and Baccarat crystal stemware on the dining table.

A short time later, Mom pulled a pan of her homemade lasagna out of the oven. Dad ladled portions of his layered salad onto chilled salad plates. The buttered garlic bread was in the top rack of the oven waiting to be toasted. Half an hour passed, then another, followed by another. Mom put the lasagna back in the oven to warm and went back to Susan's bedroom. She returned, saying everything was okay, and that Susan was *almost* dressed. Another half hour went by.

"Everyone, just be seated," Mom said. "Laurie, you sit in one of the big chairs in the living room since you're the birthday girl. Susan will sit next to you in the other one." She'd bring our dinner out on trays as soon as Susan came out, she said.

Everyone ate and chatted in the dining room while I waited for Susan. Overall, it took Susan nearly three hours to get dressed for my birthday, the last one I would ever celebrate with her. She wore her new salmon-colored denim pants, a white top, and a gray sweater. I watched as she willed herself down the hard, tiled hallway to the living room. She gripped the railing above the stairwell as she took one tiny step at a time. She had somehow dressed herself and walked out of her bedroom on her own two feet for my birthday party. It remains one of the saddest scenes of my life.

DAD IN SECOND YEAR OF SUSAN'S ILLNESS

Susan and I ate in silence with the chatter in the dining room as background noise. I could tell by her razor-sharp focus on her food that she needed all of her energy just to get it in her mouth. It was unbearable. Like a drowning person, I looked over at the rest of the family, unable to eat. I felt guilty for longing to be with them, with the living.

I was twenty-eight. Susan was twenty-five. She died nine days later.

CHAPTER 32: OUR LOSS

"Call nine-one-one, Irene!"

Mom said she struggled to get out of the bathtub and to the wall phone in the kitchen. Dad was at Susan's bedside as blood spilled from her mouth onto her blankets and then onto his moccasins. Before she lost consciousness, he said, she managed to say, "I love you, Daddy." Dad said those were her last words.

After the emergency crew came, and after Mom and Dad saw her one final time at the hospital, Dad called the three of us with the news.

"Your sister is gone, honey."

I heard his words, but I couldn't feel my body. I told him we'd be right down.

Mom shuffled down the hallway toward me when she heard the front door close behind Jody and me. She held a wet tissue to her reddened nose. It was the first time I'd seen my mother cry over Susan. Upon seeing her tears, I finally released my own.

"Oh, Laurie, what will we do without Susan?"

I didn't know. When Dad emerged from a dark shadow in the hallway, he came over to me. He placed his hands on my face and looked deep into my eyes. It was as if he were trying to convince himself that I was still here, that I was still alive. He didn't say anything. He barely said anything over the next twenty-four hours either. None of us did.

When Mom didn't need Dad for funeral preparations, he was outside on the deck wearing his bloodstained moccasins. Tim came upstairs every few hours or so, holding his midsection. He'd cracked one of his ribs crying. Caroline and her husband drove up from Santa Barbara. The image again was of all of us as lifeless puppets on separate tracks moving around the house, this time to a very somber soundtrack.

We buried Susan on the side of a hill overlooking the beach at Half Moon Bay, the same beach where she'd first met Matt. In her late teens then, she wore a tiny bikini and had long, straight, sun-bleached hair. She spent hours watching him surf the unpredictable waves and hours filling her hope chest with items for their future life together.

A small group gathered for the burial—Mom, Dad, the three of us kids, Matt, and friends and relatives of my mother. None of my father's new friends from San Francisco attended, though I didn't think about that then.

Dad had been solemn but steady throughout Susan's long illness. When the priest motioned to the burial assistant to lower Susan's casket into the ground, something in my father seemed to snap. He bolted out of his metal folding chair and stumbled a few feet uphill to Susan's casket, where he kneeled, his eyes lifted toward the priest.

"No, please don't, Father, please don't," he said.

His voice was plaintive and slightly hysterical at the same time. It frightened me to see my father in this state. I may have cried out, "Oh, Dad," or I may have just thought it. The other mourners didn't utter a word.

Dad again looked up at the priest, tears streaming down his face.

"Please, Father, I just need to see her one more time."

This time a loud gasp erupted from the mourners, including from me. I put my hand to my mouth. Mom stood up.

"Oh, Ralph, please don't," she said.

It was unbearable.

The priest, who'd probably seen it all before, nodded sweetly to Mom as if to say, *It's okay, Irene, it's okay.* Since all priests were like fathers to her, she must have felt somewhat reassured. She collapsed back into her small metal folding chair with a thud. Father motioned to his assistant to open the casket. The mourners let out a collective gasp, or at least it seemed that way to me.

I looked over at Mom. She held her handkerchief embroidered with tiny purple flowers up to her nose and mouth. I held my breath.

At that moment, Mom's friend, Violet, seated to my right, squeezed my hand. I turned toward her.

"Laurie, it's all right, honey."

She spoke in a voice similar to the one she used when I was a little girl in school with her own daughter. I leaned my head on her shoulder.

As soon as the assistant opened the casket, Dad leaned over and kissed Susan's forehead.

The fog by then had drifted over from the beach, and the air was chilly and damp. Dad lifted his head just enough to look at Susan one more time and then rested his head on her chest. I feared there might be a tussle, that Dad wouldn't allow Susan's casket to ever be closed and lowered into the grave. The worker stood still and silent. He'd probably seen mourners like this, too.

After what seemed like the right amount of time passing, not too short and not too long, the worker gently helped Dad up and guided him toward the rest of us. Dad recoiled and turned back again. This time he didn't return to his spot at the casket. He headed up the hill above it, above us, all by himself.

I looked around. The rest of the mourners, including myself, appeared frozen like characters in a TV show set on pause.

When Dad reached the top of the grassy hill of the cemetery, he turned to gaze at the ocean. He remained there, alone, long after the burial ceremony was over. Except for our immediate family, all of the guests returned to their cars. I think we went back to the house, but I don't have any memory of that.

My parents went back to work one week after Susan died. Dad, sixty-one, still worked at Standard Oil in San Francisco, and Mom, fifty-five, at the photo lab on the Peninsula. Tim began graduate school at Santa Clara University that fall. Caroline and her husband returned to Santa Barbara.

I was twenty-eight, busy as a full-time worker at a winery in Sonoma, and now the single mother of a third grader, grieving over the loss of my sister, and still unconsciously pulled to fill the empty space between my mother and father.

CHAPTER 33: GRIEVING

"Your father and I are having a hard time, Laurie," Mom said on a phone call. "We don't seem to know what to say to each other."

Her rare admission came a few weeks after Susan died. I assured her that Jody and I would be down Friday evening after work. As usual, she opened the front door before we even turned the handle. Except for the dim light above the stove in the kitchen, the house was dark. She clutched at us.

"Oh, Laurie, thank you so much for coming down," she said.

I didn't know how to soothe my mother, or myself, over our shared loss. But I was willing to try.

"Go see your dad now, honey," she said. "He always feels better when one of you kids is here. Come along, Jody." Mam directed her to the kitchen table and a new book of word puzzles. She'd already laid out two pens next to the book, one for each of them.

The burden I felt over having parents who weren't in love with one another increased after Susan died. Even though I was nearly thirty, I still felt and behaved as if the survival of my parents' union was critical to my own survival. Largely unconscious of that fact, though, I knew nothing of healthy personal boundaries.

My parents should have been able to lean on each other in their grief. Except for mealtime at the family house, though, I rarely saw them in the same room at the same time. They both seemed to take comfort solely in their surviving children.

As usual, I heeded my mother's direction and headed out to the deck to see my father. He straightened himself up when he noticed me, just enough to pull an old, crumpled handkerchief out of his pocket. I dragged a deck chair over next to his.

We stared at the clouds and the fog and the Monterey Cypress trees he'd planted as seedlings, now over twenty feet tall. They held the sloped bank well in place, but on this day he didn't boast about what a wise choice his tree selection of long ago had been. He didn't put his hand over my hand and squeeze it as he used to. He didn't point out the new blossoms on some odd-looking volunteer plant. He didn't ask about Jody.

When he finally spoke, it was about a message he'd received from Susan. Just that morning, he said, the clouds had formed into the shape of a giant seagull. Dad reminded me of his and Susan's shared love of the book *Jonathan Livingston Seagull*. In it, an outcast seagull struggles to learn love, self-respect, and forgiveness.

I nodded but it was disingenuous. At twenty-nine years of age, Dad's vision made me nervous. Perhaps it was a sign that his grief over Susan had pushed him over the edge. Now I think how comforting it must have been for him in that moment to have felt so connected to a child recently lost, especially over a book whose story somewhat mirrored his own. I wish I'd allowed myself that kind of quiet time and space to grieve. Instead, fearing the family would unravel, I took cues from my mother and kept perky and busy.

By late fall, when thick fog chilled us out on the deck, Dad shrouded himself in Susan's navy-blue parka. She'd bought it for a hike in the redwoods she'd taken with Matt in Big Basin

State Park before she got sick. Dad's weight had dropped so much that now even Susan's parka hung limply on him.

I returned to the kitchen to watch Mom and Jody make Tollhouse cookies. As soon as they were in the oven, Jody ran down the hallway to dig into the old toy closet. Without looking up from the mixing bowls and beaters and nut chopper now soaking in the sudsy sink, Mom made an announcement.

"Your father informed me he won't be going to my office parties or choir picnics with me anymore," she said.

Mom announced big news items like this much the same way I'd always done. If I didn't get it out right away, I would lose my nerve. Her voice was in her usual chipper tone, but this time it was strained.

"What are you talking about, Mom?"

I felt angry. Dad had gone too far, I thought, especially so soon after Susan's death. Now he was being unkind. On the other hand, I also understood. Dad was uncomfortable at those chatty social events. He didn't enjoy small talk with people he didn't know. At the time, I thought, *Well, then, don't make small talk. Talk big.* Of course, doing so would have meant revealing more of himself.

Mom brushed off my question.

"Oh, he's just bored at those events anyway, honey," Mom said. "It's okay."

"But aren't you sad he won't be with you?"

"I don't want your dad to do anything he doesn't want to do, honey," she said. "I just want him to be happy."

I might have connected this attitude toward my father to my own attitude toward my father, focusing almost exclusively on his well-being. Instead, I nudged my mother to do what I wasn't able to do for myself, to focus on her own feelings.

Dad came in for lunch wearing the blood-spattered moccasins. The stains were now black. Despite Mom's disapproval, he wore them in the house for at least a year after Susan died.

"They make me so sad, Ralph," she said.

"They don't make *me* sad, Irene." His tone now was one of anger.

My mother tried to push aside her grief. Dad wore his grieving heart on his sleeve, or, in his case, his moccasins. Planted in the middle of these two extremes was me, though unconsciously so.

CHAPTER 34: MOVING FORWARD

Mom grew increasingly concerned about Dad's emotional health. In our phone conversations every few days now, she punctuated her dialogue by the two words, *your father*. *Your father* is in a world of his own. *Your father* won't talk to me or go anywhere. I don't know what to do about *your father*. I hustled down every weekend, Jody in tow.

Dad was even gaunter now, his eyes red and lifeless. He no longer zipped up Susan's baggy jacket but instead wrapped it and his arms around himself. Out on the deck, he just stared off into the distance. I knelt down beside him.

"Mom and I are worried about your health, Dad," I said. "Please talk to me."

"Honey, I'm okay," he said. "I don't want you to worry about me. Tell me what Jody's been doing."

His last sentence came out pinched, sounding as if he were just feigning interest in his only grandchild. I fiddled with my watch. I wouldn't let him distract me from the purpose of my visit.

"Dad," I said. "Can I take you to a doctor?"

His response surprised me. He had in fact seen his doctor that very week.

"He prescribed antidepressant medication for me."

Not knowing anything about antidepressants or their long-term implications, I felt hopeful.

"Oh, good, Dad. Maybe you'll start feeling better."

"I'm not going to take them, honey."

"Why not?"

"In a weird way, depression is comforting. It's like being in a small, warm, dark room. No one expects me to do or say anything. Does that make any sense to you?"

I'd never thought about it that way.

"Now don't you worry about me," he said. "I'm just going to stay here for a little while longer."

I didn't know if my father was clinically depressed or if he was just a parent in deep grief over the loss of a child. Looking back, I admire his willingness at the time to go deep into his own well of sadness. Instead of doing that myself, after completing every household and gardening and mothering task I could think of, I took on emotionally deadening tasks like organizing old files or dating and mounting old photos. I never let myself stop at that time.

In the middle of this trying time, while Mom was "beside herself with worry" over Dad, and Dad was missing in action, and I was numb to my own grief, exhausted as a single working mother, and suffering panic attacks in the middle of the night, I made another rash decision. I didn't want to be alone. I suggested to the professor that we marry, and he agreed. I married this kind man who was fifteen years older than me, and who had dark brown curly hair, blue eyes, and brown skin like my father.

This would be my third and final marriage, I told myself, as I'd also sworn about my second. I knew I could trust him. He would be faithful to me. I didn't expect romantic love anymore. Security was what mattered. Everything would be fine.

My mother chose travel. After more than a year of trying to bolster Dad's moods, it seemed to me that one day she just gave up. She joined friends on a trip to the British Isles while Dad stayed home. It was the beginning of a new life for her.

No more walls

CHAPTER 35: WALLS COME DOWN

While Mom was in Scotland in 1981, Dad invited me down for my thirtieth birthday. Mom had managed to get a call through to me that morning. No matter what, my parents were tireless about remembering and celebrating their children's birthdays, no matter how old we were.

"Oh, honey, I'm having such a good time," my mother said. "You wouldn't believe it. It's nothing like being in the United States. We saw a castle today that's over five hundred years old. I got a blue mohair shawl for you. It's so soft."

Two years after the loss of Susan, Mom's voice was excited and childlike again. I felt my body letting out a big sigh.

Dad was back on his game, too. He created yet another one of his fancy frozen concoctions, this time for my birthday dessert. He said it took him two days to make. I was impressed. Freeform swirls of whipped cream topped individual layers of chocolate, coffee, and vanilla ice cream. He deftly carved wedged-shaped pieces of this tall creation with a knife he pulled out of a bowl of hot water.

While the sweet birthday celebration was normal in our family, the state of the family house was not. In the corner of the dining room was a ladder. This wasn't normal for my parents, nor was it something I'd ever have associated with my father. He explained he was tearing down the partial wall between the living room and dining room.

I may have tittered a little. Considering my father wasn't handy with tools—except for pruning shears and leatherworking awls and bevellers—this was an ambitious undertaking for him. His steady progress over the next month would surprise me. He pounded and chipped away at the wall. He sheetrocked and painted the ragged edges. The change was dramatic. Sunlight now poured into the living room from early afternoon until sundown.

He next hired a decorator to hang shiny, silvery wallpaper covered in white bamboo shapes. The heavy, dusty beige drapes that had hung across the sliding glass doors for more than a decade he replaced with sleek black-and-white shoji screens. Under one of the outside eaves, he hung a handsome porcelain birdhouse in the shape of a Japanese pagoda. He positioned it perfectly to welcome visitors to the living room. On the newly wallpapered walls, Dad hung framed Japanese prints and pencil drawings, and driftwood wall hangings I made for him. He chose rich, serene blues, silvers, and greens for this "great room."

He next demolished an entire wall, the one that separated the kitchen from Susan's old bedroom. Susan was gone, but her bedroom would not be an empty space. The result was an open and airy combined kitchen and family room.

"It's all so gorgeous, honey," Mom said on the phone one evening. "Wait until you see what he's done with the hallway the next time you're down."

She praised Dad's new home improvements, but she didn't say anything to me about the new HRC sticker on the bumper of his VW Beetle. When I asked Dad about it, he told me that the initials stood for "Human Rights Campaign." That made sense to me. He'd always been a supporter of human rights. I didn't realize until years later that the HRC was a civil rights organization fighting for gay rights.

After nearly two years of depression, followed by a year of the remodeling work, Dad had a new spring in his step. The walls had come down. Though he was still slim overall, his legs were back to being as muscular as they'd been during his jogging years before Susan got ill. The remodeling project had been a good workout for Dad. Gone were his sweatpants, Susan's now threadbare windbreaker, and even the bloodstained moccasins. Though he'd never return to the clothing of his hippie days, the new black slacks and copper-colored leather blazers he wore to work, though slightly bohemian, were smart-looking and of the time. His eyes were clear, bright, and wide open now.

The family as a group never discussed the obvious. Dad was "coming out" all over the place, boldly displaying his new bumper sticker for all to see, tearing down walls, remodeling the family home and his wardrobe, positioning beautiful objects for the benefit of visitors, and letting light in where it had never been before.

He and I had spoken little about his sexuality since Susan's doctor first diagnosed her illness. Except for briefly telling a few friends about it during that time— "It's not a big deal," I assured them—I'd held the secret inside for six long years.

With Dad's new vigor, he was ready to confide in me once again. I was older now. After the way history had treated him and other gay people in the twentieth century, I believed he deserved my unconditional love and support. I rationalized my complicity in any way I could. At the core, though, I know I feared abandonment. If I didn't support him, he might leave. From my earliest memory on, I'd never been free of that fear. He put my faithful complicity to the ultimate test that year by mentioning a man by name to me.

"Come outside with me on the deck, Laurie," he said. "I'd like to show you something."

He pointed to the fig tree.

"See those figs at the top, honey? The deer can't reach them. I think we'll finally be able to enjoy a few this year."

He took me around to the entry garden. When he leaned down to pick up and show me a shell-studded rock, I noticed his newly tanned back.

"I found this over at the beach," he said. "It looks like an exquisite piece of sculpture, doesn't it?"

"Uh-huh."

I followed him out to the front sidewalk, far from sliding glass doors that might be ajar. I knew from experience we wouldn't be talking about figs or beach treasures out here.

"His name is William," Dad said. "And he's the nicest guy you'd ever want to meet, honey."

I wanted to envision William as being part of a fun group of Dad's progressive friends in San Francisco, all of them of course gay, but not *too* gay.

"Yeah?"

My flat-toned voice feigned nonchalance; my nervous stomach was anything but.

"We have the *greatest* conversations, Laurie," Dad said.

"Cool," I said.

Dad changed the subject.

"There's something else. I know someone who is really sick. I'm so worried about him."

The year was 1981.

"Yeah? What's wrong with him?"

"Doctors are calling it *the gay cancer*," he said. "He has these purple splotches all over."

The image sickened me. I turned away. I didn't want to hear anything more about it, though it never occurred to me then that my father, my *gay* father, might be susceptible to it. People don't catch cancer, I rationalized.

In the midst of whatever horrible disease was now plaguing

his gay friends, Dad stood tall and strong again. When he leaned against the retaining wall now, he no longer looked worn down or in need of support. His shoulders were straight and relaxed at the same time. In fact, his whole body seemed relaxed. He and Mom were now finding happiness somewhere other than in their marriage, and they weren't hiding the fact.

Mom slid open the tiny bathroom window and called us in for dinner. Dad stayed outside for a quick smoke. As I crossed the threshold to the house, I became my mother's daughter, smiling and friendly. She wanted to hear what Jody and I had been doing. I didn't tell her about my ongoing night terrors or that I'd already sought out a marriage counselor. I also left out any reference to Dad's new friend, William, and the gay cancer plaguing people Dad knew.

A few years later, on his sixty-fifth birthday, Dad retired. He was more than ready, he said, to start the next phase of his life. After his retirement party in San Francisco, he got busy with other activities. He announced he'd been putting in requests at the San Carlos library for gay literature and periodicals. He was surprised when they approved "every single book" he requested. I didn't ask him for the names of the titles. Thinking of the proper, conservative-looking librarians I grew up with, I was surprised, too. I thought my father bold.

"They haven't said no to anything yet, honey," he boasted.

He next suggested to the resource librarian that they set up an LGBT section in the library. Again, to his surprise, she assigned him the (volunteer) job of doing so, which he accepted.

Once he set up the new LGBT section, he registered for a writing class at the local community college. It had been forty-five years since he dropped out of Pasadena City College and gave up his dream of becoming an English teacher. He told me he wanted to take the class because he thought he had something to say. However, he wasn't sure anyone else, especially the writing instructor, would think so. He considered his fellow students, most of whom were in their late teens or early twenties, brilliant by comparison to him. When he turned in his first assignment, he said, he repeated to his professor that he wasn't sure he had anything worth saying. A week later, his teacher handed him back his paper with a large red *A* at the top.

"I couldn't believe it, honey," he said. "I just looked at him. Then he told me, 'Yes, Ralph, I believe you *do* have something to say.'"

Tears rolled down his cheeks when he told me this story. I gave him a cheery smile.

That year, he wrote a number of essays, stocked the local library with gay literature and periodicals, and, it seems to me now from his numerous mentions of William, regularly saw him and other gay acquaintances in San Francisco, more and more of whom he reported were also getting sick.

I prided myself on being open to hearing about my father's gay life. I even boasted to a few friends about his attendance at that year's Gay Pride parade. However, I framed it as just another one of my father's well-known civil rights stands.

CHAPTER 36: HIS BOYFRIEND

"I'd like to ask you a favor, honey," Dad said, taking a long pause.

He sounded serious. My stomach tightened as questions flooded my mind. Has he finally decided to leave the family? Does he need my help to get Mom through the transition? Is he the one with the gay cancer now? Does he need to go over some practical things with me before he dies?

It was none of those, but it would still unnerve me.

Dad flicked the bottom of his pack of cigarettes and pointed out a recently bloomed, lavender-blue iris in the front yard. Our patterns were well established. I feared abandonment if I didn't support him. He appreciated nature and slow drags on his cigarettes, both of which served as preludes and added drama to his storytelling.

"Okay," I said, though my response sounded more like a question than an affirmative statement.

"Well, then, it's about William."

He leaned down and stubbed his first cigarette out in the gravel.

"You know, honey, William really appreciates fine wines."

I now knew where this was going. The winery where I now worked was a small boutique facility, popular with wine aficionados from around the world.

"Yeah?"

"He'd love a tour of the winery," Dad said.

"He would?"

"It would mean so much to him, honey."

It sounded more as if it would mean a lot to my father. His arms moved around while he spoke. He thrust out his chest as if he were imagining showing William around the winery and vineyards himself.

I can't recall my father ever saying no to me. I'd never said no to him, either. Personal boundaries are an important part of a healthy family system, but I didn't even know what they were back then.

My father was now stepping further out of his closet and becoming more authentically himself, though still out of earshot of Mom. The more he stepped out, though, the more I sequestered myself in a closet of my own. I was now the one who had to watch my every word, especially around Mom and Tim. Dad told me that Mom didn't want Tim to know he was gay, that she would be *so* embarrassed. I think I saw a slight snicker on my father's face, though I am no longer sure of it. I couldn't stomach the fact that my mother would be ashamed.

The number of stories I kept secret grew by the day. When I spoke with my mother now, I was no longer all there with her. My focus was on making sure that a certain word or date or story didn't slip out, one that revealed something I shouldn't know.

My night terrors increased in frequency and intensity. In a recurring one, a small, closet-sized room of my own trapped me inside. There were no doors or windows. There was no way out. The four walls, plus the ceiling and the floor, gradually moved in toward me. As they got closer, my chest heaved with heart palpitations. I'd awaken screaming, drenched in sweat, and ashamed of myself for something I didn't understand and couldn't stop from occurring. My self-awareness in my early thirties didn't allow me to see a connection between the dissolution of my father's closet walls and the fortification of my own.

"Uh, okay, Dad," I said.

"Great, honey!"

Dad smiled. He may have even jumped a little.

"I will let him know," he said.

Dad coordinated all the arrangements. I still hadn't met or spoken to William. I was surprised when Dad told me he wouldn't be joining us at the winery. I didn't even think to ask him why not. Maybe it was a strategic move on my father's part. The idea of arriving with a probable lover at his daughter's workplace may have crossed a line even for him. It also would have made the visit harder to explain to my mother, not that I planned to do that anyway.

I fidgeted at my desk all morning. The winery owner sat cattycorner from me between the front door and my desk. I wondered if he could tell I wasn't working. Just in case, I punched some random numbers into the large calculator and hit the equal sign. A paper tape glided out of the top. I tore off the phony tabulation and "filed" it in a lower drawer.

That was the day Dad's "friend" visited the winery.

A panel of glass separated my office from the wine cellar below. I watched as the winemaker's assistant stepped off his ladder and climbed down inside the wine tank. Using a tool that resembled a giant potato masher, he punched down the thick, dry cap of grape skins that floated to the top during the fermentation process. The summer's record heat had ripened the grapes early that year. From before sunup to a few hours after dark, the high-yield tonnage in the gondola trailers poured into the wine cellar. In between glances at the reflection of the front door in the glass, I kept an eye on the worker in the open tank below. The strong fumes sometimes made them dizzy.

According to my father, William wanted to learn more about the winemaking process. A small, hands-on winery like this was a perfect fit for that. He could observe the methods up close.

Mary Beth, the tasting room manager, had scheduled a pairing of wine and chocolate for noon that day. Awaiting today's visitors was not only the thrill of witnessing the annual grape crush but also the sampling of handmade chocolate truffles. The realization that hordes of tourists would soon be flocking to the tasting room calmed me a little. Long conversations with William in the middle of such a frenzy would be difficult.

For the past hour, the tall metal ledgers and sturdy paper cards I used to track vendors and wine orders by hand sat untouched next to my clunky adding machine. A few minutes after twelve noon, I caught William's reflection in the glass. I watched him pause before knocking. His gaze wandered up the steep bank of grapevines just outside my office door. His body moved like a robust but slightly jumpy young man's. Seated in my office chair, I jumped a little, too. I opened the door just as William knocked.

"William?" I said.

He nodded. I smiled.

"Welcome," I said. "Please come inside."

He extended his hand before I could turn around.

"Hello, Laurie," he said. "It's so nice to finally meet you."

I was surprised to hear him call me by my nickname, but it of course made sense. My father called me Laurie. William's word, "finally," struck me, too. I wondered just how long he'd known Dad.

After shaking my hand, William placed his other hand on top of mine. My hand was now sandwiched between both of his. I smiled as I slipped it out of his grasp. I glimpsed his white, classic sports car in the parking space at the bottom of the steps as I closed the door behind him. The car reminded me of the vintage Cadillac with the flashy tail fins that Mom made Dad return to one of the men in his office. I mused about a possible connection between gay men and stylish vintage cars.

William surveyed the hectic winemaking scene below while I surveyed him. His short graying hair came down just above his ears. A diamond stud pierced one of them. I couldn't remember which ear, if pierced, was supposed to signal one's homosexuality.

I guessed William to be in his early fifties. That would have made him about fifteen years younger than my father. Just like old straight men going after younger women, I thought. William had tucked his snug, salmon-pink polo shirt into his creased, distressed black denim jeans. I noticed how his tight shirtsleeves strained under his bulging biceps. I thought, *Oh, no, he looks so gay.* I don't know what brought me to this immediate conclusion, but maybe it was the *San Francisco Chronicle* photos of the husky, jeaned "buckaroos" in the annual Pride parades.

I pointed out the frothy slurry of grape juice and skins to William. Large hoses pumped this must from the outdoor wine press to the steel tanks in the cellar. The workers punched down the caps with those large "potato mashers" every few hours.

William swooned. "Ooh, I just love that yeasty, grapey smell," he said.

"Let's go down to the cellar now," I said. "It will be even stronger there."

I let out a nervous giggle. On the way down the stairs, I told him about the long hours the crew had been working.

"We won't want to bother anyone," I said. "But you can look all you want."

Truth be told, I didn't want coworkers questioning me about the nature of my relationship with a man who was "obviously gay."

"That would be great," William said. "Your dad is very proud of you, you know."

I think I grimaced. He sounded so familiar. Still, I could see why Dad liked him. He was polite and friendly, in contrast to how I must have appeared to him that day. I guided him over the wide hoses and electrical cords and around the loud pumps. The winemaker burst through the large cellar door opening as we passed by.

"Oh, hi, Rick," I said. "I'm just showing someone around."

I introduced the two of them. Rick acknowledged William with a slight wave and trekked off without so much as a double take at him. I guessed I was worried about nothing. We moved out of the way and stood against the side of a tank while I described the frenzied tasks going on all around us. William's pretty iridescent, powder-blue eyes darted around. They were smaller than my father's but similar in color. He scanned the warehouse-like room and the view outside through the large cellar door. His gaze stopped at the giant pile of dried seeds and stems shooting out one end of the grape press while the juice flowed in the opposite direction. He pointed at it.

"What do you do with those?"

"We spread them out in the vineyard," I said. "They make great mulch. Here, let me show you."

I hustled William out the cellar door. In the noonday sun his skin looked so fair and freckled, much like my mother's. I wondered if he'd been a redhead when he was young, or a Titian blond, as my father would have insisted.

I shook my head and pointed up to the hillside vineyards behind the winery, now mostly a mottled mosaic of yellow and scarlet leaves. Gnarled, leafless woody trunks were visible on the steepest slopes where the temperatures had reached the highest.

"This scene is stunning, Laurie," he said. "You know, it looks like a Renoir painting."

What, are all gay men this way?

I thought back to our family field trip to the de Young Museum when I was a little girl. Dad had been as awestruck at seeing an original Van Gogh painting as William was by this viticultural "art" on the hillside. I realized in that moment that I had never been around another man like my father. The contrast between Dad and the fathers of my friends was glaring.

"Let's go over to the tasting room now," I said. "I'm sure you're ready to have a taste!"

"Uh, okay, Laurie," William said.

He tore his gaze from the vineyards. I marched him across the driveway, the only sound the loud crunching of gravel under our shoes.

Through the tasting room's open door, I caught sight of not the usual dozens of visitors but only a few. In my hurry to get the tour over, we'd arrived at the tasting room before the daily rush. Mary Beth popped out from behind the varnished redwood burl bar when she heard us.

"Hey, hi, Laura!" she said. "Who ya got with you?"

Her loud, cheery voice grated on my nerves today. Before I had a chance to say anything, she thrust her hand out to William.

"Hi, I'm Mary Beth. Welcome!"

William perked right up, probably relieved to meet at least one gracious person that day.

"Thank you very much. I'm William, and I'm happy to meet you."

I edged myself up on a bar stool and watched as the two of them got right to it. Mary Beth described how the chardonnay got its smoky edge from the new French barrels because the cooper burns the inside of them. She filled William in on the ideal sugar and acid levels of the grapes that went into the Cabernet Sauvignon Reserve.

William sipped, spit, and cooed his way through each taste of the current offerings. He asked about how a particular wine might compare to the wine made by the grapes crushed that day. He asked how the builders constructed the wine cellar so deep into the rocky hillside. "Dynamite," Mary Beth explained.

She moved on to her recommendations for wine and food pairings—chardonnay with lemon-dill salmon; cabernet sauvignon with grilled, marinated venison; and for dessert the sweet white Riesling with blue cheese.

"And speaking of dessert," she said.

She pulled out a tiny, silver platter with half a dozen dark chocolate truffles on it. Grabbing hold of a truffle with a tiny pair of silver tongs, she handed it to William on a napkin along with a glass of merlot she'd already poured.

"First take a tiny bite of the truffle," she said.

William complied.

"While it's melting in your mouth, take a sip of the merlot."

He closed his eyes and when he opened them, they were lit up.

"Okay," William said. "Now I'm in heaven."

He again reminded me of my father. I wondered if all gay men were polite, appreciative, and enthusiastic—or if this was just the kind of gay man Dad liked, someone like himself.

"Hey, Laura, how do you know William?"

"Uh, he's a friend of my father's," I said.

She turned to William.

"Cool!" she said. "I love Laura's father."

William smiled but thankfully moved on.

"Can I purchase a few bottles of this fantastic wine?"

Mary Beth got to work bagging a few bottles of wine, gave William my twenty-five percent employee discount, and even threw in a few chocolate truffles in a red cellophane bag at no charge. William thanked her repeatedly.

A few tourists sauntered into the tasting room, just the cue I needed to usher William back to his snazzy little sports car.

"I can't tell you how grateful I am for your time, Mary Beth," William said. "It's been a big treat for me."

"I'm glad you came by!" she said.

When William and I reached his car, I stuck out my hand to

shake his. If he was anything like my father, I knew to expect a hug and made sure it didn't happen. It was then that I noticed something flash over William's face. It looked to me like kindness. Maybe he understood my inner conflict. I wondered if he regretted the visit. In any event, he didn't make a move to hug me. He shook my hand but held it a little longer than most might. William was a sweet man.

"Thank you so much, Laurie," he said.

He bent down to get into his car, closed the door, revved up the engine, and drove down the narrow dirt road back to town and to San Francisco.

I felt awful. I was much nicer than this person he'd just met, this beloved daughter of his good friend or lover. I still wasn't sure.

That evening I got a call from Dad, a rare occurrence. They still had only one phone in the house, and it was in the kitchen, not private at all. He wanted to know how everything went. Mom must have been at choir practice.

"Things went well, Dad, but . . ."

"But what, honey?"

He knew me well.

"Well, everybody could tell he was gay, Dad," I said.

I had no evidence of this whatsoever.

"I didn't know how to introduce him," I said.

The whiny tone of my voice annoyed even me. There was a long pause. I knew my words had stung him. I wanted them to. I felt like I had betrayed my mother by spending time with my father's lover. But I regretted my words.

"Honey, he's just a good person, just someone who is interested in wine," Dad said.

My stomach clutched. I could tell he was hurt. There was something else, though, something much worse. In the tone of his voice was a soft, almost aching sound. It seemed to emanate from somewhere other than his vocal cords. I'd never heard that sound coming from my father. I wonder now if it emanated from a long-ago time.

"I know he is, Dad," I said. I took a deep breath. "But please don't send any more of your gay friends to the winery."

As the words escaped my mouth, I wished I could retrieve them. I couldn't believe I'd even uttered them. For a long time, Dad said nothing.

"Okay, honey, I won't," he said.

This was the first boundary I think I ever set with my father. It was clumsy, unkindly stated, and I didn't feel at all good about it.

Mom called me the following weekend to hear about my week. I picked my words carefully, never mentioning William.

CHAPTER 37: A BUDDY

M y father no longer gushed about the great talks he was having with his gay friends, though he'd already toned it down after my remarks about William's winery visit. Our conversations now included regular updates on the ticking time bomb initially called the gay cancer. In 1982, the Center for Disease Control renamed it AIDS, Acquired Immune Deficiency Syndrome, to reflect the fact that it wasn't isolated to the gay community. Still, gay men in San Francisco, New York City, and Los Angeles were the ones dying from the disease at an alarming rate.

"You just would not believe it, honey," he said. "They're just wasting away."

At the same time, evangelical televangelist Jerry Falwell preached that AIDS was "the wrath of God upon homosexuals." In 1983, President Reagan's communications director, Pat Buchanan, joked, "The poor homosexuals—they have declared war on nature, and now nature is exacting an awful retribution."

The situation was grimmer by the day. President Reagan didn't speak the word AIDS in public until 1985. By then tens of thousands of Americans had died of the disease, most of them gay men. Hundreds of thousands were already infected. Federal support, financial and otherwise, was slow in coming.

Nationwide pronouncements of homosexuals getting what they deserved played on the nightly news. The obituaries of those who died of the disease filled pages of the *San Francisco Chronicle*. However, around my mother and brother, I didn't speak of AIDS or stand up for those who were sick and dying as I normally would have. If I did, I concluded, I might accidentally out my father to my brother. To my mother, I might out myself as knowing Dad was gay. In retrospect, I look at my assumptions at the time as misguided. Compassion for the sick is not complicated. I was now the one twisting into different shapes for family members.

Living in the Bay Area at the beginning of the AIDS epidemic felt like living inside an old newsreel, the kind I saw in movie theaters as a kid. When I watched the historic footage of the 1945 mushroom clouds over Japan, I already knew what was coming. I knew it would be horrific but there would be an end to it. In the early years of AIDS, no one knew if or when it would end.

Studies now show that in the early 1980s, HIV, the virus that causes AIDS, had already infected nearly half of the gay men in San Francisco. With little or no help coming from the federal government, San Francisco locals stepped up. Elected officials found needed funding in the city's budget. Home care programs were set up. Local spiritual and medical practitioners provided one-on-one support to those without means to pay for it. Those who were well took care of the sick.

As one of the well, my father volunteered for what he called the AIDS Buddy Program. It may have been a program of the Shanti Project in San Francisco. His job, he said, wasn't to be a nurse or a housekeeper. It was to be a friend. Dad blossomed in this chaplain-like role.

"There is no hope for them," he said.

because it matters..
we ask you to volunteer

Shanti Project

Our community's in crisis — and you can make a difference.
Are you someone who can open your heart to a person with AIDS?
Can you offer compassion and understanding to their friends, family and loved ones?
If so, Shanti Project is the place for you.

Shanti Training

Our next training will be held May 11, 12, 13/18, 19, 20.
We ask that you be able to make a one year commitment of 8 hours a week.

For further info, please call 558-9644

Shanti is a word meaning "inner peace."

SHANTI FLIER SOLICITING AIDS VOLUNTEERS

What puzzled me at the time was how my father's face glowed when he reported this gloomy news. Maybe it was the result of spending time with gay men like himself and of being able to comfort them. I felt proud of him, even though the images and terms he used horrified me—sunken eyes, purple splotches covering gaunt bodies of frightened, desperate men without their families at the end of their lives.

Some of the men left children behind when they died, fathers like my father, children like me. Dad was one of the lucky ones. So was I.

To my surprise, Dad brought up his volunteer work at dinner one evening at the family house.

"All I can do is hold their hand," he said.

I avoided Mom's eyes. She and I still hadn't spoken about the fact that I knew about Dad. My older sister and I had spoken briefly about it on her rare trips home. Tim was the only sibling who didn't know. After dinner I approached Dad, this time without an invitation. He was outside smoking a cigarette.

"Dad, it's getting weird for me around Mom," I said. "I don't know what to say sometimes."

"Your mother knows, Laurie," he said. "I told her you know."

"You did?"

"Yes, honey. I also told her that you know about the day she found out."

My mind raced. *Is she angry with me for knowing? Does she think I look down on her for staying in the marriage? Can we all talk about this as a family now?*

I could feel myself twisting into a pretzel again.

CHAPTER 38: ETERNITY

On the morning of Christmas 1986, my father gave my mother a gold eternity ring. Embedded with a continuous line of diamonds and emeralds, it held special meaning for my mother. She was sixty-two, my father sixty-eight. They'd been married for forty-four years. She squealed when she saw it.

"Ralph!" she said. "Oh, honey."

I didn't understand the symbolism of the then newly-marketed rings. But she did.

"You see, Laurie, the continuous line of stones represents never-ending love."

She delivered her explanation with a perky delivery and a big smile. Dad sat on the nearby couch with a gleam in his eye. I was confused. All my life I'd scoured my parents' gestures for signs of love for one another. Mom ran to kiss Dad when he arrived home from work. In photos, she's often grabbing his arm and leaning into him in the one-sided affection of theirs.

Even though this eternity ring wasn't physical affection, it was a grand gesture on my father's part. He preferred pearls, turquoise, and other semiprecious gemstones mounted in artistic settings. Here, he picked out an exuberant though conventional ring for his wife, something he knew would mean the most to her.

He still didn't kiss or embrace her, though. I wasn't kissing or hugging my third husband, either.

CHAPTER 39: PULLED BACK IN

"Your father's in San Diego, Laurie."

Mom spoke in clipped words on the phone. Her voice was high. She sounded as if she could hardly breathe. I'd barely gotten *Hello* out of my mouth when she blurted out the news. I wonder if she thought she might lose her nerve if she didn't get it out quickly. I knew something was wrong. With the exception of family vacations when I was little, Dad rarely traveled out of town. At that point he'd flown in a plane only once in my lifetime and that was only a short trip to Bakersfield to see Grandma and Grandpa Hall.

"What do you mean, Mom? What's he doing there?"

"He flew down there with some new *friends* of his."

From the way she emphasized the word *friends*, I knew what she meant. Before I could say anything, she switched topics and asked about Jody, my job, and our vegetable garden. Then she said good-bye and hung up.

Based on the year, 1986, Dad may have been attending the First International AIDS Vigil of Prayer in San Diego, though he never spoke to me about it. The Metropolitan Community Church (MCC) of San Diego, a gay church founded in San Francisco in 1970, hosted the vigil.

A few days later, Mom called again.

"Your father hasn't returned home yet," she said, her voice even more shrill. "I'm getting really worried, honey."

"Do you want me to come down, Mom?" I said.

"No, honey, I know you're busy with Jody," she said. "I'll call Tim."

Tim, now married and a first-time father of a baby girl, lived in a city in the East Bay, less than an hour's drive from the family home. He and Mom shared similar but lighthearted interests, like movies, long drives out into the country, and tours of model homes. I wondered what would happen when the two of them talked this time. I didn't have to wait long to find out.

Tim called me that evening. He'd spent Sunday afternoon with Mom.

"I know Dad is gay," he said. "Mom told me."

He said Mom was anxious but unforthcoming when he arrived. When he pressed her to tell him what was wrong, she said that Dad was "at an AIDS conference in San Diego," that he was "hanging around with gay men," and that "it's become a real problem."

"I had no idea what she meant," Tim said. "I jokingly asked her, 'What are you saying, Mom, that Dad's gay?' She hemmed and hawed for a few seconds. I was shocked when she said yes."

Mom must have been at a breaking point. I'd known Dad was gay since 1975. It was now 1986, eleven years later. Tim's next words didn't surprise me.

"Why didn't you tell me?" he said.

I could tell he was hurt.

"Did you think I couldn't handle it?"

I didn't think that at all. Our mother was the one who supposedly didn't want him to know.

"I really don't know, Tim," I said. "I just felt all tangled up inside. Dad's secret became my secret."

I flailed. I remembered how frustrated I felt when I asked

my mother why she didn't talk about her father. She was three when her parents split up. She never knew him. However, he lived until 1946, the year Mom turned twenty-two. She had plenty of time as an adult to contact him. Why didn't I tell Tim about Dad? Why didn't Mom try to locate her father?

"It was as if he didn't exist, honey," she said. "Nana never spoke of him. It was as if he were dead."

I didn't understand when she told me this when I was little, but I do now. Dad's secret was something he and I alone spoke of.

That is not entirely true. I told Jody about her grandfather's sexual orientation when she was a sophomore in high school, two years before Tim knew. My disclosure came because of a comment she'd made to Dad. He relayed the scene to me. He and Jody were talking at the family kitchen table during one of the summertime weeks she spent at their house. They were discussing something—Dad couldn't remember the details— and Jody mentioned a boy in one of her classes who was gay.

"I couldn't believe it, honey," Dad said. "It was as if it were the most normal thing on earth to know a boy who was gay."

"Yeah, she and her friends talk that way, Dad," I said.

"Well, I had no idea," he said. "I asked her if she thought being gay was something strange, or if it was a bad thing to be. She shook her head nonchalantly. I cannot tell you how happy I am to have my own granddaughter talk that way."

Jody learned the truth from me later that week. She was as nonchalant as she'd been with her grandfather. Of course, I felt obligated to tell her not to mention it to Mam, someone to whom she was very close. Now Jody had joined us in the closet.

After Mom told Tim, everyone in our family now knew Dad was gay. However, only two of us would ever speak about it together at one time. Dad and me. Jody and me. Tim and Mom. We never spoke about it as an entire family. Ever.

Dad was the one who told me what happened the night he returned home from San Diego. The house was dark. He found

Mom at the kitchen table in a chair facing the front door. She was shaking, he said, and had been crying.

"She was beside herself, Laurie," Dad said.

I hated hearing this, but I didn't stop him.

"Then she said, 'I can't take this anymore, Ralph.'"

"I told her I wasn't doing anything wrong, that I was just having fun with my friends," he said. "She just kept repeating, 'I can no longer live like this, Ralph.'"

My poor mother. My poor father. I kept repeating those phrases in my head. I wasn't thinking, *Poor me,* for being in the middle of this. I wasn't telling myself I had the right to say, *Stop telling me what the other parent is saying.*

"I told her . . . No, I actually yelled at her, 'Okay, Irene, I'll stop everything. I'll stop it all. But I won't ever be happy again.'"

How rash and childish, I thought.

Now I wonder why Dad didn't take her up on her ultimatum. She was in essence giving him an out. She told him she couldn't live that way anymore. Dad had found his community, and beyond that a calling to help his ailing brothers. Mom was traveling the world with her friends. They had plenty of money.

Instead, Dad shut himself down once again. Maybe he couldn't envision giving up his marriage after four decades. Maybe he felt he owed it to Mom for being dishonest from the beginning about who he was. Maybe he was afraid he'd be all alone without her, as I felt when Jody's father issued a similar ultimatum to me almost two decades earlier. I chose her father, then left him. Dad chose Mom. And from all appearances, he was in the marriage for the long run.

Later in the week, Tim asked Dad to meet him at a restaurant for lunch. Some time later, he relayed the details of the conversation to me.

"I told Dad I knew he was gay," he said. "He turned white as a ghost and his mouth dropped open. Then I told him I was entirely fine with it. He said he was so relieved."

Dad told Tim some of the stories he told me, that he knew he was gay from an early age, that the young Baptist minister was gay, too, and that the police in Los Angeles had twice arrested him for being gay.

I asked Tim if Dad told him about Stanley. Tim shook his head no, so I told him the story.

"Dad probably didn't think I was ready to hear that the big love of his life wasn't Mom," Tim said.

◇　◇　◇

A few years later, a serious illness landed Dad in the hospital.

"Honey, you'd better come down soon," Mom said. Her tone was flat and serious.

"Is it Dad?"

"Yes, he's fading fast, Laurie."

"What do you mean he's fading, Mom? What's wrong with him?"

She wouldn't say.

The nurses on the sixth floor of Sequoia Hospital in Redwood City directed me to an isolation ward when I arrived. I later found out it was the AIDS ward. Mom was at Dad's bedside. The color of his skin was an ashen gray. The whites of his eyes were yellow. He lay there, sunken into his hospital bed looking deflated and resigned. I took his hand and thought of the AIDS Buddy program, though I remained naïvely unworried about Dad contracting the disease.

I asked Mom to join me out in the hallway and pressed her again for details.

"Why is he yellow, Mom?"

"Well, honey, he has . . . uh, he has hepatitis," she said.

Well, okay, I thought. There's a name for it. But I didn't understand why she was so nervous about telling me. I would learn later than gay men are at an increased risk of contracting Hepatitis B. Now I understand why he was in an isolation ward. Doctors would have known in 1990 that a man sick with Hepatitis B was probably gay and therefore could have AIDS. Both would have landed him in an isolation ward. Though I did not know any of this at the time, my mother's secrecy was a signal that she was uncomfortable about something.

I was surprised when she called a few days later to tell me that Dad was out of the hospital. He didn't die after all. Though he'd recover from hepatitis, over the next few years he was plagued with ulcers and other stress-related physical ailments. Mom stayed home and cared for him as each new illness plagued his system.

Dad never returned to those energetic days of his in the 1980s. However, he did recover from subsequent illnesses and regain some degree of vigor, just as he'd done after the bankruptcy and after Susan's death. But now he funneled his energy into solitary activities like cooking, gardening, listening to music, and reading. He rarely went out and, from what Mom told me, they rarely spoke. When they did, she said, it was about practical household matters and their remaining three children.

What a grim existence, I thought, but I no longer tried to intervene.

Dad spoke little to me now. He'd answer my questions but that was about it. He was seventy-six. Mom was seventy. She loved him when he was happy and healthy—as long as he was not openly betraying her, I assumed—*and* when he was morose and silent. She did not appear to hold onto any long-term animosity toward him for his sexual orientation or infidelity. When he entered the room, her eyes still lit up.

Dad quit the AIDS Buddy Program. He also dropped out of his writing class at the community college. He destroyed the essays he'd written for the class. Before then, whenever I asked about his writing, he'd say, "Oh, one day you'll see them, honey."

I never did.

A HAPPY MOMENT, 2003

My father's beloved tea set

CHAPTER 40: PRECIOUS TEA SET

My father never again stayed out overnight. He never flew anywhere again nor mentioned William. When I visited, I'd find him sitting at the kitchen table, sorting through mail, or smoking cigarettes out in the garden, pulling weeds here and there, wearing tattered sweatpants and threadbare denim shirts as he did during Susan's illness.

Sometimes I caught him listening to contemporary songs on the stereo: Bette Midler's "The Rose," or "Teach Your Children" by Crosby, Stills, Nash & Young, or "Suzanne" by Leonard Cohen. Other times it would be melancholic songs from the past: "He'll Have to Go" by Jim Reeves, "Scarlet Ribbons" by Harry Belafonte, or Patti Page's "Tennessee Waltz." Unless asked, he didn't speak up at family gatherings anymore. When asked, he answered using as few words as possible.

He didn't ask me to talk to him in private anymore, except for one time. He whispered that he had something he wanted to show me. *How many more secrets could he possibly have?* I wondered. I followed him back to the master bedroom and then into his closet while the rest of the family finished their dessert out in the dining room. He asked me to hold out my arms. He carefully pulled down a medium-sized white box from a back shelf, gently placed it in my arms, and slid back the lid.

Layers of thin tissue paper covered whatever was inside. I wished we could have sat down somewhere and placed the box on a table. But I could tell by how firmly Dad's feet were planted on his closet floor that he wasn't about to leave. He pulled back the tissue and unveiled the contents, one by one. My eyes widened when I saw the porcelain teapot with the large, delicate rose protruding out one side. I'd never seen anything like it. Dad held it close to his chest. It was so over-the-top, not something I'd ever pick out for myself. Just in case he'd purchased the set for me, though, I was careful about what I said.

"Wow, Dad," I said.

Using his fingertips, he pulled back another layer of tissue to reveal a matching teacup. It was as if he were un-swaddling a newborn baby.

"Isn't this the most beautiful thing you have ever seen, honey?" he said.

That was debatable, but I was happy to see him smiling over something again.

"They *are* beautiful, Dad."

Though I tried to sound enthusiastic, my words came out more as comfort, which they were.

"They are a bit much, though, aren't they?" he asked.

His chin dropped to his chest. I could imagine this set displayed behind the glass doors of the handsome black lacquer china cabinet he'd purchased as part of his major house remodel a decade earlier. A voice in his head must have been telling him no, he could not display it in full view. People would know.

"Would you like them, honey?"

I took a deep breath. I would not be saying *no* to him.

"Uh, sure, Dad," I said. "But you love them. Are you sure you don't want to keep them here at the house?"

"Go ahead and finish your dessert now," he said. "I'll wrap them back up and put them in the trunk of your car. You can take them home with you."

I joined the rest of the family back in the dining room. Dad snuck out the front door with his marvelous, pink rose tea set, soon to be leaving the family house for good.

Luis, taken by Laura, 1991

Laura, taken by Luis, 1991

CHAPTER 41: LUIS

started college in 1988, the same year Jody did. I was 37. During her first semester, she met and fell in love with a bright, handsome, and hardworking young man. Fortunately, she didn't inherit my fears about men being untrustworthy. In sticking with the one she loved, she schooled me on the subject.

One hot summer day, Jody found herself double-booked. I was on summer break. She called to see if I could meet a contractor at her house. She had forgotten about a dentist appointment that she'd scheduled at the same time. I had received my BA in Landscape Architecture from UC Berkeley a few weeks earlier. Graduate school wouldn't be starting for another few months. I had the time. The doorbell rang at the appointed time.

"Hi, I'm Luis," he said. "You called about a bid?"

Cute, friendly, and a little shy looking, this contractor was all business. He had a grid-lined notepad in his hand, a heavy-duty measuring tape on his belt, and a flat yellow pencil with a dull point tucked behind one ear. He looked past me through the living room toward the sliding glass doors that led to the backyard.

I invited him in and handed him the patio drawings as he walked by. He moved quickly, his biceps bulging beneath the short sleeves of his faded red T-shirt. I paused at the threshold of the back door. From a squatting position, he leaned over to take measurements. The back of his shirt rose up a few inches above his blue jeans.

I grimaced. I was forty now and still married to my third husband whom I didn't love. I didn't want to have any sexual feelings for any man again. No more marriages. No more divorces. And at least in college, I wasn't a failure. I looked forward to graduate school and a meaningful profession afterward. However, the stirring this contractor caused in me wouldn't let up. His businesslike demeanor that first day told me that I'd stirred up nothing in him, though. No lightning bolts struck him that day.

Jody says she fell in love with Rob at first sight. My mother said the same thing about my father. My father said that about Stanley. Two decades earlier, I had felt something strong for Jay, but I'd squandered my opportunity out of fear of abandonment.

I had a mother and a daughter who both believed themselves worthy of the best, the fetching blue-eyed soldier, the bright, polite college boy. Instead, I chose safety in Bill, and with the others after him, as my father had done with my mother. I gave up Jay to avoid heartbreak. Dad gave up Stanley to avoid jail, or worse. Dad and I had both led secret double lives with other lovers.

Days went by. I couldn't get Luis out of my mind. When he poured the concrete patio, I was there. I watched him drag the wide concrete hose to one side of the wooden forms and then to the other, barking out orders in Spanish to his workers. He leaned over the quick-drying mixture and troweled it smooth. Like an artist, I thought. Like Dad's baseball-playing ballet dancers.

After three weeks of just happening to be at Jody and Rob's house while Luis was there working, and fantasizing about him the remainder of the time, shame got the better of me. I berated myself for my promiscuous past and my selfishness. No way would I be making an announcement about leaving yet another husband, a steady and kind college professor, no less, and running off with a cute contractor who'd bewitched me. Not to mention that Luis paid no attention to me whatsoever.

On Luis's final day on the job, when he sprayed acid over the concrete to expose a top layer of pebbles, I left Jody's house determined that my fantasy remain just that. On my drive down to an urban design conference at Stanford University a few days later, though, the stirring struck me again. I'd been excited about the conference because of its theme of how teenagers experience their neighborhoods and cities, a theme I would further explore in my master's thesis two years later. The farther south I drove and the farther away from Luis, though, the more I felt the same physical sensation of the walls in my nightmares closing in on me. At that moment I heard a voice in my head that said, *I don't want to die without experiencing this at least once.* I began sobbing like a teenage girl and had trouble seeing the road ahead of me through my tears.

A few miles before the Golden Gate Bridge, my foot seemed to lift off the accelerator on its own. I pulled my car over to the gravel shoulder of the freeway, kicking off a cloud of dust. Cars zoomed past at high speed a few feet from me. I froze, unable to will myself forward to the conference and a life focused on my new profession, nor back to the unknown.

One thing I knew for sure, though, was that whether or not Luis was available and a suitable partner for me, I could not go on living the way I'd been living. Dad had chosen security over true love. No matter what, I told myself, I would no longer allow my fate to be the same. I could no longer pretend to myself or to anyone else that my marriage was built on true love.

My body trembled with the knowledge of what I believed I must do. I drove on the shoulder to a freeway exit and pulled into a gas station. After dropping a few quarters into a pay phone and hearing two or three rings, Luis picked up. My heart raced.

"Uh, hi, this is Laura, Jody's mom," I said. "Would you like to take a walk on the beach with me sometime?" The last sentence came out as one long word.

Luis said yes. We made plans to drive out to the coast early the following week. I continued on to the conference, my body no longer trembling.

By the time I received my master's degree in landscape architecture, I was three times divorced and living with Luis. During our early years, my anxiety and baseless suspicions about his almost certain infidelity were high, as usual. My nighttime shrieks rattled both of us. Luis hung in there with me. I hung in there with me. I stopped sniffing for perfume scents on his neck and snooping around in his wallet and shirt pockets for women's phone numbers. About five years after we moved in together, my night terrors came to an end.

In 2009, seventeen years after my heart quickened upon opening Jody's front door to him, Luis and I were married under the gilded copper dome in San Francisco's City Hall, the same spot where one year earlier the first same-sex marriages in California took place. It had taken me a long time to get there, too.

"You weren't ripe before," Luis told me one day.

"Huh?"

"Just like an avocado."

"What are you talking about?"

"Avocadoes don't ripen on the tree," he said.

"Uh . . ." I stuttered.

"They only ripen after they've fallen to the ground."

CHAPTER 42: MOM SPEAKS

Mom was at her usual perch at the kitchen sink. Her gloved hands attacked a pile of dirty dishes. I sat at the kitchen table, the large kitchen island between us, our typical safe spots for delicate conversations. Dad was outside smoking. She and I hadn't officially acknowledged to each other that she knew I knew Dad was gay. And that I knew she knew that.

"Mom," I asked. "Why did you stay with Dad after you found out he was gay?"

She jerked her head toward me, her jaw clenched. She turned off the running water but kept her rubber gloves on, the steam from the hot soapy water rising and encircling her.

I remembered that look. She had that same one when I asked her the definition of *fuck* decades ago. But I was now forty. This time she wouldn't be sending me off to the bathroom to wash my mouth out with soap.

I remained silent. She rested her gloved hands on the edge of the sink. Minutes went by before she spoke.

"I wanted you kids to have a father," she said. "*I* never did."

Her eyes were wide, and her high voice was pinched. She sounded as if she were defending herself in court.

Did she think I was accusing her of being foolish? I wondered. Did I sound as if I, her thrice-divorced daughter, considered myself the wiser one in marriage? I didn't feel that way at all. I felt only compassion for her. She had endured her entire adulthood as the straight wife of a gay man. She deserved better. I grimaced at the thought of her sacrificing herself so that my siblings and I would have a father in the house.

She kept her hands resting on the sink but turned her body toward me.

"You know, Laurie, I know I don't talk about it much, but it was hard growing up without a father."

Her tone was strong and louder than her normal soft, sweet voice, as if she were ready to set the record straight. I stood up and leaned over the dividing counter. I was ready for this. I'd been ready for a long time. In that moment, I felt so much love for her, this fatherless child who married a man who in a way also abandoned her.

"I know, Mom. Do you remember him at all?"

"Well, I remember sitting on his lap. . . ." she said, her voice trailing off.

This was new information. I held my breath. Mom looked off into the distance through the windows.

"He had brown shiny shoes," she said.

She turned back toward me.

"It's the only memory I have of him."

"Oh, Mom," I said.

"He never even said good-bye."

I couldn't imagine that. I couldn't imagine not having a father, my father. I couldn't imagine Dad leaving without even saying good-bye.

Mom's father, the grandfather I never knew, lost everything in the stock market in 1927, two years before the Wall Street crash of 1929.

"We lost our gorgeous home in Minneapolis where I was born, the one Nana loved so much," she said.

My mother was three years old at the time, the youngest of three children. The family moved to a nearby apartment for a few months before Nana and their three children boarded a train to California.

"We couldn't afford a place of our own," Mom said. "Times were hard, honey. It was right before the Depression."

They moved in with my great-aunt and -uncle in the former Vallemar train station in Rockaway Beach (now part of Pacifica), just south of San Francisco.

"I loved all the animals there," she said. "But things got harder as I grew up."

In photos taken of my mother at the time, she's cuddling kittens, feeding goats, and walking dogs.

"Nana never spoke of him, honey," she said. "It was as if he never existed."

There are no photos of her with her father. I couldn't imagine what it must feel like to be an adult without ever having seen a photo of yourself with your father. I too might have felt he never existed. No wonder my mother considered it of paramount importance that her own children grow up with a father.

With the help of an unexpected inheritance from a bachelor uncle, Nana was able to build a house on the Peninsula for herself and the three children, the same house where my mother lived when she met the handsome soldier at the USO dance. Mom loved her beautiful new high school, Sequoia High, but grew weary of hearing her girlfriends speak of their fathers.

"They'd say, 'Oh, my *father* said such and such,' or 'My *father* and I did this.' I wondered what it would be like to be one of them, to have a father." She sounded bitter and sad at the same time.

Mom was giving me hard evidence of the importance of fathers to her. I understood. Still, I didn't like the idea of her staying in an unhappy marriage so that I could have a father in the home. Knowing Dad, he certainly would have remained a part of my life, though not a part of hers.

Maybe that was the key, or at least part of it. I surmise that Dad may have been a father-like figure for her, too. He was twenty-four when they met. She was a seventeen-year-old, fatherless high school senior. Dad was in charge of the money throughout their marriage. He gave her shopping money when she asked. He bought her clothes. He picked out our houses and cars. Then again, many couples who married in the 1940s had similar arrangements.

"Seeing your father for the first time . . . oh, honey," Mom said. "He had the most beautiful blue eyes."

Mom's eyes lit up as if we weren't talking about her *gay* husband. But I never tired of hearing the fable repeated over and over.

"He looked like a movie star," she said. I knew that.

Though she was close to her uncle, there had been no other father figures in her life up until then. Born Irene Alice, she was tall and thin and loved to dance, much like Irene Castle, the famous ballroom dancer of the early 1900s after whom she was named.

"I didn't have much experience before I met your father, honey," she said. "Well, except for Harry Davis."

The two of them dated casually in the first half of her senior year. One day he invited her to travel with him to Los Angeles to meet his mother.

"I was excited to travel, to see Los Angeles," Mom said. "Nana didn't like the idea at all. But she let me go anyway."

Harry proposed to her on the trip.

"I was so surprised, honey," she said. "I told him I wasn't ready to get married. I just wanted to see Los Angeles."

Of course, he wanted to marry her. That was obviously the point of the trip, I thought. He brought her to Los Angeles to meet *his mother*. How could she not have known? When she met Dad, though, she knew she wanted to spend the rest of her life with him.

"Your father wrote me such *beautiful* letters during the war," Mom said.

I couldn't help but wonder if she was trying to build the case that Dad loved her *then,* or maybe that he wasn't gay *then*. I was getting impatient. I didn't want Dad to walk in on us just yet.

"Mom, did you ever tell any of your friends when you found out?"

"Oh, no, honey, I would have *never* done that," she said.

This was incredulous to me. I did a quick calculation in my head. The year was now 1992. She'd found out in 1957 and had now been carrying this secret for thirty-five years.

"Why not, Mom?"

"Oh, I would have been too embarrassed," she said.

She carried my father's shame while putting her effort into preserving the family system as it was. Then again, I was doing the same thing. For years I told few about my father's secret. My focus, though unconscious at the time, was on healing the unhealable bond between my parents, not on shining the light on the central issue, that a mixed-orientation marriage would forever remain that way.

"Didn't you ever want to talk to *anyone* about it, Mom?"

I should have been asking that same question of myself.

"Well," she said. "I did speak once with Father O'Donnell about it."

Fully aware of the Catholic Church's view of homosexuality by then, my eyes widened.

"He said your father was just going through a phase."

She spoke calmly and matter-of-factly, as if she had hoped the priest's words might have been true.

"A phase?" I said.

"Father told me to focus hard on the marriage and it would pass."

I tried not to sound angry, though I recalled my mother's magnificent new hairstyles every Friday on Birch Avenue around the time she discovered Dad's secret.

Though it must have been a relief for her to hear the priest's reassuring words, I hoped she now understood that this wasn't possible. I wouldn't be joining her in her fantasyland. It had been more than three decades, after all, and Dad was still gay. She said nothing more about the priest's advice, though.

"Would you do it again, Mom? Would you marry Dad if you knew?"

She'd swooned over my father my entire life. Those blue eyes. Those white teeth. His beautiful love letters. The way he took care of us kids. The way he wasn't like the other husbands. I'd fully prepared myself for her to answer *yes*.

"Oh, *no*, honey," she said.

She pronounced the "no" as if there were a dozen *o*'s in it. Her voice was clear and strong.

Wow. I thought she would have said something truer to character, that she'd have loved and married Dad no matter what. But she didn't say that. I felt proud of her. She wasn't as naïve or as self-sacrificing as I'd assumed she was, at least not on this topic.

LAST PHOTO OF MOM, AGE EIGHTY-ONE, 2005

MURAL IN MOM'S FINAL BEDROOM

THE WEDDING DAY PHOTO ON MOM'S NIGHTSTAND
THE DAY SHE DIED

CHAPTER 43: CANCER STRIKES AGAIN

While my mother toured France in 1999 and took photos of stone arches, window boxes filled with red geraniums, and small children in their crisp school uniforms, Dad, now in his early eighties, was touring new houses near our home in Sonoma County after a visit with Luis and me. He gushed about the reasonable prices.

"Now all I have to do is convince your mother," he said.

I sensed a coming tug-of-war and my spot once again in the middle. Mom called me soon after she returned from her travels and pleaded with me not to encourage Dad. But I knew that at their ages, they'd likely benefit from close proximity to at least one of their children.

"I know your father wants to move up there, honey," Mom said. "But I love our home. I love San Carlos."

"I know you do, Mom," I said.

San Carlos had been her home for sixty-two years, since 1938. She currently held the title of the longest-standing member of the choir in the history of St. Charles Church. All of her close friends, who numbered in the dozens if not hundreds, still lived there. Dad's friends from work lived in San

Francisco. He felt marooned in the hills of San Carlos. I proposed a compromise.

"Why don't you just move into one of those new senior apartments downtown, Mom? Dad might have an easier time there and you'd still be in San Carlos. It's flat there. He could walk without tiring. He could hang out in the park, people-watch."

"Oh, no, honey," she said. "I'm too young for *those places*." She was seventy-two.

I weighed the pros and cons. If they lived a ten-minute drive away instead of a two-hour one, Luis and I could quickly be there when they needed assistance. And I was happily settled in my profession. Over the prior decade, I'd worked with local city planning departments on the design of their towns' common spaces and was often successful in building bridges between opposing community factions. The timing was good for me to start tending to my parents' old-age needs. But sympathizing equally with the parent who wanted to move closer to one of his children and the one who wanted to stay in her beloved home and hometown, I decided not to lobby for either position.

Mom put up a good fight, I could tell, because no decision was forthcoming for months. Then, just as she did before with all of the family moves, she yielded. The dour mood Dad had been nursing for years lifted. He was closer to family—me—now. He again had a blank canvas in a new house. From the beginning of my parents' marriage, he'd made most of the interior decorating and landscaping decisions. He planned to do the same here.

Soon after they moved in, he mounted shoji screens on the windows and decorated the living room with a brass Japanese lantern, a stacked Chinese wedding basket, antique blue-and-white ceramic charger service plates, and a tansu-style chest he bought from Gump's of San Francisco. He replaced the suburban front lawn the builders installed with drought tolerant shrubs and groundcover and, of course, gravel and driftwood. Once again, he was the only one on the block doing this.

Mom, accustomed to acquiescing to Dad on everything related to their homes, now numbering seven, let him have his way with most of it here, too. But this time she'd claim a space of her own. She assigned herself the master bedroom and bathroom. Maybe she considered it her consolation prize for allowing such a painful move on her part.

For the first time in their marriage, my mother made the decisions about paint colors, window coverings, and wall decorations, there in her separate bedroom. She leafed through catalogs and spent her afternoons at the local mall viewing flowery bedspreads and chintz throw pillows and shams. There would be no dark-colored, silk bedspreads, uncomfortable contemporary chairs, or Asian antiques in her realm.

She decorated the tops of her dressers with framed photographs of her four children, three granddaughters, and two great-granddaughters. One large photo of her wedding day stood sentry above all the others. In it, she wore a large round hat and a wilted gardenia corsage. Dad stood handsome and erect in his formal military uniform.

Neither of my parents got the marriage they would have wanted for themselves. Nevertheless, here in this new house, with separate bedrooms and separate areas of their own in which to express themselves, they settled into what appeared to be a living arrangement acceptable to both of them. It was a small victory, and I as their middle-aged daughter enjoyed the view.

Despite Dad's initial excitement about the move, once his decorating duties were complete, his gloomy mood returned. Everything about his life, though newly ornamented, was, after all, still the same. By contrast, Mom embraced her new home and town despite her initial reluctance to move there. She attended local Mass on Sundays with a majority of Spanish-speaking parishioners and sang in the choir. She volunteered to take photos of newborns at a nearby Kaiser Hospital. Children and photography remained two of her most cherished interests.

She gave tours of her new bedroom to visiting family and friends, pointing out the colorful mural of an open garden gate she hired a local artist to paint. Even though there were no people in the mural, it reminded me of an old photo of my mother that Dad took in Carmel during one of his rare wartime furloughs. In the photo, Mom is leaning on a wooden gate smiling a sweet, shy smile and wearing a short-sleeved, polka-dotted summer dress. Her wavy red hair is blowing in the breeze. Dad loved this photo, naming it "the girl at the gate." Now here she was, the older woman at the gate.

After a few years of settling into a new home and a new town, Mom approached me with a request.

"I would like to have a talk with you, honey," Mom said. "By ourselves. I want to set some things straight."

Wow.

There was a seriousness in her voice, an urgency. She was now eighty-one; I was fifty-four. I'd been ready to talk for decades and had only received a few snippets from her about her life with Dad. I did not think to ask why now. It was nearing Mother's Day. I suggested we go out for brunch in Healdsburg. As a child, she had spent summers with her grandparents there while Nana worked in San Francisco. The river town held fond memories for her.

"Oh, I would love that, honey," Mom said.

I was jumpy when I picked her up that Sunday morning. She looked pretty in her soft yellow sweater with the silver-and-turquoise brooch, something I had given her one long-ago Christmas or birthday. I knew she'd intentionally worn it for me. Whichever child visited her would find their particular gift displayed on her sweater or ear lobes. Her pretty, now-platinum hair resembled a soft halo around her face.

We drove to a small French café. As soon as the server placed our croissants, tiny bowls of sliced strawberries, and mugs of hot coffee and milk on the table, my anxiety got the best of me.

"What was it like, Mom, when you first found out Dad was gay?"

By the scowl on her face, I knew I'd seriously erred in my timing. Maybe I had misread her message. Maybe she didn't want to talk about her marriage after all. Or maybe she didn't want to talk about it over croissants and berries on Mother's Day inside a charming café.

"Oh, honey, let's not spoil Mother's Day," she said. "We'll talk about that another time." She held up her coffee cup for a refill.

How I wish we could have had that conversation. The following week I took an afternoon off work to take her to a doctor's appointment. She told me it was important. Her physician, unbeknownst to me, had performed a biopsy on her the prior week.

"You have a rare form of bladder cancer, Irene," he said.

I gasped. The doctor collapsed into his chair.

"And there's no cure. I'm so sorry."

I was having a hard time breathing. This did not fit my mental picture of when my parents would die. Mom was six years younger than Dad. He'd had multiple internal surgeries, hepatitis, hospitalizations for pneumonia, and long bouts of depression. He'd been smoking cigarettes for more than sixty years. *How could he possibly outlive my mother?* After all, she was optimistic, energetic, a world traveler, a non-smoker, a non-drinker, someone whose mother lived to be 97 and grandmother to 101, and someone who woke up each day forgetting any bad news from the day before.

The doctor's eyes glistened with tears. Mom sat up straight and clear-eyed. My throat stung.

"How long, uh, how long does she have, Doctor?"

"No more than six months," he said.

Tears stung my eyes, but Mom was quiet and stoic, undoubtedly making checklists in her mind. I kept firing questions at the sweet doctor.

"How, uh, where did my mother get this?"

He recovered enough to answer.

"Laurie, it's a rare cancer," he said.

He used my nickname. Mom must have talked to him about me.

"There has only been one study. . . ."

The study showed a link between Mom's type of cancer and a chemical used in the photo developing process in the 1940s, the same era in which she took and developed photos of German prisoners-of-war at Fort Ord. Dad hadn't wanted her to move down there. He implored her to continue living in Nana's house in San Carlos until his discharge. This was one time he hadn't prevailed.

"Okay, let's get going, honey," Mom said.

She thanked and hugged the doctor, whose shaken appearance made him look as if *he* were the one losing a family member.

Mom charged out the door ahead of me. She had things to do. I banged my knee on the corner of a metal cabinet on the way out.

CHAPTER 44: THAT JACKET

"You know, Laurie," Mom said. "Your father made that jacket." I could tell by the sense of urgency in her voice that she had secreted this information inside herself for a long time. She did not have to tell me which jacket she was talking about. I knew. She had worn the odd-looking (to me) swing coat throughout my childhood.

Mom and I never had *that* talk, the one where she would "set things straight" about Dad. However, she seemed determined to get this particular news out before she died. Bedridden now, she made her announcement with clarity and without emotion. She was wearing her pink satin bed jacket with the small, baby-blue floral designs and Peter Pan collar that Dad had bought for her for their honeymoon sixty-four years earlier. I chuckled to myself about my mother's delivery, as blunt and direct as I'd always been with her. Her eyes darted toward her closet.

"My initials are inside," she said.

"Huh?"

"*Your father*, he embroidered my initials inside. . . ."

Her eyelids drooped. She said what she wanted to say. I wondered why this deathbed admission seemed to hold such importance for her. I slipped into her closet and peeked at the lining of the jacket. There they were, Irene Alice Hall's initials, *IAH*.

I wondered why I hadn't noticed them before. Had she purposely hidden them from us? If we had known as children, did she think we'd have assumed our father was gay? Or did Mom just want me to know of her appreciation for her husband and the stylish coat he made for her more than five decades ago? I'll never know for sure.

Hospice workers streamed in and out with their pain-relieving patches and reluctance to make any predictions. After I pleaded with one of the workers, he pulled me aside. Based on his experience, he said, Mom wouldn't last for more than a few days. I was relieved to get the facts, given all the silence and pretense surrounding Susan's illness and impending death. I took a leave of absence from work and moved into Mom's pretty bedroom, napping around-the-clock on a little rattan couch in full view of my mother and her pretty mural.

Mom let loose a few more facts during a video interview of her and Dad that Tim recorded a few days before she died. The interview began as the two of them had begun, at the USO dance in 1942.

"Mom, tell us again about the time you and Dad first met," Tim said.

Despite her overall weakness and the fact that she had relayed this story to us dozens of times before, her eyes lit up. I was now in my mid-fifties and had known for more than three decades that Dad was gay. Still, the hair on my arms stood up. I could never get enough of their origin story.

"I fell for your father like a ton of bricks," Mom said. "Just like that. He was the handsomest man I'd even seen. He had big blue eyes and white teeth. . . ."

Dad blushed and rolled his eyes before jumping in with his exaggerated version of the fairytale.

"There were about two hundred soldiers, seven girls, and this tiny little orchestra," he said. "I told my buddy, 'Let's get outta here.'"

He glanced over at Mom, his eyes twinkling.

"The cook, who was dancing with *your mother*, yelled out to me, 'Hey, Hall, where ya goin'?' Uh, I forget his name. . . ."

"Pete," Mom said. I found it sweet that she recalled his name. Between the two of them, they completed the story.

"So I yelled back at Pete, 'We're getting outta here. There's no one to dance with.'"

After a dramatic pause, Dad kept going.

"And then I heard. . . ." His voice cracked.

"And then I heard the sweetest voice say, 'I'll dance with you.' And, Tim and Laurie, that's how it all began."

I expected the next sentence to contain the words, "Titian blond," and I would be right.

"She had the most gorgeous hair I had ever seen," he said. "It was sparkling and beautiful—Titian blond, *not red*—and shiny and gorgeous. That was the first thing I noticed."

He spoke this as if we had never heard it before. Mom smiled at him and placed her hand on his arm. She glowed. In that moment, she did not look sick at all. She looked like someone in love for the first time.

"The second thing I noticed was how much I enjoyed talking with her. She was very different from the girls I had known."

Mom jumped in before I could ask him what he meant by *different*.

"I knew I wanted *your father*," she said. "He stood out like a star to me."

Here were my parents, sixty-four years after they first met, recreating that romantic evening in 1942—the blue eyes, the Titian blond hair, the sweet voice, the pretty blue eyes and white teeth—as if nothing had occurred to tarnish that memory. As if Dad weren't gay at all.

Tim then asked them to describe their honeymoon, a story we'd also heard many times. Mom loved the courtyards and Spanish architecture of the Mar Monte Hotel on the Santa Barbara coast. They strolled through the darkened downtown. Due to a wartime blackout, most stores were closed.

"I wanted to get back to the hotel," Mom said. "But your father wanted to go to a movie!" Given what she would later discover in Dad's locked box, she still sounded surprised by his reluctance to consummate their marriage that first night.

Dad's cheeks flushed.

"I didn't *want* to see a movie," she said. "I had a pretty, white satin nightgown I wanted to put on."

Dad looked down at his hands and fiddled with them.

"Was it your first time with a man?" Tim said.

"Oh, no, Tim, I had lots of boyfriends in high school," she said.

"No, I mean . . . well, you know," Tim said.

Mom eyes widened as if this were the most insulting question Tim could have asked her.

"Oh, my goodness, yes!" Mom said. "Your father was the first."

Tim didn't ask Dad that question, nor did Dad offer anything further.

"I finally talked him into going back to the hotel," Mom said.

Dad remained silent. Mom then described the searing heat in Dad's hometown of Fellows, where they traveled the next day, and how soon their honeymoon was over.

"Your dad then left for Alaska," she said. "We didn't know when or if we'd ever see each other again."

Mom closed her eyes and said she was tired. I helped her walk back to her bedroom

Four days before she died, when she no longer could get out of bed, I told her that Jody and her family were on their way from Virginia to see her. They'd be arriving the following day.

Mom smiled but then her look turned serious. I knew this look well. She was making plans again.

"Look at this, Laurie," she said.

She pointed to a few drops of blood on her sheets, the pretty set she'd picked out for herself when she and Dad moved into the new house near us.

"Go to Macy's right now. Pick up some new sheets for me, would you?"

My incredulity must have shown on my face.

"*Please*, Laurie."

"Are you sure, Mom?" I said.

At most, she was a few days from death. I didn't want to waste any of our final moments together shopping.

"I don't want the girls to be frightened," she said, *the girls* referring to her two great-granddaughters, then ages thirteen and nine. Yes, I thought, still and always her focus would be on the children. I couldn't imagine how we'd change the bed with Mom in it, though.

"They need to be just like these, honey," she said.

She pointed to the detailed edges of the flat sheet. I wasn't paying much attention. All I could think of was that this would be the last time she'd see Jody, the last time she would see her great-granddaughters, and soon the last time I'd see her. I really didn't want to take the time to go shopping. Nevertheless, she was insistent.

"See, Laurie, the edges are scalloped."

She pointed to the embroidered, half-moon shaped edge.

"And they are *off-white*. Not white. Remember that. Find the exact same ones."

Off I traipsed to Macy's where I got a little impatient with the perplexed salesclerk.

No, they have to be off-white! And the scalloped edges have to have little holes in them!

When she rang up the sale, I apologized to her.

I did well enough with the selection, it seemed. Mom didn't complain. The home nurse and I were somehow able to get the new sheets on Mom's bed before Jody and family arrived. When they did, all three girls—Jody, Amanda, and Cassie—hustled directly to Mam's bedside. Mom perked up as each gave her a hug.

"Look at all that beautiful hair," Mom said.

So typical of her, even now, to hand out a compliment to her visitors.

The next day, the day before she died, we celebrated Cassie's tenth birthday. Mom loved celebrating family birthdays. She loved baking birthday cakes, and she loved eating them. I brought the store-bought cake into her bedroom so she could see it. By then she'd been unresponsive for perhaps four or five hours.

"Mom, here's Cassie's birthday cake."

I spoke in the sweetest voice I think I'd ever used with her. This would be the last family birthday Mom would ever celebrate. The hospice workers told me that even when the dying cannot move or see anymore, they could still hear, almost to the end.

Mom heard me, and to all of our surprise and with great effort on her part, she shot straight up in bed.

"Okay, I'll get up."

But her eyes remained closed.

"Mom, it's okay," I said, speaking as I would to a young child. "You don't need to get up."

"Oh, good," she said. She fell back down onto her pillow.

She'd always made so much effort for her family, to ensure that her children were okay, that no one was frightened by blood or bad news, that everyone's birthday was properly celebrated and photographed, that we'd never hear her utter a bad word about our father, and that her children were loved and protected by *two* parents the way children should be. It seemed she'd be doing this until her final breath.

THE ONLY PHOTO OF MY MOTHER'S
SPECIAL JACKET

Later that afternoon, Mom called out for me. I'd fallen asleep on the rattan couch near her. I jumped up, concerned about her pain level.

"I'm here, Mom," I said.

"Take the diamonds, Laurie," she said.

Just like that. *Take the diamonds.* This must be her final business, I thought. I brought over the tooled Italian leather jewelry box to her bedside, the one Dad bought for her in the early years of their marriage. Mom handed me the diamond and emerald eternity ring, her prized possession from her beloved husband of sixty-four years.

CHAPTER 45: THEIR FINAL SCENE

From my earliest memory, I feared my father would leave us. Whether that stemmed from the fact that my father was gay and led a life apart from my mother, or that my mother had grown up without a father, I spent much of my life hopeful for any sign of a strong bond between my parents. When I glimpsed it, I felt safe no matter my age. These moments were few and fleeting. But on my mother's final night of life, both she and my father unknowingly gifted me with my lifelong dream.

With the exception of my father, we had all said our final good-byes by late afternoon the previous day. I'd asked Mom if she wanted to tell me anything else, anything at all. I hoped to hear more of her side of things, something that might help me understand her or myself a little better. She shook her head. I let it go. It was how she wanted it to be.

"But please take care of your dad, honey," she said. "He is much worse off than you think."

Her concern for Dad in her final hours shouldn't have surprised me. I nodded. She gave me a serious look.

"Honey, *promise* me you will look after your dad," she said.

"Of course, I will, Mom. I promise."

I didn't know what she was talking about. Although Dad was now eighty-eight, he seemed to be doing pretty well. He'd been out in the kitchen most of the past week holding court with Mom's visitors while she lay dying in bed. At times, I felt annoyed by how jovial he sounded.

On what would be my mother's final evening, I could tell she wouldn't last much longer. She hadn't spoken for more than twenty-four hours. I planted myself at her bedside. The night sky outside was dark, and the lights in her room were low. As far as I knew, my father hadn't been in her room even once that day. I wondered if my parents might end up this way, apart at the very end. I willed myself not to intervene. It was *their* marriage, I told myself, their *lives*. It was time for me to let go of the fable.

I needn't have worried.

Dad, in his dramatic fashion, must have had it planned out the whole time. As I filled my glass with water in the kitchen, I watched as my father lumbered down the dim hallway to Mom's room, bent over his cane. Maybe he'd been waiting for me to leave her room. I hadn't considered that. I tiptoed behind him. I didn't want to interrupt anything, but I longed to see my parents together for what I knew would be their last time.

Dad walked straight to Mom's pink, tufted vanity stool next to her bed. I told myself to leave then, that they deserved privacy with their final good-byes. But I couldn't tear myself away from the doorway. Dad leaned in close to her and placed his tremoring hand on top of one of hers. He called her by the nickname she went by more than six decades earlier, her name the night they met.

"*Rus-ty*," he said.

His voice was singsong sweet, sounding as if he were speaking to a child. I wonder if that was how he felt. Maybe he'd always felt that way about her.

Mom didn't open her eyes or even stir.

"I am so glad you said yes," Dad said.

It was a story I'd heard so many times in my life, about his telegram from Seattle in 1942 with the words, *Marry me, dearest.*

"I'd do it all over again," Mom said.

Even from the doorway, I could hear my mother's statement loud and clear.

Dad jerked his head up. He may not have expected her to say anything. I certainly didn't expect *this* response. After all, she had recently told me she *wouldn't* do it again if she had known he was gay.

But he promised to spend the rest of his life with her, and he had kept his promise. Was this Mom's way of acknowledging that? Or was it as simple as her love for him, even now?

Her words to Dad were her last. Well, nearly. Either my father with his diminished hearing couldn't understand her, or maybe he didn't believe what he'd heard.

"*What* did you say, Irene?" he said.

He leaned in closer to her. This time she gave it all she had.

"I'd do it all over again."

She was loud and almost insistent in tone. She wanted him to hear her.

Those were the last words I heard my mother speak, that she'd do it all over again. Dad's loud sobs jolted me. I hurried down the hallway to Tim and his family in the kitchen. Tears streamed down my face.

"She said she'd do it all over again!"

The startled looks on their faces startled me in return. Here I was, sleep-deprived, already grieving for my mother and now in middle age acting like an insecure child. No one said a word. Nevertheless, I felt elated knowing that my mother did not regret her life. On the other hand, maybe she just wanted Dad to believe that, to know he hadn't hurt her. Either way, I witnessed this tender love scene between my parents in my mother's final hours.

As the early morning light streamed through Mom's sheer curtains the following morning, I awoke with a start and rushed to her bedside. Her eyes were closed, but I could still hear her breathing. Moments later, a drop of blood dripped from her mouth just as had happened in Susan's final moments of life.

"Oh, Mom, oh, Mom," I kept repeating.

In all the time I had spent by her side as she lay dying, I had not prepared words for this eventuality. But then they came to me.

"Have fun with Susan, Mom," I said.

That image even made me happy. Then, finally, "I love you, Mom."

With that, she opened her eyes and looked straight at me, or rather through me, it seemed. She mouthed the words *I love you*, then closed her eyes and took her final breath. I couldn't move. After not being able to talk with her about so many things, here we were alone, in her final moment, expressing our love for one another.

My mother was one month shy of her eighty-second birthday when she died in her pretty, youthful room with representations of everything and everyone she loved in her life displayed around her. The photo nearest to her in her final moment was the one of her standing next to Dad on their wedding day, her handsome husband with the blue eyes and white teeth.

Tim rushed in, I think somehow knowing. I went to Dad's bedroom and jostled his shoulder.

"Dad," I said. "Mom's gone."

He rose slowly out of bed without looking at me or saying a word. He slipped on his robe, grabbed his cane, and padded to her room as if I wasn't even there. I followed him.

"Oh, Irene," he said, his arms outstretched at the foot of her bed.

He spoke in such a tender, fatherly voice. Tim and I left the room, left our parents alone at the end. This time I wouldn't eavesdrop.

Tim and I sat in silence in the kitchen. Dad joined us not too long afterward. He had work to do. In his typical book-keeper's way, he had already made a list of the things to do when Mom died.

We planned her memorial service at the local Catholic church where she had sung in the choir for the past five years. Tim planned to speak and welcome mourners when they arrived. The volunteer coordinator from Kaiser Hospital, where Mom had taken photos of babies as a volunteer, asked to speak. The choir director had already picked out my mother's favorite hymns.

I focused on Dad's well-being, though he did not seem to need my support. He selected the venue and menu for the reception. He did not say anything about Mom's memorial service, though, or about any tribute he may have planned.

On the day of the service, he sat on the aisle side of the front row pew. Two attendants wheeled Mom's casket up the aisle. It looked like a fancy pink-and-white birthday cake, the casket she'd requested before she died. I peeked over at Dad to see if he would roll his eyes over the expensive, frilly casket that was *just going into the ground, Irene*. But he didn't.

The priest said some words, which I don't remember, and then invited the others to speak. I couldn't fight the lump in my throat and remained silent. As the priest moved to close the service, Dad stood up. I chuckled a little knowing how much he enjoyed the sense of drama his last-minute moves evoked.

Hunched over, Dad fumbled with his cane and nearly dropped it. Gentle murmurs erupted from the small crowd, ones that reminded me of the murmurs at Susan's burial when Dad stood up and pleaded for her casket to be opened one last time. When Dad reached the first step and wobbled, Tim jumped up and escorted him to the lectern. I wondered what he was going to say. *What could he possibly say about the woman he married to be safe and with whom to have children?*

He told a story. I prepared myself for hearing Titian blond one more time. However, this time the story wasn't about romance or love. Or maybe it was.

"Whenever I spoke with someone who knew Irene," he said, "they would tell me, 'Oh, she is *so* sweet.' In fact, many of you today told me that."

He spoke slowly, with plenty of dramatic pauses but with obvious purpose as well. I could tell he had rehearsed it and was enjoying the mourners' rapt attention.

"Well, I want to tell you something," he said.

His eyes twinkled. A slight grin came over his face.

"She has said the same thing about all of you."

That was the point he wanted to make. I didn't see him shed a tear that day. He didn't say how much he loved Mom or how much he would miss her. Now I think he spoke to the quality of hers that meant the most to him. She had been kind to him, this gay husband of hers whose infidelity and dishonesty spanned their entire marriage. As for Dad, he kept his promise to her, and in a way to me, too. He remained Mom's husband until death parted them sixty-four years later.

Mom's happiest memory, Pacific Grove, 1945

DAD AND THE BULLWHEEL IN THE OILFIELDS, 1942

DAD AND TIM JOG ON
THE GOLDEN GATE BRIDGE, 1981

CHAPTER 46: A SINGLE MAN

The day after the funeral, I drove up to Santa Rosa to see my father. My mission was clear. However, he'd hear no talk of a housekeeper or a home nurse. He wouldn't discuss a move to a place where someone else would do the cooking, cleaning, and gardening.

"I can take care of everything myself, Laurie," Dad said.

"But *Mom* said—"

He shushed me.

I had to admit that my father looked like a new man, all jaunty and busy, with recipes on the countertop and already a trip alone to the grocery store. He didn't seem to be in mourning at all. It was so at odds with how I was feeling, stunned and blue without my chirpy, loving mother as our family's cornerstone.

Even though Dad's bubbly energy seemed disrespectful to Mom, it was still welcome. He was talkative. He smiled. His depressive mood appeared to have disappeared overnight. He turned away all offers of help, from meals to laundry to shopping to driving. He would drive himself in his 1966 VW beetle wherever he needed to go.

I readied myself for the phone calls I felt sure were forthcoming. However, when I received a call from him a few days later, it wasn't a plea for help. No. Not at all. In fact, he'd met a man, a young one. This could not possibly turn out well, I thought.

As Dad described it, on one of his evening strolls through the neighborhood, he walked past "this really nice man." Greg, probably in his early forties, Dad said, was out at the curb picking up his mail.

"I complimented him on his *gorgeous* azaleas."

I thought about their four-decade age difference.

Greg nodded a thank you, Dad said, and then tucked his bulky mail under one arm and pointed out some of his other plants now in bloom.

From the way Dad told it, the two of them immediately clicked over blooming shrubs. At first, they chatted a few times a week after Greg got home from work, and then only for a few minutes on his driveway. Soon their conversations extended to the weekends, though. One warm summer evening Greg invited my father in for a cold drink. Dad gushed about their growing friendship.

"He is *so* interesting, honey!" he said. "We talk about *everything*!"

Dad's cheeks glowed. I imagined the worst. My widowed father, eighty-eight and a half, was frail and living alone. The newspaper warnings from AARP and public health agencies about elder abuse and swindles hadn't slipped by me. I wondered if this young man might ask my father for money. Or maybe he'd hurt him physically. Or worse. If Greg were gay, he might break Dad's heart.

I called Dad after work the following evening.

"Is Greg gay?" I said.

Dad didn't hesitate.

"Yes. He's gay, honey."

I was about to ask him how he knew, but I didn't. Dad's voice was animated, clear and youthful sounding. He no longer whispered to prevent Mom from hearing. He even seemed to enjoy talking on the phone. I was now the one who ended our calls.

When Dad confirmed the obvious to me, I froze. I hadn't prepared a follow-up. If I had, I might have warned him about their age differences, or advised him to be careful about his bank account. As if he didn't already know he was an old man. As if he were not already watchful over his money.

By the following month, Dad's cheery demeanor was gone. I drove up on a Saturday to take him out to his favorite Chinese restaurant for lunch. When I knocked and got no answer, I let myself in. There he was, hunched over in his kitchen chair, his face ashen. I asked about Greg, but he said he'd rather hear about me. I got busy talking.

My urban design company was now in its ninth year. I knew Dad liked hearing about it. Tim told me he bragged about me in their conversations. I worked long hours and was often out of town on business. I enjoyed bringing communities together, when I was successful, over the design of their towns and parks. At times, the various factions remained firmly stuck in their uncommon visions for the future. I despaired of them as I'd despaired of my parents' unlikely pairing. I had a lifetime of peacemaking aspirations, a profession as a facilitator, and an ability to see things from both sides. But none of these would bring Dad and Greg back together.

Over pork fried rice (Dad's favorite) and eggplant with garlic sauce (mine), Dad opened up to me. One evening when Greg's house lights were on, he said, his knocks at the door went unanswered. This had been going on for more than a week now, though it was the first time he'd mentioned it to me.

"Maybe he's just busy, Dad," I said.

Before the words were out of my mouth, I realized how silly I sounded. Dad exhaled a resigned sigh.

"No, honey," he said. "That's not it."

Oh, Dad.

"It's actually okay, honey," he said. "I understand. What would he want with an old man like me anyway?"

"Dad, I'm so sorry."

I reached across the table and held his hand. He slipped it out of mine and went back to his rice. The year was 2006. By that time, I knew enough about gay culture to understand the romantic challenges elderly gay men face in finding love. Dad wanted to go back to where he'd left off seven decades ago, when he was a young man in love with Stanley. But he was no longer young. I looked over at him, his focus now on willing his trembling hands to transport the rice from his bowl to his mouth without spilling it.

Where were all the lonely, elderly gay men, I wondered. When I got back to my computer, I did some research. A volunteer at the Senior Center of Santa Rosa told me they had no special gatherings for gay men and referred me to the Spectrum LGBT Center in Marin County. A kind staff person there told me that Spectrum had not yet established a section in the North Bay. However, the Unitarian Universalist Congregation in Santa Rosa was "pro-gay." Perhaps my father could find a companion there, she suggested. I called Dad and gave him the address, doubtful he'd feel confident enough to attend a service.

Even though he'd long ago given up on church and religion, to my surprise he drove himself there the following Sunday. He called me that evening. After the services, he said, an elderly gay man came up to him. They arranged to meet for lunch the following week. However, when I spoke with him the evening of his lunch date, he told me the connection hadn't gone anywhere.

"I can't see myself with such an old man."

His tone conveyed no sense of irony. I kept my mouth shut.

Dad never went back to the church. Soon the calls Mom had predicted started coming in.

"Honey, I'm sorry to bother you," Dad said.

I'd just arrived home from work. The breathless, staccato tone of his voice frightened me.

"I made a big pot of clam chowder," he said.

Uh-oh.

"Yeah?"

"While it was simmering, I went out for a cigarette," he said.

"Did it boil over, Dad?"

"Yes, honey. I'm sorry, but it's all over the floor."

I drove right up and let myself in. He wasn't exaggerating. It was not only all over his linoleum floor but all over the stovetop and the lower cabinets as well. He'd tried to clean it up himself but hadn't made much progress. Reaching the floor without falling over was nearly impossible for him now.

Dad sat with his shoulders curved forward in his kitchen chair, gritting his teeth and looking embarrassed. I made him a ham sandwich and got to work with the cleanup while keeping an eye on him. His denim shirt now sagged over his increasingly bony frame, well over his lap. My mother's warning about his fragility rang in my ears. He wasn't eating well and might set the house on fire.

The next time I visited, Dad had a bandage on the top of his head and a large purple bruise on his lower arm. He looked as if someone had beaten him.

"Dad! What happened?"

That morning, he said, he'd fallen down on his sloped driveway while retrieving his newspaper. I decided not to badger him about using his cane or walker. Before Mom died, she told me he was embarrassed to be seen with either of them.

"I couldn't get up, honey," he said. "I bled all over the concrete."

After about ten minutes on the ground, a man driving by noticed him and stopped to help. Knowing my father's dramatic storytelling, I hoped it had only been a minute before help arrived. But I wouldn't let this happen again.

"Dad, it's time to get some help," I said.

This time he didn't fight me. Maybe he could tell by the tone of my voice that this was now nonnegotiable. By then he must have known that the independent, gay bachelor's life wasn't in the cards for him. It took only a few short months after Mom's death for him to realize for himself what she had long known. Day-to-day life at home without her was infeasible.

We researched assisted living facilities online. One nearby catered to gay elders, but construction on it wouldn't begin for another two years. Dad would soon be eighty-nine. In the end, he chose a senior facility one mile from my house. The rustic set of buildings was nestled in a small redwood grove. His small apartment included a deck that overlooked the stately trees and the raised vegetable plots that some of the residents tended. Like most senior facilities, women were in the majority.

At first Dad appeared enthusiastic about the move, just as he'd been with all of the other moves in my lifetime. It was yet another blank slate. It was also a chance for a new life without everyday household chores that were for him now fraught with danger.

Once we moved Dad in, he affixed a glossy blue-and-gold Human Rights Campaign decal to his walker. I took that as a healthy sign. He wore both his and Mom's turquoise-and-abalone shell necklaces now, and his chunky silver bracelet. The abalone rings and the rings made from sterling silver spoons adorned fingers on both of his hands. All of his jewelry now hailed from the 1960s and '70s, from the Summer of Love, from before Susan got sick, from the time he came out to me. He complimented a staff member on her handmade tie-dyed shirt, one with all the colors of the rainbow. The following week she brought him one, and he wore it regularly.

Dad acknowledged the staff by name and thanked them for whatever they did for him that particular day. He told them long stories about where he got his jewelry and about his children's college degrees. He complimented them on the food. I knew because they told me. When I walked down the hallway with him, the staff looked as enamored with him as the nurses in the hospital had been the last time he was there.

He asked Luis to hang up photos, posters, and artwork from past family homes on his walls. When we first moved him in, we'd left them on the floor leaning up against his living room walls. Though Dad's mind seemed fuzzy and distant to me much of the time now, when it came to decorating his walls he proceeded as always with a laser-like focus. He must have had it all planned out ahead of time, I thought.

He pointed to a photo Mom had taken of him in 1975 as he jogged across the Golden Gate Bridge. He was fifty-seven then, lean, tan, and wearing a big smile. He asked us to mount it at the end of his short hallway.

"Oh, no, a little higher," he said to Luis, and then added, "Yes, that's perfect."

He smiled a satisfied smile. Visitors to his apartment would now have an extended view of this happy, strong jogger. This *young single* jogger.

Next, he selected the photo Mom took of him in his Army uniform on their first visit as a couple to his family home in Fellows. There he stood in front of the old, giant bullwheel from his 1920s childhood. This hand-hewn part of an oil rig sat against a backdrop of the flat, dusty oilfields he'd detested as a child but now spoke of in wistful terms.

"Oh, honey, that bullwheel was as beautiful as the wooden sculptures at the San Francisco Museum of Modern Art."

I nodded.

"Can you put it right by the front door?"

"*Here*, Dad?" I said.

"Yes, right there, honey!"

It would be the first thing visitors would see, this strong young soldier in front of the rustic relic from the oilfields of his childhood. My mother had snapped the photo in 1942 while on their honeymoon, but no visitors but his own children would know that.

On the adjacent wall, Luis nailed up an early 1900s panoramic photograph of Fellows. Hundreds of oil derricks dotted the flat, treeless landscape. A large photo my mother took of Dad on a Mendocino bluff overlooking the Pacific, in his blue jeans and white shirt with rolled-up sleeves, came next.

He then selected the one Mom took of him sitting on the redwood deck at the old house in San Carlos. Potted plants surrounded him. Mounted above his head in the photo stood the driftwood and pop-top sculpture he'd made from trash he collected at the beach. An enlarged, framed photograph Mom had taken of his prized red amaryllis went next to his TV. He wanted his framed print of the Gettysburg Address mounted above his computer. I read the words anew. This print had hung on the walls of all of our family homes and now hangs in mine.

Four score and seven years ago, our fathers brought forth on this continent, a new nation, conceived in Liberty, and dedicated to the proposition that all men are created equal.

Dad pointed to two Sierra Club posters, and then to a wooden, antique hat stretcher. Luis mounted the stretcher above the light switch at Dad's front door. On this unusual piece of hand-carved oak, Dad stuck a reddish-brown seedpod from his collection of dried leaves, stalks, and pressed flowers from our old houses. I felt a little smug when he pointed to the beaded, macramé wall hanging I'd made for him when I was in high school. In his new life, I was welcome. Sort of.

The last item he pointed to was a tiny, framed print of Thomas Gainsborough's *Rustic Children*, a late 1700s painting of a Victorian-era mother and her two children.

Soon, we had adorned every wall of Dad's tiny apartment with photos of himself, his garden, his childhood landscapes, crafts I'd made for him, a Gettysburg Address poster, and the small print of classical art I suspected came from Clarence.

"That's it, Laurie," he said.

I stared at what remained on the floor. He had not pointed to a single photo of Mom or any of his children. There were some references to his past, but nothing revealing the fact that he had a family, that he had me.

"Are you *sure* we're all done, Dad?"

He nodded casually, as if he hadn't just jettisoned all evidence of his family from his newly single life, and in the presence of his second-born, no less.

"I have to get down to the dining hall," he said.

He liked arriving to meals early so he could get extra servings of canned fruit cocktail at the salad bar. It had been a long time since that fancy dinner party in the 1950s when he'd created his elegant, grape-studded ice cream confection.

"We'll clean up while you eat, Dad."

I stared at what he left *out* of his decorating scheme. His wife. His children. Over the course of just a few hours, he'd erased us from his life. I plunked myself down in his recliner and stared at his walls. A single, young, vital, gay man with no children or grandchildren was how he projected himself now. A time before Mom. A time before all of us.

I told myself how wonderful it was that he'd finally be leading an authentic life. My heart hurt, though, knowing that the love and kindness of a woman and four children could never be enough to make up for a life lived in hiding. I understood. I was fifty-seven, not a child or even a young adult anymore. I was fatherless while my father was still alive. My earliest memory. My lifelong fear.

Luis and I packed up all evidence of the life Dad lived with Mom and the four of us kids. When I got to the small, framed photo of my parents standing in front of City Hall after their 1942 wartime wedding, I balked. Though feeling silly about my insecurity, I couldn't bring myself to drop it in the discard box. Mom had kept this photo on her nightstand for sixty-four years. Like a nervous, small child, I scurried into my father's bedroom and placed it on his chest of drawers.

I shouldn't have. The items now on his wall were what *he* chose of his life to remember at the end of his life, what *he* wanted visitors to see. Luis and I left for home before Dad returned. When we next spoke, he didn't mention the wedding photo. He didn't remove it, though. He would have known I was the one who put it there.

In the end, Dad's apartment reflected him and him only—his passion for equality in the Gettysburg Address poster, environmentalism in the Sierra Club posters, and his wife's photography, though only of a younger him and his garden, not of her. It was the opposite of what her final bedroom looked like, filled with photos of her husband, children, grandchildren, and great-grandchildren.

Dad sent me an email a few weeks later.

I think your mother would look approvingly at my apartment.

I had to laugh. How could he think Mom would be happy to see no photos of herself in his apartment—except for the one I'd pushed on him—or of us kids? Maybe, I rationalized, he was focused on what she'd think of his interior design, about how talented he still was. After all, despite the unfulfilling nature of the marriage, Mom had always been an appreciative audience of Dad's artistic expressions. Now, at the sunset of his life, it seems he still sought her recognition.

A few days later, Dad told me he heard Mom speaking to him. She called him from another room, he said, just as she'd done throughout their life together. To emphasize the point, he spoke the way she did, in her high, singsong voice.

"Ra-alph."

I had a hard time reconciling Dad's family-free bachelor pad with his sweet words about my mother. The expression on my face during this time must have been one of constant bemusement.

For a few months, Dad appeared content in his new living quarters. The staff cleaned his room and did his laundry. He went on at length about how delicious the food was while I wondered about his taste buds. He outfitted his small deck with the potted succulents, driftwood, and colorful perennials he had us bring over from our other family homes. Moreover, staff members were *so* nice, he said. They must have thought the same of him, I thought. So many of the other residents appeared drugged, distant, and uncommunicative. Even I scurried past them in their wheelchairs on my way to Dad's unit. But soon the familiar refrain started up once again.

Dad grumbled about the low number of men in the facility. Those who did live there weren't friendly, he said. No, he told me, nor did he think any of them were gay. Weekly bingo, card games, and idle chitchat held no interest for him. They never did. He complained how nobody wanted to discuss the potential for the first woman president (Hillary Clinton) or the first black president (Barack Obama). Nor did they want to discuss climate change, the degrading environment, or the same-sex marriage debate that was now going on at the national level.

Dad's best friend at the facility was a friendly, outgoing woman who likely had a crush on him. She invited him out to lunch along with her daughter. She lent him CDs of Israel Kamakawiwoʻole's mellow music. Repeatedly, he showed off his ability to pronounce the singer's multisyllabic name.

Then came the call. He was ready to move again. By then, he was so weak and gaunt I couldn't imagine him ever moving again. Even his paperwork had gotten away from him. Piles of magazines, junk mail, requests for donations, and partially filled-out tax forms covered his dining table. April 15th was fast approaching. Dad resisted any help with organizing, recycling, or filling out his tax return. Being on top of the family paperwork had always been a point of pride for him. I tried to refrain.

It was, however, time for another serious father–daughter talk. I remembered how Dad had moved us into a new house every few years during my childhood. I never heard my mother express any interest in moving. I could hear him now, pleading with her.

"Irene," he'd say. "It would make me *so* happy."

I suspected he'd soon try that one out on me.

He was sitting in his leather recliner when I used my key to get into his room. Even though his neck pillow was in place, and his head and his eyelids hung low, he lifted his head up when he heard me.

"You don't have to get up, Dad," I said. "I just want to talk with you about something."

He rubbed his lips together. They were cracked and dry. I retrieved his water-filled, blue tin cup from the refrigerator and placed it on the side table next to him. I sat down on one of his favorite chairs from the sixties, the contemporary, molded-plywood, Norman Cherner chair. When I was little, I considered them artistic, maybe even stunning, but unbearably uncomfortable. They were still uncomfortable.

"Dad," I said.

I was aware of the weightiness in my voice.

"You've lived in a lot of houses over the years."

He didn't look away from me—a good sign, I thought. His blue eyes still twinkled a little, though the whites of them were dull. He gazed off, just a little beyond me.

When we both caught each other's eyes again, I continued.

"Dad," I said. "I'm wondering something."

"What is it, honey?"

His voice sounded as caring and kind as it had been when I was little.

"Do you think there is something else that could bring you happiness now?" I said.

I took a deep breath.

"I mean, besides a new place to live?"

I was nervous. He'd always put up such a good fight when pushing for a new house. I hoped I wouldn't have to tell him no. However, from the attentive look on his face, I could see that my wording had at least piqued his curiosity. Perhaps the perspective I offered had never occurred to him. He turned to look at the redwoods beyond his deck, or at least in that direction. He didn't say anything. I didn't say anything. Then his head dropped, and he nodded off again. I was used to this by now.

I tiptoed toward the door. It squeaked a little when I opened it. Dad rustled around in his recliner.

"I will think about what you said, Laurie."

I looked at him and smiled but didn't say a word.

"I *will*, honey," he insisted.

"Okay, Dad."

He'd always pushed back hard in these types of conversations before. I walked out feeling somewhat assured of a good outcome.

At two o'clock in the morning, the phone rang. It was Dad. He had been getting confused about whether it was night or day, so I was accustomed to his disoriented calls at odd times. But on this very early call, he sounded surprisingly clear and focused. He asked me to come over as soon as I could. I sweetly noted the time and said I'd come over the following evening after work.

"That will be fine, Laurie," he said.

He sounded different to me, clearer and calmer.

When I arrived the next evening, he was in his recliner as usual. He began speaking before I even took off my jacket and sat down.

"Honey, I now understand what you said about moving—"

I was so surprised that I interrupted him.

"You *do*, Dad?" I heard my voice rise.

"Yes," he said. Not "yeah" or "uh-huh." It was a very clear "yes."

I pulled the chair over close to him and sat down, hardly noticing the chair's hard, unpadded seat this time.

"I wanted to let you know that God has been talking to me," he said.

He spoke deliberately. I felt like I was ten years old again out in the pool yard with my young, articulate father. I was hopeful.

"Yeah?"

"Yes. He told me my life was meant to be the way it was."

I let out a sigh.

"He told me I'm a good person," Dad said.

My eyes filled with tears. I leaned back in the chair, my jacket still on and my purse still slung over my shoulder.

"Yes, you are, Dad," I said.

We looked into each other's eyes for a brief moment before Dad's gaze again extended beyond me. The room was dim now, illuminated only by the outdoor lights shining through the sliding glass door. I got up to switch on a light. But when I looked back at Dad, he was asleep. I switched it back off, tiptoed out, and locked the door behind me.

CHAPTER 47: FINAL QUESTION

I returned the next day after work. I no longer knocked. Dad was folded over in his recliner, asleep. He resembled a curled-up cat. His back, now rounded, no longer held him up. I turned on the light and adjusted his neck pillow so that he could see me.

"Hi, Dad."

"Oh, hi, honey," he said.

"I'd like to ask you another question," I said. "Is that okay?"

"Sure, honey."

He blinked his eyes and licked his dry lips. I grabbed his water cup out of the refrigerator for him.

"Here, Dad, take a sip."

I readied myself for my question. Looking back now, I can think of dozens of questions I wish I'd asked him in his final days: *How did you feel in the immediate hours and days after you told me you were gay? What did you mean when you said I could see things from both sides? Is there anything else you'd like me to know about your life that you haven't already shared? Is there anything you'd like to ask me? What in your life has made you the happiest?*

Instead, I asked him only one question, and it was a negative one.

"Is there one thing you most regret about your life, Dad?"

His eyes opened wide. They appeared so blue, something I hadn't seen in a long time. I loved that color of blue, a cornflower blue. He gazed off into the distance, which was not far in his little room. It seemed far away, though.

"Yes, Laurie," he said. "There is."

He fiddled around with his sweatshirt and adjusted himself in his recliner.

"I regret not trying harder to find a way to live a life with that sweet young man, Stanley Hughes."

He spoke this long sentence clearly and without pause. Afterward, he smiled.

Despite understanding the implications for my own life in that scenario, I smiled, too. I could see from his faraway look that he was back there now with Stanley, back in Pasadena. He was openly and happily in love with a man who loved him back.

Even though Dad's skin tone was pallid and his body bent, I was surprised to see that he no longer looked old to me. He was a young man again. Seeing how he'd decorated his apartment, with no evidence of his children, or of my mother other than in the wedding photo I had foisted upon him, I wasn't surprised by his answer.

"Stanley really was special, wasn't he, Dad?" I said.

He gazed up at me, his beautiful blue eyes now as clear as the sky.

"Yes, honey, he truly was."

His eyes widened with that faraway look again.

"And he felt the same way about me, honey," he said. A long pause followed.

"Yeah?"

"He wrote me a letter. . . ."

"He did?" This was news.

"He wrote it right after we met," Dad said. "I was on my way home to Fellows."

Dad's mental faculties seemed remarkably clear now. I decided to stop filling in his long pauses.

"He wrote, 'After you left, I tried listening to the radio . . .'"

Dad choked up. Yet he looked radiant and happy at the same time. After a few minutes, he regained his composure.

"He wrote, 'I tried playing the piano. I tried reading a book. But I could do nothing . . .'"

Dad glanced down at his hands as if he were holding the letter.

"'But I could do nothing but think of you.'"

He got these last words out quickly before he teared up again. My eyes and smile remained on him.

He dug out an old, wadded up, yellowed handkerchief from the pocket of his faded gray sweatpants and brought it to his face. I recalled the crisp feel of the bright white monogrammed linen handkerchiefs of his when I was little. After using one, he'd fold it in half and then in half again before carefully slipping it back into his pocket.

"I sure wish I had that letter now," Dad said. "It was in that box, the one your mother found that day. It was on her bed when I got home."

I took a deep breath, wondering what was worse for my mother, the sexy photographs or that love letter.

"I went crazy, honey, yelling at your mother . . . I tore up the letter into tiny pieces."

His head dropped as if something heavy had fallen on it.

"I *sure* wish I hadn't done that," he said.

Here was my father, now ninety years old, surrounded by photos of his handsome youthful self, the relics of a time before all of us kids, and photos of the dreary oil town where he lived when he'd first met Stanley. In this moment, gone was the anxiety I'd suffered when he and I spoke privately in the garden of the family house. Gone was my hope that he'd stop telling me how unhappy he was. I no longer felt unfaithful to my mother. Now I wanted more information. There wasn't much time left.

"Dad, do you know what happened to Stanley?"

I fantasized about a possible end-of-life reunion between the two old men, former lovers who'd been caught in the cultural crosshairs of the 1930s.

Dad cleared his throat and sat up a little more, as much as he could anyway. He was clearly enjoying this. So was I.

"You remember Clarence, honey?"

Of course, I did. I nodded.

"Well, he told me that Stanley never recovered from the breakup," Dad said.

When I asked the question, I never suspected the story could get worse.

"He said that Stanley became reckless and irresponsible."

Dad didn't offer any details and I didn't ask for any. I didn't want to imagine Stanley in jail or dying from AIDS at a young age.

"But he did call me, years later," my father said.

I gasped.

"You're kidding, Dad!" I said.

From the gleam in my father's eyes, I knew he wouldn't be nodding off or taking a cigarette break anytime soon.

"I was working at that motel," he said. "Remember, honey? That one over by the airport?"

It wasn't a time I wanted to remember. I tried to push down the image of my formerly proud, elegant father who wore Brooks Brothers' suits, fancy shined shoes, and stylish hats to work. I didn't know how he dressed as a night clerk at a motel in the scary, industrial part of South San Francisco, and I didn't want to know.

"I picked up the phone at the motel one night and I couldn't believe it, honey," he said. "It was Stanley."

"You're kidding."

By now, I was getting suspicious about Dad's memory. Was this call from Stanley a fantasy he'd created for himself? He seemed so clear and certain of the details, though.

"I was so happy to hear from him," Dad said. "And he was in *San Francisco*!"

Sweet images of a romantic rendezvous between these two middle-aged men at the time flooded my mind. Yet our family life had remained the same. Mom and Dad remained married. Something must have gone wrong.

"He called to tell me that Clarence had died," Dad said.

Stanley, he said, was at the San Francisco International Airport when he called Dad. Dad could see the airport from the windows of the *sleazy* (Mom's word) Bayside Motel where he worked.

"I begged him to delay his flight, honey," Dad said. "I asked him to please, *please,* at least have a drink or a cup of coffee with me."

Dad's arms were flailing now.

"But he refused," he said.

What a dreadful ending to this story, I thought.

"What do you mean he *refused*, Dad?" I said. "What exactly did he say?"

"Oh, he said something about having to catch a flight."

This didn't make any sense to me. Stanley should have called him earlier in the day.

I imagined how Dad must have experienced this. He'd just filed for bankruptcy at the time. He'd lost our prestigious modern house on the hill. His wife, the mother of four school-age children, had to get a job, something she would have never chosen to do while the four of us were still at home. The family was deep in debt. Dad had just lost a good job at the VA Hospital because he was gay. How humiliating it must have been for him to be night clerking at a motel that served as a temporary shelter for drug addicts, prostitutes, and alcoholics, and hearing Stanley's refusal to see him on the phone.

Yet, Dad didn't seem all that broken up. Instead, I was the one who was shaken and teary. My annoyance about this missed connection between two old lovers might have been because it was news to me. By contrast, Dad would have had more than four decades to reflect upon it. His voice sounded melancholic but resigned. After all, he had chosen his own future that fateful day after the arrest.

I wondered why Stanley might have refused to see Dad that day. He may have continued to lead an openly gay life after their breakup. If so, it is likely their long-ago love affair was less important to him than what Dad saw through rose-colored glasses from the closet.

Alternatively, Stanley may have resented the now safe family man who wanted to relive his early days. He wouldn't have known the difficulties Dad had faced over the years, or that the man he knew as Duane now went by Ralph. Or maybe Clarence had been right. Maybe Stanley *had* gotten reckless. Maybe he looked terrible. The two of them would have been in their late fifties by then. Maybe he had some arrests of his own and felt ashamed of the life he'd led. On the other hand, maybe he still felt stung by my father's abandonment.

While my mind was in overdrive, Dad nodded off again. As soon as I saw his eyes close, I draped the afghan over his lap, the one from the 1950s with the blue, gray, and pink squares. These colors in the afghan had always seemed an odd combination to me. They were not the cheery greens and yellows that typical 1950s homemakers chose at the time. In the centers of the gray squares were intricate, Asian-looking designs.

I had criticized the color scheme to Mom years earlier. It wasn't like those I saw in friends' houses.

"*Your father* crocheted the squares, honey," she said. "But I connected them all together."

That is what my mother did. She kept us connected. She held us all together despite everything. The co-created afghan was now warming my father in his final days.

THE OILFIELDS OF DAD'S YOUTH WHERE
HIS ASHES WERE SCATTERED, 2008

LAST PHOTO OF DAD, AGE NINETY, 2008

CHAPTER 48: GONE

Dad's eyes lit up when Luis and I entered his dim hospital room that early morning in July 2008. Despite having banished all photos of his children from his apartment, he reached out his arms to me as if he were greeting a celebrity.

"Do you know how beautiful you are, Laurie?" he said. I never tired of his welcome.

An ambulance had brought him to the hospital a few hours earlier. He was in pain. After running some tests, his doctor diagnosed him with a life-threatening intestinal blockage.

Over the past few weeks, Dad had insisted bladder cancer, the same type of cancer that ended my mother's life, was the cause of his pain. He pointed to an area on his lower back.

"See, honey," he said. "It is the same place your mother pointed to."

The doctor assured me that Dad did not have bladder cancer. Still, I didn't fight Dad on this. He seemed oddly comforted by the thought of sharing the same fatal illness as Mom's. His insistence moved me since, with the exception of the wedding photo I added on my own to his apartment decor, no other indication of my mother existed there.

Out in the hospital's hallway, Dr. Kumra advised me that he was duty-bound to offer my father a surgical procedure for his intestinal blockage. If successful, he told me, it could extend Dad's life, but for only a few months at the most. Given Dad's advanced age of ninety, I could not believe we were even having this conversation.

Before I had a chance to respond—not that it would have made a difference anyway—this handsome young doctor with olive skin and dark chocolate brown eyes was on his way to my father's bedside. Dad had told me many times how much he *just loved* Dr. Kumra.

"He is the *nicest* person, Laurie," he said. "You just *have* to meet him."

Now I had. This pleasant and handsome doctor of perhaps forty years leaned over and looked straight into my father's starstruck eyes. He described the complicated internal surgery to Dad using medical terms unfamiliar to me. I'm sure the terms were unfamiliar to my father, too, but Dad didn't seem to mind. Not at all, in fact. He beamed under the spotlight of Dr. Kumra's rapt attention.

Luis and I looked on from the other side of Dad's metal hospital bed. I might have even huffed a little. Even if he wasn't going to take this seriously, at least I would.

Dad's eyes locked onto Dr. Kumra's as he described the complicated final measure that *could* be performed if Dad so chose. The doctor's voice was loud and clear, and his tone was firm.

"Ralph, I want you to know something," he said. "It will be a *really* rough road if you decide to take it."

I was sure I knew what Dad would say. I'm sure the doctor and the nurse who were standing at his side knew, too. *Why bother at this point?* Or, with my father's typical, dramatic flair, *I have lived a long life, and I am ready to die.* Or, my favorite, because it would be so in character for my father, *Why waste the money?*

But he didn't say any of these things. Instead, a big grin broke out on his flushed face. His blue eyes danced under the orange-yellow overhead lights. He even tried to sit up a little. I could see that rather than being devastated by the grim news, he was reveling in it as the sole focus of Dr. Kumra's attention. Finally, he responded.

"I look forward to the gravel!" he said.

What are you talking about, Dad?

Dad enunciated his words as clearly as he did when I was young. He spoke them in a confident almost jovial voice. My head spun.

I looked over at the doctor and the nurse for a sign. But they looked as stunned as I was, a reaction I thought must be rare in a hospital setting. It took me a moment to understand that Dad's reference to the gravel corresponded to the "rough road" Dr. Kumra predicted ahead for him.

Dr. Kumra shrugged his shoulders and leaned a little toward me for direction. I didn't know what to say. Should I support my dying father's wishes, or was Dad just posturing before the fetching doctor?

In the end, my direction wasn't required. Dad began to convulse. At the doctor's order, the nurse injected a drug into his intravenous line to slow the convulsions.

I followed Dr. Kumra out the door to discuss what was going on. It was soon clear to me from his hemming and hawing, and his heavy use of medical terminology, that this was the end. I rushed back into Dad's room and took his hand. I told him that everything would be okay, using the same sweet voice he used on me when I was a little girl with a sore ankle or as an unwed teen. That tone worked on me, but my words now only seemed to increase my father's agitation. He lifted his right arm and pointed toward the opposite wall.

"Laurie!" he said. "*Turn* it."

His breathing was labored, and his tone was one of impatience. My chair was crammed into a tiny space between his hospital bed and a large, beeping patient monitor behind me that flashed red and yellow lights. I turned my eyes in the direction my father's arm was pointing. All that I could see on the wall was a standard hospital clock. I turned back at Dad, confused. He continued to wave his arm, the one unencumbered by the intravenous tube attached to his bruised left wrist.

He bellowed out a second request. This time he sounded angry.

"Turn it *back*, Laurie," he said.

His eyes flared. I was getting nervous. Would he die with his last words to me misunderstood? Maybe the time on the clock is wrong, I thought. Dad had always been a stickler for accurate time. I thought of his down-to-the-second jogging stats he posted on the refrigerator door back in the late sixties, after he'd landed the solid job at Standard Oil, after the intoxicating Summer of Love and before Susan got sick.

Maybe the clock was broken, I thought. But how would Dad even know the correct time now? I checked my watch. I looked at the clock and then back at my watch. They showed the same time, a few minutes before three o'clock in the afternoon. I turned toward Dad, my forehead now scrunched up.

"*What*, Dad?"

"Move it back, honey!"

He rotated his arm counterclockwise. His face was beet red now.

"The *large* hand, Laurie!"

"Uh, okay, Dad," I stuttered. "I'll take care of it."

I could hear myself talking to him in that high voice adults use when they're blowing off a child's request. He shot me a look.

"Okay, Dad, I *promise*," I said. "I'll do it."

This time my voice was respectful and serious, though I

wasn't exactly sure of what I'd promised. He calmed down and closed his eyes. A male nurse appeared in the room and wheeled my father's bed down to a private room at the end of the hall. I thought it unfortunate that Dad wasn't able to appreciate his handsome, muscular escort.

Soon Tim arrived with his guitar in tow. He sang some of Dad's favorite songs—"The Rose," "Amazing Grace," and "Mockingbird Hill." I remembered my father singing the last one to us in the kitchen when we were little, telling us that it was his father's favorite song.

When the sun in the morning peeps over the hill
And kisses the roses 'round my windowsill.
Then my heart fills with gladness when I hear the trill
Of the birds in the treetops on Mockingbird Hill.

It was twilight in Santa Rosa now. Tim strummed his guitar. I thought of all the times Dad bragged about Tim's singing to anyone who would listen. I hoped he could hear Tim now. Dr. Kumra advised me to go home to get some sleep now that my brother was there. I could come back in the morning, he said. It would be like Mom's final night, he said. I'd be there early to say good-bye to Dad just as I had with her.

I kissed my unconscious father on his forehead, and then fell asleep in the car while Luis drove us home. A few hours later, in bed, I stirred from a dream. Off in the far distance I saw a bright horizontal light. A thick, heavy darkness slowly overtook it until it was just a thin line of light, like the line of light under the kitchen door that I feared going out when I was a toddler. In my dream the light flickered a few times, slowly dimmed, and then went out completely.

Even as I was dreaming this dream, I understood its significance. After all, it was what I'd feared since early childhood. I wasn't surprised when the phone rang, and it was Tim. As a toddler, I was distressed when the light in the kitchen went out, when my father left for work. I thought he would never come back. Until now, he always had.

Dad died on July 28, 2008, at the age of ninety, my final words to him a promise I'd turn back the clock. It would be three years before I started fulfilling that promise by going back in time. It would be another five years before I realized I was doing just that.

CHAPTER 49: WHAT I DIDN'T KNOW

thought I knew everything about my father. He lived for nine decades, and I was there for nearly six of those. He answered every question I ever asked of him. And I asked a lot of them. Nevertheless, a few years after Dad died, I grew curious about his wartime letters, the ones over which my mother had swooned. *Could I learn more?* I wondered.

I pulled out her box. From the company logo on top, I assumed Mom had used a box from the photo lab where she worked during the war. Printed below the logo was the warning, "Open only in photographic darkroom."

These letters had been in the dark for a long time, at least for me. Mom had lined the letters up in chronological order. Bringing the first letter to my face, I inhaled its sweet, musky aroma. Dated May 27, 1942, my father wrote it one month after the USO dance where my parents first met. It reminded me of his smell when I was a little girl sitting on his lap. I started reading the letters, now a faded brown color.

My darling,
It would be impossible to find the proper words to tell
you how very much this past month has meant to me.

So began my parents' unconventional sixty-four-year love affair. How proper and tender were his first written words to her. My eyes welled up, knowing what was in store for this young hopeful couple.

In almost spiritual terms, Dad described his feelings about their chance meeting.

Whom shall I thank, Rusty, for sending my com-
pany to Belmont? Can it be just simple luck, or is there
really such a thing as a guiding star? When I consider
on what a narrow balance our meeting hinged, I can
only think there <u>must</u> have been an intervention by Fate.

This was one of Dad's common ponderings, how much chance meetings change our lives. The USO dance then. The crippled man in the restroom in Pasadena a few years earlier. The charismatic preacher in Fellows, who told Dad at eighteen that he wasn't alone, and who then introduced him to Clarence, who in turn introduced him to Stanley.

Later in the same letter, he declared his abiding love for my mother.

I tried last night, but I'm afraid I didn't succeed
very well, to tell you how dear you are to me; how
greatly I cared for you from the first night I saw you.
I'm not good at words, Rusty; you'll have to attempt
to read between the lines. If you do, you'll find there
the words which I can't seem to grasp but which will
say to you that my heart is yours and that—I love you.
Yours Always, Ralph.

I had witnessed this struggle of my father's in my lifetime. He could say in writing what he had a difficult time saying in person. I never observed him telling my mother in person that he loved her.

Dad not only professed his immediate love for this naïve high school senior he had just met, but he also sounded giddy about the overseas, wartime experience awaiting him. It had been eight months since Japanese forces had bombed Pearl Harbor.

> *We shall soon be underway. It's all very exciting, and I know it's going to be a thrilling adventure . . . Looking forward to the day when we return. Please wait for me, my dearest.* (June 18, 1942)

I knew by now it would be a cold and dreary time for him, but at least he wouldn't be on the battlefield.

In the first letter he wrote Mom from Alaska, he didn't reference drills or shooting practice. He wrote about a symphony.

> *Tonight, my dearest, if I could be granted just one wish for one hour, it would be to hold you closely, to hear you say you love me—while we listened to Tchaikovsky's Pathétique. I love you, Rusty, with all my heart. Yours always, Ralph.* (July 22, 1942)

I had to laugh. I doubt many soldiers wrote love letters home like this. It sounded so much like Dad, dramatic and full of imagery. About his reference to Tchaikovsky, some accounts suggest that he was convicted of homosexual sex with a minor while he composed *Pathétique*. Some historians consider this symphony Tchaikovsky's farewell to life. I wondered if my father knew this history and if he too saw a parallel in his own life, though I was probably reading too much into it.

Skipping past a dozen or so more blue envelopes with the purple three-cent stamps on them, I pulled out a small, yellowed envelope with the words, "WESTERN UNION TELEGRAM" in large type on the front. Inside was an even yellower piece of paper, neatly folded in half. I'd heard about this telegram all my life. Could this really be it?

I carefully slipped out the brittle paper using my thumb and forefinger.

Seattle Wash 1150A Sept 8, 1942
Miss Irene Utman
Unexpected furlough. Arrive Frisco tomorrow. Marry
me, dearest.
Love Ralph.

Over the prior few decades, I'd grown weary of my father's repeated stories of the past, of the sexual experiences of his youth and young adulthood, of his arrests and unfulfilled life. I did not want to know that the four of us kids weren't enough. I didn't want to know that he didn't love my mother *that* way. Yet here was a twenty-four-year-old soldier writing romantic prose in elegant handwriting to a Titian blonde who called out to him from across the dance floor, someone to whom he would propose marriage after knowing only five months. I knew what was to come. Still, it seemed such a beautiful love story. In 1942, it pulled my mother in. It pulled me in now. I found myself rooting for them.

As the war dragged on, Dad appeared cheerful as he romanced his girlfriend from afar. Nevertheless, I could read between the lines.

Never stop, Irene, being the angel you are, pure,
loving, charming. Promise me. I cannot think of you as
being ever anything but good, so markedly contrasting

to what parts of my life have been, and it is only your influence that causes me to make an attempt to lead a life good in thought and deed. If it were not for you, sweetheart, I should be a complete failure as a man. Your affectionate husband, Ralph. (June 25, 1943)

Dad saw himself as a bad man doing bad deeds, though he was optimistic about the goodness of my mother whom he seemed to put on a pedestal, and as someone who might keep his given nature at bay. I remembered how ashamed I too was of my behavior, of my teen pregnancy, my promiscuity, my failed marriages.

In a letter Dad wrote a few months earlier, he was clear about the self-hatred he often felt, though my mother wouldn't have then known why.

There's that restless, dissatisfied, other self of mine that is continually trying to make itself heard. Though I hate myself for allowing it, occasionally I lose the battle—with the result that I fall far short of the standards that my wife and friends and family have set for me. As it is, every success I shall ever achieve will owe its thanks to you, for it is only your love that provides me with the incentive to destroy the old no-count self. I dedicate my life, every breath of it, to you, Irene, to your happiness. (April 3, 1943)

Dad must have been doing his best at the time to annihilate the person he was when he was born. I hadn't known this. I assumed that from the beginning of his marriage to my mother, he expected to be leading a double life. If he had said something to me like, "I did everything I could to extinguish my homosexuality, but I wasn't successful," I would have viewed him less as a dishonest husband and father and more of a man on

a heroic—though impossible—journey. Much like him on the *gravel road* about which he'd spoken in the final hours of his life. The rough road.

A few months later, Dad seemed to be trying to convince not Mom but himself that his new life was the right one.

> *If we succeed in defeating this threat to our American way of life—and we shall succeed—and I come home to you at last to find our love unchanged, I shall ask no greater reward for my small efforts as long as I live. You and life together is such an overwhelming wealth that I would be an ingrate indeed if I desired more.* (June 29, 1943)

He'd always desire more, even at age ninety on his final day. Dad took it even further in the next month, fantasizing about a place where there would be no one else but the two of them.

> *Believe me, darling, I feel if we two could take ourselves to some land where there was no one but ourselves, our love and our life together would soon make of our new world a Shangri-La.* (July 21, 1943)

Shangri-La is the happy, imaginary place isolated from the outside world that author James Hilton wrote of in his 1933 novel, *Lost Horizon*. I don't know if Dad ever read that novel, but I wonder if he was trying to conjure up a place where he would be isolated from other *men*. He sounded so desperate.

The Army didn't allow World War II soldiers to bring their correspondence home with them after the war, so my mother's letters were destroyed. Nevertheless, I could tell by my father's half of their written conversations that their long-distance relationship, at the least, was idyllic. Signs of trouble showed up, though, when they met in person during Dad's rare furloughs.

Maybe I was not very successful in showing you my love, but it is there, believe me darling. (Feb. 15, 1944)

Hints of in-person problems came up again when Mom visited Dad in Fort Ord on their second anniversary, in 1944.

Dearest heart, please believe that I love you very deeply. I adore you. If sometimes—too often, I know—I don't feel too well and I act strangely, please forgive and forget. (Sept. 11, 1944)

Those times, when Mom wasn't someone on the other end of a romantic letter, were plainly hard for him. He'd picked in her the ideal person to marry, though. She was good at forgiving and moving on. However, from what Dad wrote the following spring, even her powers of positive thinking eventually seemed taxed.

As for my being a bad boy if you aren't with me, please don't think of that. I am resolute in everything I told you. I have no desire to go out and be gay. With your love guiding me, I could not do anything which would be unfair to you. (April 25, 1944)

I was surprised to read the word *gay* since in the 1940s it wasn't in common use. It is probably safe to assume that Dad was referring to Mom's concerns about extramarital affairs he might be having with women, much as my concerns had been from the time of those earliest dinner parties. It seemed all of my mother's friends wanted to dance and pet him. On some level, my mother and I must have both known early on, even though we didn't yet know the gender of his preferred partners.

Dad's repeated reference to the healing, guiding influence of Mom's love saddened me for both of them. He tried valiantly to repress his true nature. I had assumed his primary goal was only to keep it secret. Letter by letter, I began to rewrite the story of my family, to turn back the clock.

Decades after my father wrote his wartime letters, and two years after Susan died, he wrote Mom a letter addressed to the Cannons Hotel in England where she was traveling. At home, he was jogging, getting healthier, and staying out late after work.

Dear Mrs. Hall, It has been a few years, hasn't it, since I last wrote a letter to you? But in my mind, it was only yesterday. A blizzard outside and all my thoughts going to a lovely red-haired girl a million miles away. I want you to know I still feel as I did then and, although I never say it, I do love you very much. I hope you will be having a wonderful time and seeing enchanting sights every day. —Love, Ralph. (June 1981)

Just as in wartime, and with another vast physical expanse between the two of them, he fashioned a romantic letter to her. He acknowledged that he never expressed these words aloud. Calling her *Mrs. Hall* in his salutation may have been an act of reassurance to her. After my mother died, I found that long-distance letter in a pink quilted box in her top drawer, a written testament of love from what even she acknowledged at the time was her increasingly distant gay husband.

CHAPTER 50: IN HIS GREAT-GRANDDAUGHTER'S WORDS

I had never seen the TV show *Glee*. However, I knew that it dealt with a host of social concerns including homophobia and bullying. While on a visit to Jody's five years after my father died, my granddaughter Cassie started up a recording of the show. She was seventeen. I settled into the sofa to watch it with her.

In the episode we watched, an engaged gay couple—one a high school student and the other in college—discuss their plans for the future. The older one encourages the younger one to believe enough in himself to apply to the arts college of his choice, which he does. In that moment, I realized what scant attention I had been paying to how today's youth, including my own grandchildren, viewed homosexuality.

Two years prior, Jody told both of her daughters that their great-grandfather, Papa, was gay. Jody waited until Cassie, the youngest, was in high school to tell her, just as I'd done with Jody decades earlier.

Cassie paused *Glee* when I asked her how she felt when she learned about Papa. She shrugged the typical teenage shrug and said it was "no big deal." I hadn't finished processing her nonchalant reaction when she started up *Glee* again.

"This is quite a show, honey," I said. "Do all the kids you know watch it?"

She pushed PAUSE again on the remote.

"Uh-huh."

Before she had a chance to turn the recording back on, I jumped in again.

"Do you know any gay people at school?"

"Yeah," she said.

Cassie scooched up a little from her lounging position. She must have known that my questions wouldn't be stopping any time soon.

"Are any of your good friends gay?" I asked.

"Uh-huh."

It was such a non-issue to her. It was as if I'd asked her if the sky was blue. At the next commercial break, I started in again. This time I hoped for more than one-word responses.

"Have you witnessed any prejudice toward gay people at your school?"

Cassie, resigned to more questions, put down the remote.

"Well, I've heard some people say it's weird or gross," she said. "But I've never seen anyone bully or tease gay people. It seems like if they're uncomfortable around them, they just ignore them."

"Have you asked them to explain why they're uncomfortable?"

"Yeah," Cassie said. "They say things like, 'It's just not right.' But they're probably just repeating what their parents say. Some of them bring up sayings from the Bible. But I can't remember what they are."

"If you saw someone harassing a gay person, would you speak up?"

Cassie pondered this for a moment.

"I would if it was a friend [who was doing the harassing]," she said. "But it'd be hard for me to speak up in a group of strangers."

I admired her frankness.

"Do you think there are any gay teenagers at your school who are closeted, like Papa was?"

"Well, I know one boy who I *think* might be gay," she said. "He dresses really well and is friends with lots of girls, not guys. But I'm not sure that has anything to do with being gay. But it kinda seems like it does."

I had nothing to add to this.

"What do you think of same-sex marriage?"

She sat up even taller.

"I had to do a paper on that in my government class, Grandma!"

"*Really*, honey?"

I tried to imagine getting that kind of assignment when I was her age or seeing her great-grandfather's reaction if he were alive today. The only paper I remember writing in 1968, when I was Cassie's age, was a dry description of Brazil's exports. I think I drew a rubber tree as part of the assignment.

"Yep," she said. "I had to research arguments for and against same-sex marriage."

"Are you for it, honey?"

"Yes," she said. "I support it."

"Why *is* that, honey?"

"I don't believe the government should be involved in someone's personal love life," she said.

"What would you say, then, to those who don't support it?"

"Well, I *know* people don't like to be told they're wrong," Cassie said. "But the world is changing."

Is it ever, I thought to myself. I could see the world changing right before me, in the eyes and the words of my youngest grandchild.

Cassie now needed no encouragement to keep going.

"When Papa was young, there was no social media like there is today. Ideas are easier to spread now. There's constant exposure on TV—*Glee, Ellen* . . . It's not an unknown anymore. It seems like every time Papa came out, he got pushed back into the closet."

What a telling image, I thought. Mine had always been of my father *retreating* into the closet, just as an overpowered enemy might walk backwards into a fort or another hiding space. Cassie's perspective provided me with a new view of my father's story. Homophobia *did* keep pushing her great-grandfather back into the closet.

"He was scared," she said. "So he had to pretend."

"Uh-huh," I said.

"What do you think now about Mam and Papa's relationship, how they pretended for sixty-four years to be in a heterosexual marriage?"

"Well, Papa always seemed happy to me," she said. "He seemed family-based."

Cassie was twelve when her great-grandfather died, so she had a good idea of who he was.

"He was, Cassie," I said. "He told me he always knew he wanted a family."

"But given everything," she said, "he and Mam must have been really close to be able to support each other for so long. You know, without the romantic side."

I nodded.

"Is there anything you'd like to say to those who believe homosexuality is evil or sinful?"

"Yeah," she said. "I'd like them to be more open-minded, to not have tunnel vision about it. And to acknowledge what I have to say. To take the time to listen to me like I listen to them."

"Anything else you'd like to tell them?"

"Yeah. I'd ask them, 'What makes your happiness more valuable than theirs?'"

What a logical way to put it, I thought.

"If Papa were alive today, is there anything you'd want to say to him?"

She looked off in the distance, through one of the windows in the family room, as if she were talking to him.

"Yes," she said. Her voice was clear and strong. "I'd tell him that I understand why he didn't fight harder. You know, to live a different life."

"You do?"

"Yeah, Grandma," Cassie said. "He wanted to stay alive."

With those words, she summed it up far better than I ever had. It was about survival. Her grandfather wanted to live.

STANLEY, LOS ANGELES, 1937

CHAPTER 51: FINDING STANLEY

Stanley was an almost mythic figure for my father. I knew so little about him, though. Dad's recordkeeping skills and his penchant for rarely throwing away anything of any value were legendary in our family. Even though he'd torn up Stanley's letter from the 1930s, I had a feeling he must have left some kind of trail. I started digging.

From a storage box in our garage, I pulled out my father's earliest photo album, a small one covered in alligator skin and with frayed, tasseled cords threaded through two tiny metal tubes in its binding. Mounted neatly on the pages were small black-and-white photos from, it appeared, the early 1930s to the year 1940, the year of Dad's arrest. Dad met Stanley in the 1930s, within this period. I knew I'd probably never see Stanley's image if it weren't in this little brown photo album resting in my hands.

I flipped through the four dozen pages. There was my father as a young teenager with his thick, curly hair slicked back. As an older teen, he is standing close to girls, often with his arms around them. In one photo his left arm wraps around a boy, though each is leaning awkwardly away from the other. There are photos of Dad and his teenage friends in swimsuits tanning themselves on the beach. Graduates stand sober by themselves in gowns and as couples in formal attire, perhaps for a dance. Dozens of tiny school photos of Dad and his friends fill in the leftover spaces. Except for those of my father and his family, I knew none of the subjects in the photos.

I pulled each out of its four pasted paper corners and checked on the back for dates or names. Most were blank. I already knew that Dad's next photo album, chronologically, tracked his army days and early relationship with my mother. This would be my only chance to find Stanley.

As I neared the final pages of the album, I stared at six photos of a young man, all by himself. In one, he sat on a tree trunk wearing wrinkled pants, a long-sleeved shirt with its sleeves rolled up, and a tie. His head dipped down in a shy smile. His thick, shiny hair was combed straight back.

In another, this same young man stood in a forested area in front of a tall observatory. Another shows him posing on the front walkway of a residence. He is dressed in a white double-breasted jacket, white pants, and white shoes. He holds his hands behind his back and smiles a shy smile. "A lover must have taken these," I said out loud.

Other than those of my father, these were the only photos in the album of a man by himself. They were also the only ones of a man looking so lovingly at the photographer. I concluded that the photographer must have been my father.

When I turned the page, I found similar poses of my father—on the same tree trunk, in front of the same observatory, one in a tie and white shoes, and with the same happy, relaxed smile. In one, he stands near a shallow, pebbled creek bed, a big smile on his face and his arms behind his back.

On the next page was another photo of the young man on a beach, standing in front of a Mediterranean-style building, and posing barefoot on a beach with six-pack abs and a big grin. I identified the building as the Cabrillo Beach Bath House, built in 1932.

These two young men were together in the same places taking photos of one another. Cabrillo Beach is located in Los Angeles County, the county where Dad and Stanley met and attended college together. There were no other photos like these. I had found Stanley.

One by one, I slipped the photos out. Most contained wording on the back, though not in my father's handwriting. The photo taken near the creek bed carried a lover's words on the back.

> *In Oak Wilde in Arroyo Seco Canyon, July 5. Duane, from the looks of this picture, you should have a screen test! Yah—*

This must have been Stanley's writing. I blushed at the obvious infatuation.

On a photo of my father in a dark-colored silky shirt, pleated pants, white belt, and white shoes, and with his head tilted slightly, Stanley had written:

> *Ah—(sigh) it must be the scent of the white flowers.*

It's not apparent what he was referring to, but perhaps it was Dad's smile, Duane's smile.

On the photo of Stanley in his white, double-breasted suit, Dad wrote:

> *In our driveway. July 18, 1937.*

Even though my father never said as much, maybe the two of them lived together for a short period before Dad's second arrest, perhaps at Clarence's house.

Only one photo shows the two young men together. It's a double exposure, though. This pre-digital-camera processing error results in something called "ghost images." In a double exposure, one print contained two separate photos, one developed on top of the other. In this one, Stanley is ghostlike, barely visible behind my father. Despite the fact that I would never have been born if the two young lovers had remained together, I couldn't help but smile. Here they were, so long ago, two happy men in love. Dad wouldn't have known when he mounted this photo that Stanley would remain a ghost-like figure for him for the rest of his life.

The final photo on the album's final page shows Stanley standing tall in his sports coat and shy smile in front of a telescope tower. I understood that with this photo, Dad's openly gay life was over. I flipped the album cover shut and looked at the cover of Dad's next photo album. Printed in gold color on its cover is *R Hall*. Still visible to the left of *R Hall*, but ghost-like, is *Duane*. Dad must have rubbed out the name he was given at birth. With this photo album forward, my father rubbed out his true self.

Mounted on the first two pages of this album are photos of my mother and father at Fleishhacker Zoo in San Francisco, where the army stationed Dad's unit during the war. No more Stanley. No more Duane. From that point on there would only be Ralph, Irene, and the four of us kids in the family photo albums.

Dad also kept a scrapbook from his earlier years. The second to the last item he mounted in it is a photo of jazz bandleader Les Hite. When I found out that the theme song of the Les Hite Orchestra was "It Must Have Been a Dream," I thought that my father's two years in Los Angeles with Stanley must have felt like a dream. A Pacific Greyhound Lines bus ticket to Greenfield Corners, California, is the final memento mounted in Dad's scrapbook. It carries the caption, "To L.A. March 11, 1941—Enlisted in US Navy."

When Dad pasted this in his scrapbook, he would not have known that the Navy would turn him away due to his arrest, that they would turn *Duane Ralph Hall* away. He would also not have known that the army would accept him under his new name, *Ralph Duane Hall,* three weeks later.

I thought of all the times I'd asked my father why he changed his name. It is the only question I remember asking him where he avoided an honest or consistent response. Hemming and hawing, he came up with a different explanation every time. How much energy it must have taken him all his life to keep his stories straight, to look straight.

The last dozen pages of Dad's scrapbook remain blank. From that point on, he would have a new name and a new life, a closeted one, and soon a female life partner in my mother. Photos of their four children filled the newer photo albums, none of which he'd display in the final place he lived.

ME AT AGE TWO, 1953

EPILOGUE

*R*ich spicy aromas coming from the kitchen drew me
downstairs that warm summer evening. My algebra
homework would just have to wait. Dad breezed into
the high-ceilinged, light-filled room; his face covered
in a shiny smile.

He wore creased, snug Levi's and a soft muslin
shirt whose pockets he'd embellished with colorful geometric patterns. After latching the heavy entry door
shut, he hung his Panama hat on the iron wall hook.
His shoulder bag he tossed onto the coffee-colored
leather sofa. It landed with a soft plop.

Dad headed straight over to Stanley, my other dad,
who was stirring a large pot of sauce on the stove. He
didn't at first notice me standing on the bottom step
of the stairs.

Upon seeing Dad, Stanley placed his spoon on the
colorful, ceramic spoon rest they'd purchased at an art
show the prior week. He blushed a little as he welcomed
Dad's embrace. Dad chattered about the talented street
artists he'd passed on his way to the bus station at Seventh
and Mission earlier that evening after work.

Dad's twinkling eyes betrayed him as he fumbled for something in his pocket. Soon, out tumbled a chunky, silver chain bracelet into his hand. He lifted Stanley's arm, now freed from spoons and potholders, wrapped the bracelet around his wrist, and snapped the clasp shut. I heard some giggling and cooing, after which Dad turned to me.

"Oh, hi, Laurie, how was school today?"

"It was good, Dad," I said. "My art teacher said he really liked my pastel drawing."

"Terrific, sweetie. I loved the way you blended the greens and blues together."

He looked back over his shoulder at Stanley. "I'll be right back," he said.

"You'd better be!"

Stanley jiggled his new bracelet a few times before returning his attention to his savory sauce. Dad hurried back to the master bedroom to freshen his face and slip on some sandals before dinner.

A few days after I found Stanley in my father's photo album, this scene appeared to me while walking the hills of San Francisco. A peculiar feeling of warmth and security filled me. Temporarily freed up from the anxiety that has been my near constant companion, I glimpsed a childhood free of the fear that my father would leave us. The bond between my two parents—my two dads—was primary in this make-believe family. *They* were the executive committee. Their bond with their children, with me, was secondary. I wasn't Dad's confidante. Stanley was.

Nevertheless, after the soothing scene ended, I asked myself why I wasn't untethered by it. After all, Mom wasn't in it. Stanley had replaced me in Dad's eyes. As I watched them, though, I wasn't picking at my fingers, nor did my head feel the pressure of an oncoming migraine. I'd slept peacefully through the night before. My shoulders were relaxed, not bearing the weight of decades-long attempts to soothe and bone my mismatched parents. I wasn't the bridge connecting a mother and a father's unfulfilled marriage. I was the child of a strong, loving bond. I was just a child. Only a child.

In my parallel reality, I wasn't subjected to a father's tales about how unfulfilled in love he was. The father he was in my vision would never be a ninety-year-old man grieving a life spent in the closet. He wouldn't be an elderly father and widower who would erase all evidence of his family, a family that had been formed out of fear.

I would never have felt sorrow over my straight mother's unrequited, one-sided love for my father. Instead, I would be moored by my parents' solid bond, not unmoored by its weakness. I would have had a strong, healthy model for my romances, not one based on dishonesty, infidelity, and fear.

I was born the child of a closeted gay father. After he came out to me, I became the closeted child of a closeted gay father. I gauged my behavior and language through the prism of his secret. Now I glimpsed a new prism, one unclouded by a legacy of secrets and shame. The giggles, the shy smiles, and the affectionate bear hug between my fantasy parents came first. I wasn't Dad's confidante or ally. He was my father. A soothing warmth enveloped me. It felt like the way a home should feel—loving, safe, and secure.

After turning back the clock to examine in retrospect the details of my family and my life, I can finally say that I know what security feels like. I know that my mother and my father, despite their unlikely pairing, were honorable people who did the best they could during a dishonorable time in our history.

I am fortunate to have been born of them.

THE END

ACKNOWLEDGMENTS

My story began to pour out of me after responding to a ten-minute writing prompt, titled, "My father's clothes." For that I have to thank longtime *San Francisco Chronicle* columnist and writing instructor, Adair Lara. My writing coach, Betsy Rapoport, took it from there, reminding me to find myself in the story. As a child in my family who focused on the needs of others, that was hard for me. But she never gave up. For my soul sisters, also daughters of closeted fathers—you wrapped me in your arms while we shared the common language of the closet. I couldn't have come this far without you. For Missy, the one who walked alongside me every step of this journey, quietly witnessing every breakthrough and backstep, my gratitude for you is way beyond measure. For Erin, a most magical being, whose insights kept the light on for me when all seemed dark, I love you. For Hatt, whose words in our neighborhood coffeehouse triggered the vision I had of growing up the child of two happy fathers in love. For Tim, the one who lived this reality with me all these years, for your brotherly love, friendship, fact-checking, and unshakeable support. For the sandmen, those apparitions who appeared to me in a vision one day when my family's story was too heavy for me to bear alone. I hope I can write your story one day. For Jody, who somehow managed to survive her teenage mom and thrive as a stable adult and strong, loving wife and mother. My love and respect for you is eternal. For my grandchildren, whose mere existence keeps me motivated to heal our family's past. For Luis, whose steady love, quiet strength, and native wisdom supported me from the very beginning. For my parents for everything. I would not have chosen a life other than the one with you.

ABOUT THE AUTHOR

Laura Hall was born and raised in a small city on the San Francisco Peninsula. After receiving her BA (summa cum laude) and MA in Landscape Architecture at University of California, Berkeley, she went on to teach for the school's Extension program and build an urban design professional practice where her projects included community facilitation in northern California communities and rebuilding plans for Mississippi Gulf Coast towns after Hurricane Katrina.

Author photo © Luis Velez

SELECTED TITLES FROM SHE WRITES PRESS

She Writes Press is an independent publishing company founded to serve women writers everywhere. Visit us at www.shewritespress.com.

You Can't Buy Love Like That: Growing Up Gay in the Sixties by Carol E. Anderson. $16.95, 978-1631523144. A young lesbian girl grows beyond fear to fearlessness as she comes of age in the '60s amid religious, social, and legal barriers.

Blue Apple Switchback: A Memoir by Carrie Highley. $16.95, 978-1-63152-037-2. At age forty, Carrie Highley finally decided to take on the biggest switchback of her life: upon her bicycle, and with the help of her mentor's wisdom, she shed everything she was taught to believe as a young lady growing up in the South—and made a choice to be true to herself and everyone else around her.

The Coconut Latitudes: Secrets, Storms, and Survival in the Caribbean by Rita Gardner. $16.95, 978-1-63152-901-6. A haunting, lyrical memoir about a dysfunctional family's experiences in a reality far from the envisioned Eden—and the terrible cost of keeping secrets.

I'm the One Who Got Away: A Memoir by Andrea Jarrell. $16.95, 978-1-63152-260-4. When Andrea Jarrell was a girl, her mother often told her of their escape from Jarrell's dangerous, cunning father as if it was a bedtime story. Here, Jarrell reveals the complicated legacy she inherited from her mother—and shares a life-affirming story of having the courage to become both safe enough and vulnerable enough to love and be loved.

Implosion: Memoir of an Architect's Daughter by Elizabeth W. Garber. $16.95, 978-1-63152-351-9. When Elizabeth Garber, her architect father, and the rest of their family move into Woodie's modern masterpiece, a glass house, in 1966, they have no idea that over the next few years their family's life will be shattered—both by Woodie's madness and the turbulent 1970s.

The Sportscaster's Daughter: A Memoir by Cindi Michael. $16.95, 978-1-63152-107-2. Despite being disowned by her father—sportscaster George Michael, said to be the man who inspired ESPN's *SportsCenter*—Cindi Michael manages financially and heals emotionally, ultimately finding confidence from within.